Departing from Java

NIAS–Nordic Institute of Asian Studies
NIAS Studies in Asian Topics

NIAS Press is the autonomous publishing arm of NIAS – Nordic Institute of Asian Studies, a research institute located at the University of Copenhagen. NIAS is partially funded by the governments of Denmark, Finland, Iceland, Norway and Sweden via the Nordic Council of Ministers, and works to encourage and support Asian studies in the Nordic countries. In so doing, NIAS has been publishing books since 1969, with more than two hundred titles produced in the past few years.

UNIVERSITY OF COPENHAGEN

norden

Nordic Council *of*
Ministers

Departing from Java

Javanese Labour, Migration and Diaspora

Edited by Rosemarijn Hoefte and Peter Meel

Departing from Java: Javanese Labour, Migration and Diaspora
Edited by Rosemarijn Hoefte and Peter Meel

Nordic Institute of Asian Studies
Studies in Asian Topics, no. 66

First published in 2018 by NIAS Press
NIAS – Nordic Institute of Asian Studies
Øster Farimagsgade 5, 1353 Copenhagen K, Denmark
Tel: +45 3532 9503 • Fax: +45 3532 9549
E-mail: books@nias.ku.dk • Online: www.niaspress.dk

A CIP catalogue record for this book is available from the British
Library

ISBN: 978-87-7694-245-8 (hbk)
ISBN: 978-87-7694-246-5 (pbk)

Typesetting by Donald B. Wagner
Printed and bound in the United States
by Maple Press, York, PA

Contents

Tables

Maps

Figures

Acknowledgements

This volume is the outcome of a workshop organised over 4–5 November 2013 by KITLV/Royal Netherlands Institute of Southeast Asian and Caribbean Studies, Leiden University and Universitas Gadjah Mada. We are particularly grateful to Bambang Purwanto and Sri Margana for generously hosting this workshop in Yogyakarta and for KITLV's financial support.

We want to thank all workshop participants for their lively and well-informed presentations and interventions. We are beholden to Budi Agustono, Ron Hatley, Christopher Joll, Olivia Killias, Joska Ottjes and David Reeve for sharing their research insights with us, Henk Schulte Nordholt for his useful suggestions, and the anonymous reviewers for their constructive comments.

Finally, we want to thank Gerald Jackson for enthusiastically embracing this publication.

Rosemarijn Hoefte and Peter Meel
Leiden, June 2018

Contributors

Pam Allen is Adjunct Associate Professor of Indonesian at the University of Tasmania, Australia. Her teaching and research area is Indonesian language, literature and studies. In addition to publications on Indonesian literature, her recent research projects include a study of the Javanese diaspora in Suriname and New Caledonia. She publishes in Indonesian as well as English, and is an accredited translator. She also works and publishes in the area of literary translation.

Rebecca Elmhirst is based at the University of Brighton in the United Kingdom, where she is currently Reader in Human Geography. Her research interests lie in feminist political ecology, and the everyday politics of natural resource governance, displacement, resettlement and migration. Much of her work draws on extensive field experience in Indonesia, where she co-researches with colleagues from universities and community organisations. She is co-editor of the journal *Gender, Technology and Development*.

Rosemarijn Hoefte is Professor of the History of Suriname after 1873 at the University of Amsterdam and a senior researcher at KITLV/ Royal Netherlands Institute of Southeast Asian and Caribbean Studies in Leiden. Her main research interests are the history of post-abolition Suriname, migration and unfree labour, and Caribbean contemporary history. Her most recent monograph is *Suriname in the Long Twentieth Century: Domination, Contestation, Globalization*. She is also the editor of the *New West Indian Guide*.

Widaratih Kamiso is a Lecturer in the History Department, Faculty of Cultural Sciences, Gadjah Mada University (UGM), Yogyakarta, Indonesia. She received a Bachelor of Arts degree from UGM in 2008 and a Master of Arts from Leiden University in 2012. Her research interests include maritime history, migration history and travel writing. She is currently a Ph.D. candidate at Christian-Albrechts Universität zu Kiel, Germany, researching European travel writing on the East Indies around the 17th century.

Amarjit Kaur is Emeritus Professor of Economic History at the University of New England in Australia and is a Fellow of the Academy of the Social Sciences in Australia. She previously taught at the University of Malaya. She has held visiting positions at Harvard and Columbia (USA); Oxford, Cambridge, University College London and the London School of Economics (UK); and the International Institute of Social History (Netherlands). Her most significant contributions are in Malaysian and Southeast Asian labour history, including *Proletarian and Gendered Mass Migrations* (co-edited with Dirk Hoerder), *Wage Labour in Southeast Asia: Mobility, Labour Migration and Border Controls in Asia* (co-edited with Ian Metcalfe) and *Economic Change in East Malaysia*. Amarjit is currently working on cross-national labour migration and forced migration in Southeast Asia, linking governance, the humanitarian crises and the political economy of South-South relations.

Peter Meel is Director of Research of the Leiden University Institute for History. His teaching and research focus is on Caribbean history, primarily the political and cultural history of Suriname following World War II. Based on archival research, oral history and literature study, his publications centre on nationalism, class, ethnicity, political culture, regional/global integration, and processes of migration, diaspora formation and transnationalism.

Nurchayati is Lecturer at the Department of Psychology, Universitas Negeri Surabaya. Her research focuses on gender and migration, gender and work, life history and psychological anthropology. She is co-author of 'Indonesia: Middle-Class Complicity and State Failure to Provide Care' in *Women, Work and Care in the Asia-Pacific*, edited by Marian Baird, Michele Ford and Elizabeth Hill (Routledge, 2017). She is also the author of 'Bringing Agency Back In: Indonesian Migrant Domestic Workers in Saudi Arabia', *Asian and Pacific Migration Journal* 20 (2011).

Wayne Palmer is a lecturer in the Department of International Relations at Bina Nusantara University. Before joining the University, he was Centre-in-Charge for a non-government organisation that provides paralegal assistance to migrant workers with labour, immigration and criminal cases in Hong Kong. His book – *Indonesia's Overseas Labour*

Migration Programme, 1969–2010 (Brill, 2016) – provides the first detailed, critical analysis of the way in which the programme is managed and how that fits with other developments within the Indonesian government. His current research project focuses on institutional capacity to enforce migrant workers' rights in Indonesia.

Rachel Silvey is Professor of Geography and Planning at the University of Toronto, and the Richard Charles Lee Director of the Asian Institute, Munk School of Global Affairs. She is best known for her work on Indonesian women's labour and migration, both internal and international. She has also published widely in the fields of development studies, cultural geography, feminist geography and diaspora/transnational studies. She is currently involved in a long-term project, funded by the US National Science Foundation and the Social Science Research Council of Canada, on Asian labour migration to the Gulf States, the role of religion in shaping migration dynamics, and the politics of citizenship and settlement.

Agus Suwignyo is an Assistant Professor at the History Department Faculty of Cultural Sciences, Gadjah Mada University (UGM), Yogyakarta, Indonesia. He received his doctorate degree in History from Leiden University in 2012, writing about the institutional transformations of teacher training in Java and Sumatra 1892–1969. His publications have covered the areas of social history focusing on education, citizenship and state formation.

Robert Tierney is a recently retired academic, having taught industrial relations at Griffith University and Charles Sturt University in Australia for twenty-five years. He has also taught at several universities in China and Taiwan. His research interests include Australian labour history and temporary immigration within the Southeast Asian region. He is currently in the stage of completing research on drought and its historical impact on small farmers in eastern Australia, especially New South Wales, and on technological change, work intensification and occupational injuries and fatalities in the New South Wales railway industry. He is also working on a study of the occupational health and safety dimensions of temporary immigration in Taiwan.

Introduction

ROSEMARIJN HOEFTE AND PETER MEEL

This volume is the first attempt to systematically examine the Javanese diaspora as a global phenomenon.[1] The main features of this diaspora are the history of dispersal, marginalisation in the host country, memories and myths of the homeland, the prospect of returning, (financial) support for relatives back home, the re-creation of a culture, the formation of a collective identity forged by all these aspects, and government policies to re-inforce bonds between the homeland and its transnational (former) citizens.[2] In the words of historian James Clifford: 'Diaspora cultures thus mediate, in a lived tension, the experiences of separation and entanglement, of living here and remembering/desiring another place.'[3] The volume covers colonial and post-colonial times, and zooms in on Javanese communities in Asia, including the Middle East, the Americas and Oceania.

---

1   In a pioneering article Craig Lockard (1971) noted that little had been written about the sizeable Javanese migrant group. His essay drew together the divergent and often inconclusive data that were available on the Javanese communities abroad and analysed Javanese emigration in comparative perspective. Lockard focused on Javanese settlements in Malaysia, New Caledonia and Suriname. More recently Julia Martínez and Adrian Vickers (2012) in a follow-up article argued that compared to the literature on the Chinese and Indian diasporas there has been little recognition of Indonesians as a migrant people. Moreover, not much work has been done to link their different forms of mobility to find common patterns. In order to boost the historical understanding of Indonesian mobility Martínez and Vickers recommended that special attention should be paid to the cultural norms and habits which make it easy to move between places and to the economic and social forces that have shaped patterns of mobility.

2   See, for example, Meel 2017, esp. 231–235 for a recent discussion of Jakarta's diaspora policy.

3   Clifford 1994, 311; see also Cohen 2008, 17 and Sheffer 2003, 83.

It targets the dispersion of Javanese across and within state borders, the connections they developed with Java as a real or imagined authoritative source of norms, values and loyalties, and the stand they took when confronted with issues pertaining to social, cultural and personal boundaries they wished to establish or uphold in their host environment. How did the migrants construct a home away from home? An important aspect in this discussion is the feminisation of migration in the second half of the 20th century. Since the 1960s, for the first time in history, women formed the majority of international migrants.[4] A comparative approach will help us to yield broader insights on the myriad Javanese experiences in the diaspora.

In this volume, first, we distinguish Java as the homeland of the Javanese and consider it a unit of reference with strong socio-cultural, socio-economic, spiritual and territorial connotations. To a large extent the homeland connection determined and determines the sense of belonging and the ways of identification Javanese migrants who were physically disconnected from Java established and cultivated in their new settings. From a nation-state-centred point of view it would be correct to label Indonesia rather than Java as the homeland. However, taking Indonesia as a category of analysis is problematic and even erroneous. It would be too expansive to judiciously and meaningfully reflect on the Javanese diaspora and would inaccurately obscure the fact that as a global phenomenon this diaspora encompasses a history of many centuries.

Second, in order to identify the phases of development in the Javanese diaspora communities as well as the changes in character of migration flows, we track continuities and transformations in the ways Javanese have identified themselves and related to each other, to their homeland, and to others in their 'new' country. It is postulated that the ways of identification by Javanese migrants at the time they left their homeland were exposed to various influences from the moment they encountered fellow migrants and entered their host society. The confrontation with these new phenomena gave rise to contemplation, debate and negotiations among Javanese migrants themselves and between Javanese migrants and other ethnic groups. This process revolves around notions of sameness across

---

4   Kenny 2013, 97.

persons or sameness over time, shared consciousness, collective self-understanding and solidarity.[5] We are interested in these processes of identification and the worlds that migrants created.

Applying this perspective to the Javanese diaspora presupposes a working definition of identity. As is the case with the term 'diaspora', the concept of 'identity' has spawned a vast literature. In this volume identity is defined as a set of behavioural, emotional, mental and personal characteristics by which an individual is recognisable as a member of a group. It includes interrelated aspects of culture, language, religion and family life, but is not necessarily restricted to these. Identity formation involves acts of boundary making that are informed by institutions, power hierarchies and political networks.[6]

In this context we wish to trace the factors that played a pivotal role in these processes of identity formation, exhibiting a complex interplay between acts of self-identification and othering. What was and is the importance of demographic relations, particularly the size of the Javanese group versus that of the other ethnic groups in the host society? What was and is the role of class distinctions, occupational differences, gender, and geographic location; of the existing membership regime, such as the laws and practices determining the conditions of social inclusion and exclusion; and of the prevalent political culture, whether or not it displays democratic or autocratic tendencies in the field of administration, respecting or disrespecting minority rights, possessing or lacking an independent jurisdiction? And connected to these questions is the issue of diaspora cohesion: is it based solely on ties to the homeland or does it also reflect the political affiliations and the socio-economic and political-legal conditions and needs in the host country? Here the role of (local) human rights groups and other NGOs are of importance to help voice opinions, organise protest and offer basic assistance.

Third, in contrast to conventional diaspora studies, which are confined to the examination of connections *beyond* the nation-state, this collection of essays also includes contributions that deal with connections *within* the nation-state. Taking into account

---

5   Brubaker and Cooper 2000.

6   Eriksen 2002; Wimmer 2013.

the fundamental ethnic and cultural differences that exist in the Indonesian archipelago and the fact that Javanese moving to Sumatra or Sulawesi encounter an entirely different and basically non-Javanese environment, we link these transmigratory experiences to the diaspora discourse as well.

Finally, next to primary and secondary sources, oral testimonies are of vital importance. Interviews with Javanese migrants give voice to their considerations, choices and experiences. These testimonies inform us about the decisions to depart from Java and the tests and trials of building a life outside the homeland without losing touch with Javaneseness.

A Short History of Migration from Java

'Abraham van Batavia, the first imported slave, arrived at the Cape in 1653.'[7] With the appearance of European imperial powers an extensive system of forced migrations developed in the Indian Ocean under the auspices of different trade companies, including the Dutch East India Company (VOC, Vereenigde Oostindische Compagnie). In the words of Kerry Ward, 'The network of imperial power included the categorization of people as slaves, convicts and political prisoners.'[8] Anthony Reid states that the VOC 'introduced a new rigidity into the concept of slavery.'[9] Migrants relocated under the VOC regime provided cheap labour in the various colonial outposts. Their forced movement was organised in the headquarters of the Dutch colonial empire: the city of Batavia (present-day Jakarta). From there a commercial and legal network extended to other islands in the archipelago we now know as Indonesia, but also to Ceylon (Sri Lanka) and the Cape of Good Hope (South Africa).[10]

7   Shell 1994, xxx.

8   Ward 2009, 4.

9   Reid 1993, 68.

10 For an introduction on the impact of the VOC (and other European intrusions in Southeast Asia) see Schulte Nordholt 2016, 88–144. See Schoeman 2007 on the slave trade from Batavia to South Africa, and Ross (1983) on slavery in South Africa. Ward (2009, 27) states that forced migrations in the early colonial period are an underdeveloped theme in

4

To be sure, commerce and migration had been a feature of Javanese life for centuries. From 400 CE onwards Javanese sailed the Indian Ocean to Madagascar and in subsequent centuries to West Africa. By 1000 CE the island of Java was part of a large trading network covering the coastal regions of Africa, the Middle East, South and Southeast Asia, and China. And slavery was not a new phenomenon either: the Dutch 'took over and interacted with pre-existing systems of slavery and dependency'.[11] In colonial times, Batavia, as an administrative centre and a port of trans-shipment, 'became the hub of a flourishing intra-Asiatic or country trade'.[12] This trade included the movement of enslaved, convicts and criminals, and political and religious exiles whom the VOC considered 'rebels'. The VOC thus used forced migration as a means of social control. However, most of these involuntary migrants were not Javanese at all,[13] but because they departed from Batavia, they became known as Javanese. At the Cape each slave was given a first name as well as a toponymic identification: Abraham van [from] Batavia.[14]

One eye-catching group of forced migrants were exiles. The banishment of political or religious opponents was not strictly a colonial practice of course: it was and is a global phenomenon from antiquity to the present. The idea was that the removal of a figure, sometimes an entire family, would eliminate a rallying point for resistance, without creating martyrs through capital punishment. In the late 17th and early 18th century the VOC banished adversaries to Ceylon and the Cape in the hope of disrupting antagonistic

---

Indonesian historiography, but see, for example, various articles in Reid 1983. On Dutch slavery and slave trade in the Indian Ocean see Vink 2003 and Van Welie 2008. Ward estimates that 14,300 or 22.7 per cent of all enslaved transported to the Cape in the VOC period had Indonesian origins. Between 20 and 30 per cent were women (Ward 2009, 146).

11 Vink 2003, 149–150. According to Taylor (2016, 165) most enslaved were non-Muslims, who had been captured by Muslims and sold to the Dutch.

12 Vink 2003, 139.

13 Most of the convicts were Batavian Chinese (Shell 1994, 195).

14 Shell 1994, 229–230, 482; see also Taylor 2016, 170–172 on toponymic names. Schoeman (2007, 87) states that 'in some cases slaves were also ordered specifically in Batavia and sent out to the Cape.'

social networks and hierarchies, installing docile successors, and thus create a favourable political and commercial environment for European exploits.[15] Many of the exiles were from Java, especially Central Java, and because of their special status were often allowed to be accompanied by family members and servants.

Some of the forced migrants, from all walks of life, adapted to the unfamiliar setting and conditions and slowly managed to make a new life for themselves in the receiving societies. In South Africa the Javanese became known as Cape Malays.[16] In Ceylon the descendants of enslaved, exiles, craftsmen, convicts, soldiers and traders are now known as Sri Lankan Malays, who still adhere to the Malay language and Islam.[17] 'Java is still remembered today as the land of origin of several prominent Malay families in Sri Lanka.'[18]

These networks of forced migration from Batavia disintegrated with the contraction of the Dutch colonial empire in the late 18th and early 19th centuries. Later in the 19th century the slave trade and slavery were abolished, but this did not end forced migrations

---

15 See Ricci 2016 and Taylor 2016. The Dutch also sent opponents into internal exile in the East Indies, see Kaartinen 2016 and Margana 2016.

16 Taylor (2016, 170) notes that relationships were formed 'between slaves and former slaves from India, Ceylon, and Indonesia, but rarely between them and slaves or freed slaves whose origin were African.' According to David Reeve (2013), the 21st-century Cape Malays are a distinct and established identity within South Africa, and have established a niche through a role in tourism. The Cape Malays make up about some 180,000 people, an estimated 170,000 in Cape Town and 10,000 in Johannesburg. They are thus a tiny fragment (approximately 0.03 per cent) of the current South African population, and easily overlooked in national affairs. Malay was last heard in Cape Town in 1923, but this language left lexical and grammatical traces in Afrikaans (Shell 1994, 63). Their current identity includes a distinct area, Bo-Kaap, formerly called the Malay quarter, with characteristic, brightly painted terraces, referred to as 'Cape Malay architecture', close to the centre of Cape Town. Apart from this distinct physical existence, Cape Malay cooking is considered a particular feature of the Cape. In fact, however, Cape Malay cuisine shows little resemblance to Javanese food.

17 Ricci (2016, 95) estimates their number at 50,000; see Hussainmiya 1990 on colonial soldiers.

18 Ricci 2016, 97.

as a revived indentured labour regime was introduced in European colonial empires.[19] In the Dutch empire this involved the movement of mostly landless people from densely populated Java – and to a lesser extent other islands – to less populous, but economically booming areas in the Indonesian archipelago. Before the turn of the century, Chinese indentured labourers constituted the main labour force in these new economies. After 1900, however, the Javanese formed the largest contingent. The purpose of the colonial authorities was to reduce poverty and overpopulation in Java, provide underprivileged and poverty-stricken Javanese better prospects on neighbouring islands, and, importantly, to establish a sizeable, temporary workforce that could effectively exploit the natural resources on the so-called outer islands. State-controlled, professional recruitment agencies provided the plantations and mines with the requested labourers. Many Javanese left for Sumatra, Sulawesi and Kalimantan where they were put to work as indentured ('coolie') labourers and engaged in the cultivation of export crops and in mining. The majority of Javanese workers were put to work on the rubber and tobacco plantations in East Sumatra and on the coffee and tea plantations in South Sumatra. Smaller groups of Javanese labourers performed hazardous manual tasks in Sumatra's gold, silver and coal mines. But irrespective of their destination and the requirements they were expected to meet, all indentured labourers had to cope with forms of abuse, high mortality rates and a penal code which made neglect of duty or refusal to work a criminal offence.[20]

The Dutch colonial state was directly engaged in this indentured labour migration by providing both the administrative and legal basis of the system. Under the same system, more than 30,000

---

19 Indentured labour is frequently associated with the abolition of slavery, but it was not a new phenomenon, as in (pre)colonial Asia systems of indentured labour were widespread (Northrup 1995, 66–67). Needless to say there were also forms of voluntary migration, including Javanese pilgrims visiting the Arabian Peninsula to undertake the *hajj*, with some of them staying longer as students or religious teachers, and small numbers of well-to-do Javanese who went to the Netherlands for their education (Lockard 1971; Martínez and Vickers 2012).

20 Houben and Lindblad 1999; Breman 1987; Hayashi 2002.

Javanese indentured labourers were shipped to the Dutch Caribbean colony of Suriname to toil on the plantations there. In addition, neighbouring colonies such as Malaya (including Singapore) and northern Borneo, as well as far-away places such as New Caledonia in the Southwest Pacific, were destinations for Javanese indentured workers to drudge in mines, on plantations or in infrastructural projects.[21] Although migration was intended to be temporary, for many workers it turned out to be permanent. Javanese overseas settlements in for example New Caledonia and Suriname testify to this. Only in 1931 did political and economic pressure force the colonial government to repeal the penal sanction.[22]

In this volume we focus on labour migrations since the late 19th century, within the Indonesian archipelago (transmigration) and beyond in East and Southeast Asia, the Pacific, the Arabian Peninsula, and the Americas.

Labour, Migration and Diaspora

Labour

From the 19th century the prospect of labour has been the main motive behind the departure of people from Java and their movement to destinations elsewhere. Although personal and socio-cultural circumstances have often played an important role, triggering people to change their life and consider outmigration, ultimately the pull factor persuading them to actually leave their native soil has been

---

21 In 1825, 38 Javanese were counted in Singapore; in 1881 this city registered 5,885 Javanese, by then the largest ethnic group (Spaan 1994, 94–85). Apart from the above-mentioned countries smaller numbers of Javanese moved to Brunei, Cochinchina (Vietnam), Thailand and Australia, mostly as free labourers, although the boundaries between free and indentured labour were often blurred.

22 During the Japanese occupation of the Netherlands East Indies millions of Javanese were subject to forced labour (*romusha*) and deployed in construction and infrastructural projects in Thailand and Burma (Lockhard 1971, 42–43). Martínez and Vickers (2015, 138) state that in Australia 'the use of contract labor continued with only slight modifications, leaving the effectiveness of abolition open to question into the postwar period.'

the lure of employment and the ensuing expectation to improve their standard of living. To be sure, the colonial government in the Netherlands East Indies, as elsewhere, actively stimulated labour migration, if only to relieve the population pressure on the land.

Looking more closely at Javanese labour migration, three features stand out. First of all, Javanese moving to a new place of residence and accepting a job outside Java had to deal with different – and in the course of time often changing – labour regimes. In most cases a mix of state-sponsored and private initiatives has underlaid a configuration targeted at managing the supply and demand of labour, promoting corporate production and maximising capital accumulation, or supporting the dominant economic sectors by providing services. This applied to both the colonial and post-colonial eras and as a rule involved the recruitment and transportation of substantial numbers of labourers, who signed a contract for a fixed period of time and were expected to return to their home country after the expiration of their contract.

In some cases destinations remained the same, although the industries demanding temporary labourers changed. Late 19th-century Malaya engaged Javanese to work the rubber plantations. Almost a century later, independent Malaysia's new export-oriented industrialisation strategy requested Javanese for agricultural development schemes as well as for the construction, manufacturing and domestic service sectors. In other cases, destinations no longer had a demand for temporary labourers, for example the Dutch Caribbean colony of Suriname. In Suriname the colonial government no longer imported plantation labourers, but in the 1930s, in close cooperation with authorities in Java, introduced a scheme to stimulate agricultural colonisation by Javanese smallholders, who were to live in Java-style villages (*desa*'s).[23] In the late 20th century, new destinations with new demands emerged. Examples are Taiwan, Hong Kong, Singapore and countries in the Arabian Peninsula that have been recruiting Javanese female labourers to work in the domestic service and caregiving sectors and male labourers for the construction, manufacturing and fishing industries.

---

23 See Ramsoedh 1990; Hoefte 2011.

In terms of labour regime the transmigration projects in Java are a special case in point. They started in the early 20th century at the initiative of the Dutch coloniser, but were continued by the Indonesian government in the second half of the century. These projects were directed at diminishing the population pressure in Java by resettling poor and landless Javanese into more sparsely populated areas in other islands of the archipelago, such as Sumatra and Sulawesi, cases both examined in this volume.

A second observation is that Javanese usually entered a labour force that also included workers from various other parts of the world. In Malaya Javanese have chiefly competed with Chinese and Indians, on the plantations and in the mines of New Caledonia with Vietnamese and to a lesser extent with workers from other Asian countries, and in Suriname with Afro-Surinamese, Indians and Chinese. In later periods, Javanese in Taiwan have mainly faced Filipinos, Thai and Vietnamese as rival labourers, in Singapore and Hong Kong Filipinos and workers from South, Southeast and East Asia, and in Saudi Arabia and Dubai for the most part labourers from South Asia. In the way Javanese have handled this ethnic diversity and held their ground in their new occupational environment they have demonstrated considerable flexibility and capacity to adjust, to which many chapters in this book attest.

Ethnically mixed labour forces also contributed to strengthening the migrants' Javanese identity. Governments and employers certainly identified them as 'Javanese', but the processes of Javanese migration and adaptation to a new environment also re-enforced the common cultural ground among migrants. For example, language differences increased the sense of alienation of contract workers from their employers and non-Javanese co-workers. Adaptation and socio-cultural identity formation often went hand in hand, but uneven sex ratios sometimes made it more difficult to (re)build communities and to generate a sense of well-being and stability.[24]

For employers, workforce fragmentation provided a way to employ divide-and-rule strategies and sabotage or sustain the absence of a tradition of worker solidarity and collaboration. The opportunity for labour migrants to organise themselves and bargain for higher

24 See, for example, Hoefte 1998, chapters 6 and 9.

wages and better accommodation was limited, particularly beyond the ethnic dividing lines. Workers gave vent to protests, but mainly by subtle forms of resistance.[25] The fear of losing their income and being sent back to their home country as well as the temporality of their contract constrained many of them from pushing for better working and living conditions, apart from some notable exceptions (see below).

A third feature relates to the structural deficiencies of the labour regimes. All contributors to this volume touch upon or explicitly state that the indentured labour system has been open to acts of exploitation and abuse. The system created room for ethnic, gender and job differentiations facilitating governments, recruiters and employers to manipulate workers and wages, and benefit from the labourers' lack of knowledge about systems and processes and their limited ability to understand rights and obligations. These have primarily safeguarded the interests of the administrative and entrepreneurial classes. In the past decades legislation and immigration policies have seemingly improved, but present-day circumstances basically show how the efforts of the International Labour Organization (ILO) to promote labour standards have been thwarted by national governments that circumvent ILO conventions, even if these have been ratified by their own parliaments.

Particularly the chapters dealing with Javanese female labourers employed in the domestic service and caregiving sectors in Malaysia, Singapore, Hong Kong, Taiwan, Saudi Arabia and Dubai demonstrate that for Javanese women working outside Java labour regimes have indeed changed, but not necessarily for the better. Administrative procedures prior to the departure of Javanese to the host country indicate that contract labourers have officially recognised legal rights and suggest that receiving countries will respect and protect these rights. However, the poor training Javanese generally receive before leaving Indonesia, the social and cultural isolation they encounter at their final destination, government negligence towards their vulnerable position, and the unequal power relations they are subject to at the workplace are testimony to enduring ambiguity and arbitrariness, hampering any significant improvement of the

---

25 See, for instance, Scott 1985 and 1990.

position of Javanese labour migrants, and irresponsibly blurring the distinctions between free and forced labour.

The authors in this book more specifically point out that in both colonial and post-colonial times parties involved in Javanese labour migration have been guilty of unlawful acts or have aptly moved in the twilight zone between legality and illegality. Referring to the Malaysian case, Amarjit Kaur mentions the illegal hiring of labourers via underground syndicates and informal social networks helping workers to illegally enter a host country or stay illegally after the termination of their contract.[26] Responding to growing public disquiet in the early 21st century the Malaysian government cracked down on undocumented Indonesian labourers and incarcerated them in detention camps where they were treated badly. Foreign labourers working without a visa or work permit and domestic workers who had run away from verbally or physically abusive employers were considered to have committed a criminal offense and were subject to detainment and punitive measures, including caning.

Aspects of exploitation and violence receive special treatment in the chapters on the Arabian Peninsula. Discussing labour conditions in Saudi Arabia Nurchayati addresses the multiple dimensions of sexual harassment, a theme that figures prominently in the narratives of female labour migrants who have worked in the kingdom. Nurchayati reflects on instances of outright abuse of female workers by their employers, but also elaborates on sexuality as a source of cultural misunderstandings between employers and employees, and

---

26 Human trafficking – an extreme aberration of these illegal operations and a serious criminal offence – is not treated extensively in this volume. The June 2017 report by the U.S. State Department on trafficking in persons lists several instances of illegal trafficking involving Indonesians, for example, 'two Saudi Arabian nationals who allegedly operated a gang that fraudulently recruited Indonesian domestic workers to be exploited in Egypt.' In Indonesia, the report notes 'widespread emigration through illicit channels rife with trafficking vulnerabilities. Despite endemic corruption among officials that impedes anti-trafficking efforts and enables traffickers to operate with impunity, only two officials were prosecuted for trafficking offenses.' (www.state.gov/documents/organization/271339.pdf, accessed 31 August 2017).

mentions examples of Javanese female workers who intentionally entered into sexual relationships with their employers. Following up on this, Rachel Silvey – focusing on Saudi Arabia and Dubai – explains why countries of the Gulf Cooperation Council have remained an attractive destination for female workers despite the overwork, underpayment of wages, discrimination and sexual violence many of them have been exposed to. She argues that women in Java wish to leave their home, which they associate with experiences of poverty, unemployment and boredom. They are aware of the dangers and humiliations they might encounter in the Gulf States, but often state that they identify similar risks at home. Besides the employment opportunities, Saudi Arabia offers a special attraction as a holy land. Working 'near Mecca' would fulfill their desire to be in the company of practising Muslims, would create positive spaces of social contact and would probably be the only way to perform the hajj. Silvey argues that traditional feminist frameworks have underestimated the central and complex roles that Islam plays in sending and receiving contexts such as the Arab case.

Migration

If we consider that Javanese working outside Java departed from the island as migrants, we need to delineate the different types of migration. Javanese transmigrants going to Sumatra or Sulawesi moved within the borders of the former Netherlands East Indies[27] and after 1945 the Republic of Indonesia. Others moved to different territories in Southeast Asia – here represented by Malaysia and Singapore – and East Asia – in this volume covered by Hong Kong and Taiwan. Particularly those who worked in Malaysia and Singapore lived at a relatively short distance from Java. This allowed for the maintenance of close relations with relatives who had stayed behind and offered opportunities for circular and return migration. For those who chose to work in the Arabian Peninsula – here represented by Saudi Arabia and Dubai – return migration was part

---

27 People moving to work in the outer islands as 'coolie labourers', see p. 7 in this introduction, also moved within the borders of the colony, of course.

and parcel of the contract they had signed and a natural endpoint of their migration trajectory. Occasionally these migrants succeeded in postponing this moment by going underground or by extending their stay with a series of new contracts. For people from Java who had moved to the Pacific – in this volume represented by New Caledonia – and the Americas – here covered by Suriname – return migration was possible and many Javanese considered this as a serious option. Following World War II Jakarta no longer wished to receive return migrants in densely populated Java, whereupon most Javanese migrants decided to permanently settle in New Caledonia and Suriname respectively.

Workers departed from Java during different waves of emigration. In New Caledonia two waves of emigration occurred, one before and one following World War II. These waves differed in size, organisation and labour goals. Suriname imported indentured labourers from Java between 1890 and 1930 and free labourers and settlers between 1930 and 1939. Malaysia (including its political predecessors) has shown an intricate picture in the field of labour migration due to its political history, territorial makeup, economic resources and central position in the region. In Indonesia transmigration programmes covered late-colonial times, but also the Old Order under Sukarno, the New Order under Suharto and the post-Suharto Reformasi period, each subtly demonstrating shifts in policy goals and approaches, ranging from highly centralised and 'ethnicised' to decentralised. The other countries examined in this volume – Singapore, Hong Kong, Taiwan, Saudi Arabia and Dubai – since the 1980s have demonstrated more linear developments, notwithstanding the fact that conditions and regulations were often subject to change or bended to the detriment of migrant workers.

Usually workers from Java temporarily settled in their host country and during the term of their contract focused on coping with their new working and living conditions and meeting the demands of their superiors. Javanese workers in Malaya in some ways were better off than those who had moved to alternative locations. On account of their cultural and religious background, comparable with Malayan culture and religion, the British coloniser classified them as Malays in the census and overtly preferred them to other labour migrants. Malaysian authorities continued this administrative practice in order to preserve the numerical superiority of the Malay group. This classification has allowed Javanese to acquire Malay reservation land to take up rubber cultivation as smallholders, whereas Chinese and Indians were excluded from this opportunity. Yet, taking into account other – much more controversial – aspects of Malaysia's immigration policy, most Javanese workers have not aspired to permanent settlement.

In various ways Javanese labour migrants have demonstrated their agency in different periods and settings. Frequently manifestations of their willpower were visible to the general public and often given substantial media coverage. In early 20th century Suriname Javanese labourers were involved in strikes and uprisings at different plantations, although the majority resisted the system in more covert ways, such as feigning illnesses or other breaches of contract. In 1945, in New Caledonia Javanese labourers together with Vietnamese workers were instrumental in ending the system of indentured labour in this territory. In the early 21st century Javanese workers in Malaysia took to the streets and militantly protested against the maltreatment Indonesians experienced from the local authorities. Robert Tierney presents examples of Javanese–Filipino collaboration in Taiwan. Their joint efforts led to a rally protesting a temporary ban on hiring Filipinas and Filipinos by the Taiwanese government, and protests in favour of a public space for Indonesians to celebrate Eid al-Fitr. Similar Javanese–Filipino cooperation in the Taiwan fishing industry produced a labour union, but Javanese contributions to its operations have been small compared to the Filipino ones.

In less overt ways female domestic workers have attempted to bridge the discrepancies between their labour contract and every-day reality as much as they can. They have designed and deployed strategies to 'manage' their employers and increase their control over time, space and tasks. In this context exchanging information and experiences with fellow domestic workers has been of crucial importance. As Nurchayati demonstrates, domestic labourers pre-paring Javanese food for their employers and instructing them how to enjoy it used their culinary skills as a tool to ease communication and mitigate tensions. Wayne Palmer examines the determination of Javanese domestic workers in Singapore and Hong Kong to counter stereotypes about their ethnic group. In distinguishing between

Filipino and Javanese domestic workers employers have invariably portrayed the former as 'smarter' and 'more intelligent', on account of the fact that many of them can boast a higher level of formal education and command of the English language (something Tierney observed in Taiwan as well). The latter have developed a reputation of being more compliant and acquiescent because they respect authority figures, but despite their hard work are also considered less professional, prudent and reliable. Palmer shows that the persistence of these perceptions is mainly a consequence of the migration system that Javanese domestic workers are subject to and which precludes them from integrating into the host society.

The 'feminisation of international migration'[28] has no doubt contributed to the emancipation of successful female labourers. According to Nurchayati, Javanese women working in Saudi Arabia have a craving for personal growth. They wish to become 'better versions of themselves', which in their opinion implies better *Javanese* women. They hope to return to their communities of origin as women who can enjoy more wealth, command greater respect, exercise more influence and lead a more meaningful life. If they have been able to substantially save money they invest what they have earned in refurbishing their homes, buying plots of farmland, starting-up small businesses and offering their children a decent education. In this way they accomplish upward social mobility and obtain middle-class status. One of the consequences of working overseas might also be a strengthening of the women's bargaining position towards their husbands, parents and siblings. They frequently obtain a greater say in family decision-making and thus contribute to a transformation of existing social relations.[29]

---

28 Moreno-Fontes Chammartin 2002, 39–46. www.academia.edu/9593785/ The_Feminization_of_International_Migration?auto=download (accessed 17 August 2017).

29 Austin (2017, 282–283) reports that 'while continuing debate about migrant workers has provided opportunities [. . .] for returned migrants to build confidence in political participation, publicly performing shifts in gender relations and resistance to the normative gender regime, my interviewees felt that the gender order in Indonesia is slow to change.' Other studies report that returning female migrants find that their absence may have led to marital instability, a weakened emotional bond with their children

Diaspora

Thinking in terms of people forming transnational communities or diasporas has increasingly gained ground since the 1990s. Inspired by the Indian and – to a lesser extent – Chinese example, the Indonesian government has quite recently coined the term 'Indonesian diaspora' and lately has attempted to develop a diaspora policy, emphasising the importance of global networking and multi-level collaboration to boost the power and status of the 'big Indonesian family'.[30] The Javanese diaspora can be considered the largest segment or subcategory of the Indonesian diaspora, although Jakarta refrains from alluding to such divisions. This would contradict the principles of the Pancasila ideology, which stresses the unity of the nation, and is the philosophical foundation and justification of the Indonesian state. Moreover, it would run the risk of producing tensions and conflicts between 'family members' and thus facilitate the failure of the desired diaspora objectives.

In the eyes of the Indonesian government members of the Indonesian diaspora are pivotal in sending remittances. As various chapters in this volume testify these money transfers are mainly provided by Javanese labour migrants located in Southeast and East Asia and the Arabian Peninsula. Particularly female labourers working in the domestic and caregiving sectors and male labourers employed in the construction and manufacturing industries have managed to save money and send part of their wages to relatives back home. More than half of bank-mediated remittances to Indonesia are transferred by labour migrants in Malaysia and Saudi Arabia.

In a socio-cultural sense Javanese labour migrants have given shape to the idea of belonging to a Javanese diaspora by identifying with the Javanese way of life they are familiar with and which they intend

---

or the loss of village-based support systems; see, for example, Hugo 2002. Undoubtedly, migration in general and its feminisation in particular have changed family structures. In many villages children are living with their grandparents, as their mother and/or father are working elsewhere (Schulte Nordholt 2016, 406).

30 For the other side of the coin, see Austin (2017) for an analysis of the ambiguous role of the state in defending the rights of female migrant domestic workers in the 21th century.

to preserve. Maintaining and reproducing forms of Javaneseness in the host country, they have focused on practising their Islamic faith. Javanese domestic workers have endorsed the importance of socialising with fellow workers during family gatherings organised in the home of their employer, at public spaces such as shopping malls and in amusement parks to which they escort their host families. Conversing in Javanese, consuming Javanese dishes and discussing Javanese drama and talent shows are core ingredients of such meetings, which support and strengthen their Javaneseness, help to surmount feelings of isolation and alienation, and sustain their connections with the diaspora. Tierney draws attention to Javanese gathering at and around Taipei Main Rail Station, a tiny district known as 'Little Indonesia'. Here they engage in communal singing, traditional dancing and putting on plays. Occasionally they use Javanese song and dance at public demonstrations aiming to bring about improvements in their material or immaterial circumstances. In those cases their cultural performances display distinct political messages.

Generally Javanese domestic labourers working in a host country experience both cultural loss and cultural gain. Frequently they have to compromise and dispense with practices that frustrate relationships with their employers. Those practices often concern their duties to pray five times a day, to abstain from cooking and eating pork, and to wear white cloth. Palmer points out that the Indonesian government seems to be aware of this give-and-take attitude. On the one hand Jakarta encourages migrant workers to learn and adopt the ways of life of the host country and particularly domestic workers to observe local practices related to child raising and the use of public spaces. On the other hand the Indonesian government rejects the adoption of liberal behaviours, the more so when these involve consumerism, atheism, immodest dressing or same-sex intimacy.

Rebecca Elmhirst as well as Agus Suwignyo and Widaratih Kamiso argue that the transmigration programmes in Java have given rise to a particular form of Javanese diaspora: the creation of 'little Javas' outside Java, but inside Indonesia. Both chapters focus on the impact of state policies and the livelihood practices of migrants on the reproduction of Javanese identity and the establishment of a 'home away from home'. Whereas Elmhirst concentrates on the effects of the transmigration policies of successive administrations on Javanese culture in the diaspora, Suwignyo and Kamiso zoom in on the contribution of the social networks of the Javanese transmigrants to the development of a shared sense of belonging and attachment to Javanese culture. They add that the combination of education and socio-economic progress has shifted Javanese orientation towards their new Java-like geographical localities, thus encouraging the creation of a more hybrid identity.

A unique case in this context is Suriname. Here Javanese labourers constituted a substantial community that managed to keep in touch with the homeland. To a large extent this was due to a quarter of the labour force that had returned to Java. Since 1954 the remaining group has undergone a process of emancipation and integration which – as Peter Meel shows – has firmly positioned them in the Surinamese political arena and resulted in a Surinamese Javanese presence in all social classes, occupational groups and residential areas. The 'twice migration' or 'double migration' of Javanese from Suriname to the Netherlands around 1975 has *de facto* produced a third homeland. As a transnational community approximately 100,000 Surinamese Javanese mainly identify with Suriname and the Netherlands, but Javanese culture has not lost its significance, and Indonesia as their ancestral home is still kept in high esteem and is becoming ever closer due to more frequent and cheaper travel options and to communication technologies, including the Internet.

About this Book

The first chapters study diaspora within colonial or national borders: transmigration or the state-sponsored resettlement of millions of poor and landless Javanese families into relatively sparsely popu-lated areas on other Indonesian islands. Rebecca Elmhirst explains why the concept of diaspora provides a useful framework for exam-ining the cultural politics of these transmigration programmes, and in particular the workings of Javanese communities (little Javas) within Indonesia but outside Java. She traces the origins, practices and socio-cultural dynamics of this internal diaspora, focusing on the Sumatran province of Lampung. Elmhirst highlights the interac-tion between a changing political culture and common expressions of identity, such as discussions and practices around land use and livelihood. Finally, she examines the ways in which a Javanese transmigrant diaspora is being re-imagined in a transformed political scene where regional autonomy champions place-based sources of political and cultural authority.

Inspired by Elmhirst's concept of 'emergent identity', Agus Suwignyo and Widaratih Kamiso explore the social mobility and sense of belonging of the Javanese transmigrant community in Southeast Sulawesi in chapter two. In particular they seek to understand why both social mobility and a shared sense of belonging played a crucial role in the making of the emergent identity of Javanese migrants in their new environment. The authors combine historical research and interviews with Javanese in Kendari and adjacent transmigration localities to study the orientation and sense of belonging of the transmigrants in Southeast Sulawesi. They conclude that a new, diasporic identity, between being Javanese and being local, is developing or emerging.

The third chapter takes us to the Pacific at the turn of the 20th century and beyond. Between 1896 and 1949 almost 20,000 indentured Javanese were taken to New Caledonia. First, Pamela Allen gives an overview of the history of this diaspora. She then focuses on some of the cultural markers of this group, and following Fredrik Barth's idea of boundary maintenance she suggests that those markers are not 'definitional characteristics' of the ethnic group. In a case study of the Tiebaghi mine she illustrates the cataclysmic impact of the indentured labour system as well as the potential for cultural pluralism in an emerging colonial society. Allen concludes with a discussion of some of the individuals and organisations that keep cultural markers alive in present-day New Caledonia. She thus highlights the tension between cultural hybridity and ethnic cohesion.

In chapter 4, Amarjit Kaur traces the different labour regimes under which Javanese have moved to Malaya/Malaysia since the second half of the 19th century. In colonial times Javanese workers were hired mostly for employment on rubber plantations, but starting in the 1970s they have mainly been engaged for agricultural development schemes and the construction, manufacturing and domestic work sectors. Due to ethnic similarities between 'Malay' and Javanese and a population policy favouring 'Malay' over

Chinese and Indians, the Malaysian government has regarded Javanese as preferred foreign workers. Simultaneously, the influx of large numbers of undocumented Javanese has frequently prompted the Malaysian government to consider them 'unwelcome guests' and to subject Javanese workers to regular mass expulsions. Kaur demonstrates that Javanese as temporary migrants have been able to balance between suitable accommodation and identity maintenance, focusing on income increase for themselves and their family in the home country.

In the fifth chapter, Wayne Palmer uses a comparative approach to study the ways migration systems determine migrant workers' level of engagement with political, economic and socio-cultural institutions in Hong Kong and Singapore, prompting them to behave in ways that are partly influenced by their ethnic and national identity. He discusses how these circumstances have contributed to the formation of stereotypes about Javanese character. Palmer's main focus is on the constraints and opportunities that shape the way in which the Javanese migrants respond to life and work in the two cities. In Hong Kong employers are generally supportive of their workers' participation in social activities outside the workplace on the weekly day off. Indonesian domestic workers can join formal and informal groups which encourage and promote practices from home. Singapore, however, does not support migrants in their self-organising for political and other social purposes. Therefore, the scale of migrant activities is much smaller than in Hong Kong.

Another popular destination in the Asia-Pacific region is Taiwan, where Indonesians/Javanese constitute the largest migrant population. Indonesians are concentrated at the low end of the wage scale and are the largest group of undocumented migrant workers, who have broken their labour contracts by fleeing their workplaces. Robert Tierney analyses how the working and living conditions within Taiwan's racialised labour market give rise to inter-ethnic tensions between local Taiwanese and Javanese as well as between Javanese and other migrant nationalities. He examines the ways in which working and social conditions, together with the tensions arising from them, have been contested by Javanese caregivers and fishers, by domestic helpers and fishers from the Philippines, and by local Taiwanese organisations that are sympathetic to the island's guest workers.

Rachel Silvey and Nurchayati take us to the Persian Gulf region. Saudi Arabia, the United Arab Emirates and other countries of the Gulf Cooperation Council are a prime destination for Javanese women. As their numbers have grown, so too has a dominant narrative about the risks of living and working abroad. In chapter 7, Rachel Silvey asks what political work is accomplished by the circulation of abuse narratives in the lives of migrant women. How does migrant women's awareness of abuse affect the ways they perceive and manage their labour market precarity, the conditions of their work, their poverty and their transnational lives? She uses interviews with migrant women from Sukabumi (West Java) to sketch the everyday life of migrant domestic workers and to explain why so many Indonesian women continue to migrate abroad, despite their awareness of the dangers they may face in their host countries.

Nurchayati's ethnographic study provides more detail on female migrants from Pranggang in Saudi Arabia, a major destination for Indonesian migrants. Through the use of case studies she examines how in pursuing their goals, some Javanese women have coped with physical, mental, social and cultural challenges, and at the same time have managed to preserve or re-fashion their sense of ethnic identity. Nurchayati also traces the connections of the Javanese community in Saudi Arabia to the homeland. She argues that these women have toiled abroad not to abandon their ethnic identities in exchange for money and status but, rather, to use these and other resources to become what they see as better versions of themselves. They have used their overseas earnings to increase their well-being: they have renovated their homes, bought farmland, begun small businesses and put their children through school.

The last chapter highlights trans-imperial and post-colonial connections. Between 1890 and 1939 the Dutch colonial authorities brought Javanese labourers, the majority of whom were indentured, to work on the plantations in Suriname. Soon the Javanese became the third-largest population group in this Dutch colony in South America. Interestingly, the Javanese in Suriname constitute the only branch of the Javanese diaspora who have firmly positioned themselves in the political arena of their country of settlement. In this chapter, Peter Meel tracks the development of the Javanese population group in Suriname by analysing their major political parties and their leaders, as well as the key interests they have championed. By focusing on the four main Javanese leaders, Iding and Willy Soemita, Salikin Hardjo and Paul Somohardjo, he assesses the role of politicians in the identity-formation process of the Javanese and their efforts to realise the dreams and ambitions of their followers and of Surinamese society at large.

In the 20th century the export of labour has become a major source of income in Southeast, South and East Asia. This phenomenon has deep historical roots, but globalisation, particularly the transport revolution, has caused labour migration to explode. In 2010, an estimated 20 million labour migrants from Southeast Asia alone worked in other countries in the region, the Middle East, Europe and the Americas. As stated at the outset, this is the first volume to systematically study the Javanese diaspora as a worldwide phenomenon. We hope this volume will contribute to the Javanese/ Indonesian diaspora coming out of the shadows of the Chinese, Indian and Filipino diasporas, and will engender more comparative research on Southeast, South and East Asian labour migrations.

References

Austin, M. 2017. 'Defending Indonesia's Migrant Domestic Workers'. In *Citizenship and Democratization in Southeast Asia*, ed. W. Berenschot, H. Schulte Nordholt and L. Bakker, 265–288. Leiden: Brill. [DOI 10.1163/ 9789004329669_012]

Breman, J., 1987. *Koelies, planters en koloniale politiek: Het arbeidsregime op de grootlandbouwondernemingen aan Sumatra's oostkust in het begin van de twintigste eeuw*. Dordrecht: Foris. Translated as *Menjinakkan sang kuli: Politik kolonial, tuan kebun, dan kuli di Sumatra Timur pada awal abad ke-20* (Jakarta: Pustaka Utama Grafiti, 1997).

Brubaker, R. and F. Cooper 2000. 'Beyond "Identity"', *Theory and Society* 29: 1–47.

Clifford, J. 1994. 'Diasporas', *Cultural Anthropology* 9(3): 302–338.

Cohen, R. 2008. *Global Diasporas: An Introduction*. 2nd ed. London: Routledge.

Eriksen, T. H. 2002. *Ethnicity and Nationalism: Anthropological Perspectives*. 2nd ed. London: Pluto Press.

Hayashi, Y. 2002. *Agencies and Clients: Labour Recruitment in Java, 1870s–1950s*. Amsterdam: IIAS/IISG. [CLARA Working Paper, No. 14.]

Hoefte, R., 1998. *In Place of Slavery: A Social History of British Indian and Javanese Laborers in Suriname*. Gainesville: University Press of Florida.

——, 2011. 'The Movement of People from East to West', *Journal of Caribbean History* 45(2): 190–211.

Houben, V. J. H. and J. T. Lindblad, 1999. *Coolie Labour in Colonial Indonesia: A Study of Labour Relations in the Outer Islands, c. 1900–1940*. Wiesbaden: Otto Harrassowitz.

Hugo, G., 2002. 'Effects of International Migration on the Family in Indonesia', *Asian and Pacific Migration Journal* 11(1): 13–46.

Hussainmiya, B. A. 1990. *Orang Rejimen: The Malays of the Ceylon Rifle Regiment*. Kuala Lumpur: Universiti Kebangsaan Malaysia.

Kaartinen, T. 2016. 'Exile, Colonial Space, and Deterritorialized People in Eastern Indonesian History'. In *Exile in Colonial Asia: Kings, Convicts, Commemoration*, ed. R. Ricci, 139–164. Honolulu: University of Hawai'i Press.

Kenny, K. 2013. *Diaspora: A Very Short Introduction*. Oxford: Oxford University Press.

Lockard, C. A. 1971. 'The Javanese as Emigrant: Observations on the Development of Javanese Settlements Overseas', *Indonesia* 11 (April): 41–62.

Margana, S. 2016. 'Caught between Empires: *Babad Mangkudiningratan* and the Exile of Sultan Hamengkubuwana II of Yogyakarta, 1813–1826'. In *Exile in Colonial Asia: Kings, Convicts, Commemoration*, ed. R. Ricci, 117–138. Honolulu: University of Hawai'i Press.

Martínez, J. T. and A. Vickers 2012. 'Indonesians Overseas: Deep Histories and the View From Below', *Indonesia and the Malay World* 40(117): 111–121.

—— 2015. *The Pearl Frontier: Indonesian Labor and Indigenous Encounters in Australia's Northern Trading Network*. Honolulu: University of Hawai'i Press.

Meel, P. 2017. 'Jakarta and Paramaribo Calling: Return Migration Challenges for the Surinamese Javanese Diaspora?' *New West Indian Guide* 91: 223–259.

Moreno-Fontes Chammartin, G. 2002. 'The Feminization of International Migration', *Migrant Workers, Labour Education* 4 (129): 39–46.

Northrup, D. 1995. *Indentured Labor in the Age of Imperialism, 1834–1922*. Cambridge: Cambridge University Press.

Ramsoedh, H. 1990. *Suriname 1933–1944: Koloniale politiek en beleid onder gouverneur Kielstra*. Delft: Eburon.

Reeve, D. 2013. 'The (Disappearing) Javanese of South Africa and Sri Lanka'. Unpublished paper presented at the workshop on the Javanese diaspora, Universitas Gadjah Mada, Yogyakarta, 4–5 November.

Reid, A. 1993. 'The Decline of Slavery in Nineteenth-Century Indonesia'. In *Breaking the Chains: Slavery, Bondage, and Emancipation in Modern Africa and Asia*, ed. M. A. Klein, 64–82. Madison: University of Wisconsin Press.

—— (ed.) 1983. *Slavery, Bondage and Dependency in Southeast Asia*. New York: St. Martin's Press.

Ricci, R. 2016. 'From Java to Jaffna: Exile and Return in Dutch Asia in the Eighteenth Century'. In *Exile in Colonial Asia: Kings, Convicts, Commemoration*, ed. R. Ricci, 94–116. Honolulu: University of Hawai'i Press.

Schoeman, K. 2007. *Early Slavery at the Cape of Good Hope, 1652–1717*. Pretoria: Protea Book House.

Schulte Nordholt, H. 2016. *Een geschiedenis van Zuidoost-Azië*. Amsterdam: Amsterdam University Press.

Scott, J. C. 1985. *Weapons of the Weak: Everyday Forms of Peasant Resistance*. New Haven: Yale University Press.

—— 1990. *Domination and the Arts of Resistance: Hidden Transcripts*. New Haven: Yale University Press.

Sheffer, G. 2003. *Diaspora Politics: At Home and Abroad*. Cambridge: Cambridge University Press.

Shell, R. C. H. 1994. *Children of Bondage: A Social History of the Slave Society at the Cape of Good Hope, 1652–1838*. Hanover, N.H.: University Press of New England.

Spaan, E. 1994. 'Taikongs and Calos: The Role of Middlemen and Brokers in Javanese International Migration', *International Migration Review* 28(1): 93–113.

Taylor, J. G. 2016. 'Belongings and Belonging: Indonesian Histories in Inventories from the Cape of Good Hope'. In *Exile in Colonial Asia: Kings, Convicts, Commemoration*, ed. R. Ricci, 165–192. Honolulu: University of Hawai'i Press.

Vink, M. 2003. '"The World's Oldest Trade": Dutch Slavery and Slave Trade in the Indian Ocean in the Seventeenth Century', *Journal of World History* 14(3): 131–177.

Ward, K. 2009. *Networks of Empire: Forced Migration in the Dutch East India Company*. Cambridge: Cambridge University Press.

Welie, R. van 2008. 'Patterns of Slave Trading and Slavery in the Dutch Colonial World 1596–1863'. In *Dutch Colonialism, Migration and Cultural Heritage*, ed. G. Oostindie, 155–259. Leiden: KITLV Press.

Wimmer, A. 2013. *Ethnic Boundary Making: Institutions, Power, Networks*. Oxford: Oxford University Press.

CHAPTER 1

Departing from Java to Lampung

Locating Javanese Diasporic Practices in Indonesia's Transmigration Resettlement Programme

REBECCA ELMHIRST

Introduction

One of the most significant departures from Java in Indonesia's colonial and post-colonial history is that associated with transmigration: the state-sponsored resettlement of poor and landless Javanese families into relatively sparsely populated areas of Sumatra, Kalimantan, Sulawesi and Papua. In his monumental *History of Java*, published in 1817, Governor Stamford Raffles predicted a migration from Java to Indonesia's 'outer islands', suggesting 'the immense tracts of unoccupied or thinly peopled territories on Sumatra, Borneo and the numerous islands scattered over the Archipelago, may be ready to receive colonies, arts and civilization from the metropolis of the Indian seas.'[1] However, resettlement from Java to the 'outer islands', known originally as *kolonisatie*, began under the authority of the Netherlands Indies colonial government in 1905 as colonial policy shifted from resource and labour exploitation towards a greater concern for human welfare, endorsed in the Ethical Policy.[2] It began with the relocation of 155 families from Java to Gedong Tataan in Lampung, southern Sumatra, with the aim of ameliorating poverty and resource conflicts in Java and spurring economic development in the 'outer islands'. The post-independence term transmigration has been taken to mean: 'The removal and/or transfer of population from one area to settle in another area determined upon within the

1 Raffles 1817, 71.
2 Cribb 1993.

27

territory of the Republic of Indonesia, in the interests of the country's development, or for other reasons considered necessary by the government.'[3]

Since modest beginnings in the early part of the 20th century, to date millions of landless and land-poor Javanese (alongside others from Bali, Madura and Lombok) have been relocated from their homeland, either supported directly, through the Indonesian government's transmigration resettlement programme, or moving in its wake without direct state support. Post-independence transmigration has focused on managing national unity, strengthening administrative control in peripheral areas and fostering state-led economic development.[4] With kolonisatie and transmigration has come the creation of 'little Javas' across a range of different agro-ecological and cultural settings in Indonesia: communities often named after villages of origin, in which are found land use practices as well as socio-cultural and linguistic characteristics congruent with those of a Javanese homeland. Years on, descendants of Javanese colonists and transmigrants who have no material connection with their grandparents' village of origin, and may have never even visited Java, are seen to retain an affective sense of their Javanese identity. Moreover, living amidst people of other ethnicities, consciousness of difference in various realms of everyday life (from family life to community ritual) means that at times Javanese identities are reinforced and elaborated.

The concept of 'diaspora' provides a useful framework for examining the cultural politics of both kolonisatie and the transmigration programme, as it enables a focus on the cultural workings of Javanese communities established within Indonesia but outside Java. 'Diaspora' is a term that challenges place-based discourses of identity and essentialised constructions of the 'native' or indigenous person. Instead, the focus turns to the idea of a shared diasporic experience.[5] The history of the settlement of landless Javanese to other parts of Indonesia shares three characteristics associated with the

---

3 Definition given in Clause 1 of the *Basic Transmigration Act* of 1972, cited in Hardjono 1977, xiv.

4 Tirtosudarmo 1990; Elmhirst 1999.

5 Bhaba 1994; Clifford 1994.

histories of transnational diasporas. First, like many transnational diasporas, Indonesia's internal Javanese diaspora has a strong, if indirect, association with the state-sponsored movement of labour to serve a colonial and post-colonial plantation economy. From the 1930s onwards, kolonisatie from Java to Lampung was linked with the reproduction of the plantation economy, as the programme focused on the expansion of wet rice agriculture into forested areas of Lampung province to produce cheap food for landless colonial plantation labour.[6] Even today, the Indonesian government's trans-migration programme is coupled with the development of large-scale oil palm estates and the reproduction of a plantation workforce.[7] Second, those resettled appear to have retained a sense of 'Java' as a symbolic 'home': a source of norms and values. Obvious vestiges of Javanese culture are seen in the marriage practices, 'traditional' culture-forms such as *gamelan* orchestras and *wayang kulit* (shadow puppets) performances – and language that remain strong in trans-migrant communities. Moreover, forms of political administration, land use, and livelihood practices echo those found in Java.[8] Third, in a similar vein to cultural processes found amidst transnational di-aspora, transmigrant Javanese identities have been remade and per-haps reinforced through sometimes uneasy relationships with host communities in and around resettlement areas *within* Indonesia.

This chapter traces the origins, practices and socio-cultural dy-namics of Indonesia's internal 'Javanese' diaspora, focusing on reset-tlement from Java to the southern Sumatran province of Lampung. It draws on historical and popular textual sources, together with more contemporary ethnographic research undertaken in a trans-migration settlement founded in the early 1980s. In excavating the cultural politics of this particular aspect of the Javanese diaspora, the chapter focuses on the interplay between a changing political culture and everyday practices of identity, as the latter are expressed through discourses and practices around land use and livelihood. Throughout, the figure of the Javanese smallholder farmer features

---

6   Pain et al. 1989.

7   Potter 2012.

8   Elmhirst 1999; Hoey 2003.

in both dominant and subaltern imaginaries in colonial, New Order, and post-reform eras, and has been pivotal in the identity politics of Indonesia's internal Javanese diaspora. Various forms of iconography depict the 'typical' rice farmer, with their conical hat, wielding a hoe or driving a bullock cart. Former President Suharto made much of his Javanese farmer roots, appealing to a populist idea of a Javanese rice farmer.

The chapter begins by exploring the reproduction of Javanese identity in the Netherlands Indies' kolonisatie project, as the colonial authorities sought to encourage movement from Java and to create a 'home from home' for resettled landless Javanese. Some of these themes continue into the independence era, particularly during Suharto's New Order, where Javanese identity is forged through the planning and implementation of the transmigration resettlement programme. As a case study from northern Lampung shows, Javanese identity is also reproduced through the discourses and practices of transmigrants themselves. Finally, the chapter examines the ways in which a Javanese transmigrant diaspora is being reimagined in a changing political landscape where regional autonomy is giving renewed importance to place-based sources of political and cultural authority, which contrasts with the cultural politics of geographically dispersed communities connected by a sense of common origin.

Forging a Javanese Diaspora: Kolonisatie and Lampung's 'Little Javas'

Planned settlement schemes ('colonisation') became a feature of Dutch colonial activity at the beginning of the 20th century, when the Ethical Policy (1900) was devised to counter poverty and land fragmentation in Java brought about in part by the Dutch *Cultuurstelsel* or forced cultivation system for cash crops.[9] In 1905 the first families were moved from the densely populated and increasingly impoverished Kedu plain of Java to Gedong Tataan in Lampung, to a ready-cleared site, which surveys had deemed to be appropriate for wet rice (*sawah*) cultivation.[10] These first settler families were allocated three

---

9 Tjondronegoro 1991.

10 Pelzer 1945.

quarters of a hectare of land, deemed to provide a 'sufficiency level' (*kecukupan*) income from irrigated rice cultivation, and in this way, Lampung's first 'little Java' was created in the form of the village of Bagelen, the name taken from an existing village in Java's cultural heartland around Yogyakarta. Between 1905 and 1911, 6,500 settlers were brought from Java to Lampung, paid for by the Netherlands Indies government.[11] However, it was not until the 1930s that kolonisatie began in earnest. Resettlement at this time was a response to the Great Depression, which had brought worsening socio-economic conditions to rural Java and the dismissal of Javanese labourers from plantations in India and the Dutch Caribbean colony of Suriname. Between 1932 and 1941, 162,000 colonists were relocated to areas in central Lampung (near what is now the city of Metro), made possible by considerable investment in irrigation technologies to provide the *sawah* (rice field) that was so important to encourage migration.[12]

The emergence of a Javanese diasporic identity in Lampung owes much to the ways Javanese people were introduced to Lampung province through this programme. In particular, the reinforcement and reproduction of Javanese identity at this point is associated with how ethnicity and cultural identity were understood, interpreted and categorised by the Netherlands Indies authorities. While categories of difference among people in the Indonesian archipelago predate the arrival of the Dutch, ideas associating regions, groups and linguistic forms took hold through colonial administrative practices, and in particular through the legal system in the Dutch codification of *adat*, which encompassed ideas about custom, law, tradition and territory.[13] An idiom of Javanese 'tradition' underpinned the vision of Assistant Resident H. G. Heyting, who was the architect of the kolonisatie experiment in the early 20th century, and who saw through its expansion in the 1930s. His idea was explicitly to create 'little Javas' ostensibly to attract reluctant Javanese to come to the unfamiliar and densely forested area of southern and central Lampung, and to remain there, with livelihoods based on the

---

11 Pelzer 1945.

12 McNicoll 1968.

13 Fasseur 1994.

seemingly timeless trope of Javanese wet rice farming.[14] The promise was that Javanese institutions and cultural practices would be preserved in these new colonies, and that the sawah area (engineered and paid for by the colonial government) would be held in communal ownership without period redistribution. During this period a sense of persistent connectedness to Java was produced and reinforced in four ways, through the efforts of the colonial authorities and through the practices of settlers themselves. First, ideas of 'Javaneseness' as rooted in a particular landscape (irrigated rice fields) and mode of living (smallholder rice farming) were actively promoted through the propaganda used, particularly in the 1930s, to encourage Javanese people to become colonists. The film *Tanah Sabrang, Land aan de Overkant,* made by the Dutch film-maker Mannus Franken in the 1930s to encourage poor Javanese farmers to join the kolonisatie programme, is an interesting example, in which characters drawn from the Javanese *wayang* plays were used to create an image of familiarity for Lampung. The landscapes in the film were predominantly lowland Javanese: wet rice terraces, home gardens and so on.[15] Similarly, the poster campaigns at this time depicted Javanese farmers working Javanese sawah in Lampung. In part, the idea was to encourage Javanese people to move to Lampung by offering the promise of the social status associated with owning sawah. Much of the effort that went into recruiting migrants involved driving this point home.

Second, in attempting to recreate a fetishised Javanese landscape, other features of Javanese rural life were also transplanted, including architectural forms, spatial planning principles, adat law and institutions (tenure systems, village administration), which sat outside of local Lampung practices. Javanese colonists were provided with a plot of sawah (around 0.7 hectares in today's measurement) per family, subsidised irrigation, a home garden (for fruit and vegetables), and the domestic and agricultural tools required to get started. As Jeffrey Kingston has noted, production of export crops was not encouraged; instead, Dutch concepts of 'rural Java' were imposed on the pioneer

---

14 Heyting 1921, *De Kolonisatie van Java afkomstige gezinnen,* cited in Pelzer 1945, 200; Kingston 1987.

15 Grasveld 1988.

settlements, effectively reproducing an idealised Javanese village into which settlers immersed themselves.[16] The cultivation parameters set by the colonial authorities thus shaped the livelihood practices of Javanese colonists and, in so doing, produced and reinforced a particular Javanese agrarian identity that stood in marked contrast with the livelihood practices and agricultural landscapes of the local population.

Third, colonial authorities invoked traditional collective arrangements associated with rural Java to subsidise the cost of setting up new settlements, with the aim of engendering a sense of familiarity and connectedness for Javanese migrants. Of these, the *bawon* share-cropping system was particularly important, in which newly arrived settlers took part in the rice harvest of established settlers as a way of making a living before themselves becoming land-owning, smallholder farmers.[17]

Fourth, affective ties to Java were powerfully reproduced through the provision of a set of gamelan instruments and wayang kulit shadow puppets to each colonisation village.[18] While those provided by the colonial authorities during the expansion of kolonisatie in the late 1930s were often a cheaper version, in the 'experimental phase' of the programme, it is notable that the initial settlers in Gedong Tataan received a gamelan set from Pakubuwono X Susuhunan of Surakarta, an important figure in Javanese royalty. Later, the colony established at Metro in central Lampung received a set of wayang kulit figures from the Sultan of Yogyakarta, Hamengkubuwono VII, thus reproducing an important spiritual link with Java's geographical and cultural hearth.

While it is clear that the colonial authorities had a hand to play in fostering the shape and identity politics of the Javanese diaspora in Lampung at this time, detailed ethnographic work by Kampto Utomo in the years following Independence reveals the part played by the everyday practices of Javanese colonists themselves, not least those exhibited by migrants coming from Java without direct

---

16 Kingston 1990, 486.

17 Kingston 1990; Pelzer 1945.

18 Pelzer 1945.

government support. By the late 1940s and into the 1950s, newly arrived migrants began colonising areas north of the original colonies around Gedong Tataan, in the area that became the subdistrict of Kalirejo, Way Sekampung. By 1957, eleven villages had been created, with a population of 18,000. Land was acquired from the head of the local Lampung clan (*Marga*),[19] usually by the leader of the pioneers, who was nominated as *kepala tebang* (chief clearer). As Utomo notes, if the harvest was good, the kepala tebang was able to attract followers and thus create a village territory, standing outside of Lampung's Marga administrative structure, with its own system of organisation, predicated on Javanese practices. The kepala tebang often became *lurah* (village head), and he would appoint a *carik* (village secretary) and others to administer the village, thus replicating an idealised *pamong desa*.[20] Observing the migrant colonies in Kalirejo in Lampung in the 1950s, Utomo writes:

> The Javanese pioneer villages [. . .] had learned to live together in mutual support, independent of the Lampung social system. Controversies among them, which were unavoidable in the process of development, failed to alter the fact that they all pursued a common goal, the establishment of Javanese villages. Thus they considered themselves as a new social unity with a common basis, common norms, common aspirations, and the same 'rhythm' of life.[21]

Thus, the outcome was the creation of separate spheres or contrasting cultural ecologies between the wet-rice landscapes of the Javanese diaspora and the extended fallow/upland rice/tree-crop landscapes of the local Lampung groups. Pelzer's observations, based on research undertaken in southern Sumatra between 1940

---

19 *Marga* is the term used for the highest social and territorial grouping of people in Lampung adat, and is organised through patrilineal descent. This was given formal recognition as a form of political and administrative organisation in 1928 when the colonial authorities granted *Inlandse Gemeente* (native community) status to Lampung's Marga (Pain et al. 1989; Van Royen 1930).

20 *Pamong desa* is a term derived from the Javanese verb *momong*, literally to take care of or foster. Utomo 1967.

21 Utomo 1967, 291.

and 1941, confirms the superimposition of Javanese landscapes into the forests of Lampung at this time:

> Land that in the past was either entirely unutilised or was used only occasionally by a hunter, gatherer or shifting cultivator, is fundamentally transformed. The forest disappears, and in its place, as far as the eye can see, stretch irrigated rice fields, interspersed here and there with villages set among gardens and groves of fruit trees. The colonies are strange isles, microcosms of Java, standing in the midst of a land whose peoples still practice methods of cultivation unknown on the plains of Java for generations.[22]

By 1941 the Lampung population was about 511,400, of whom less than half comprised the original Lampung-speaking population, with the rest made up of the 'little Javas'. This increase in the Javanese population was in part attributable to natural reproduction and also to the spontaneous migration of Javanese people that followed in the wake of the transmigration programme itself. The cultural dynamics of Indonesia's internal Javanese diaspora were therefore produced through a combination of colonial social engineering that reflected idealisations of Javanese rural life, and the everyday livelihood practices of pioneers. These pioneers were drawn to Lampung by the social status afforded from becoming a sawah owner, and their actions, in establishing themselves as rice farmers in Lampung, reinforced a Javanese identity. The emerging agro-ecological landscapes of the Javanese pioneers stood in marked contrast to that of the local Lampung people.

Transmigration: Reproducing Javanese Identity through State and Diasporic Practices

The figure of an idealised Javanese farmer has continued to run through the cultural politics of Indonesia's post-independence resettlement programme. Transmigration continued in the immediate post-independence period with the resettlement of veterans from the Independence struggle and repatriated labourers from Suriname.

---

22 Pelzer 1945, 231.

But it was under Suharto's New Order presidency (from the late 1960s to the late 1990s) that transmigration became a key element of state development policy, to address a number of development objectives, including political stability, the raising of national agricultural output, regional development and nation-building.[23] Continuing a theme first developed under the Dutch, in many instances, the transmigration programme of the New Order also created 'little Javas', landscapes, administrative structures, and cultural communities often quite different from those of the people already inhabiting the designated resettlement areas. As a people dispersed from a particular point (Java, or in some instances other 'little Javas' elsewhere in Lampung), who maintain an idea of 'Java' through their agricultural practices, and who do not necessarily feel a part of the host area, the shared experience of New Order transmigration in the 1970s and 1980s continued to give shape to a Javanese transmigrant diaspora, albeit in slightly different ways from its colonial antecedent.

A number of analyses of New Order transmigration have suggested that it was a way of promoting a nationalist vision and narrative of development and progress, based on a particular model of village life and rural livelihoods, which valorised a particular version of lowland Javanese cultural identity.[24] Hans Antlöv has described Suharto's notion of himself as a divine and benevolent ruler governing from an exemplary centre. These ideas crystallise in New Order transmigration: giving it a more explicit cultural flavour than was the case for kolonisatie during Dutch colonial rule.[25] Hoey suggests that for Suharto this was a personal project: the former president's biography draws on his own remembering of Gadjah Mada's ambition to build the unity and integrity of the Majapahit kingdom, which Suharto saw as manifest in his

---

23 The New Order era, presided over by President Suharto, was characterised by an authoritarian form of rule and a disenfranchisement of the population, made possible only because this phase of Indonesia's history was also marked by rapid economic growth conjured from the country's rich natural resource base, and generally raised levels of prosperity compared to the era preceding it.

24 Guinness 1994; Hoey 2003.

25 Antlöv 2005.

archipelagic vision of Indonesia (Nusantara).[26] Efforts to realise this vision hinged on bringing a Javanese 'centre' into the country's margins: either in the form of Javanese government officials representing the state in remote areas through the administration of transmigration settlements, or through the resettlement of poor Javanese migrant farmers, who would be set up as rice-farming smallholders.

To understand how and why a particular Javanese identity was asserted through transmigration in the 1980s, it is necessary to recognise that the practices of governance which made up the programme were themselves culturally embedded. The formal institutions (such as policy frameworks and jurisprudence) and more informal conventions, habits and routines associated with transmigration almost invariably emerged from a common cultural heritage among state authorities and the bureaucrats administering the programme. Their shared values were associated with a particular idea of traditional 'Javanese' cultural values of stability and harmony, effectively to support authoritarian practices, and as strategies for the repression of change and contestation.[27] The policies and practices associated with the New Order transmigration programme were important in promoting a 'design for living', coloured by an elite Javanese imaginary, and these ran through settlement administration models, land use policies and practices, and local political structures, fostering what Dove has referred to as the 'agroecological mythology' of the Javanese.[28] To illustrate the point, observations made of a transmigration settlement created in the early 1980s in northern Lampung are instructive of the state's role in producing a diasporic Javanese identity through transmigration. Perhaps echoing the community development described by Utomo,[29] the built environment, administrative structure and village practices in this transmigration settlement are modelled on an idea of the 'village' which owes much to an idealised notion of what constitutes a 'Javanese' village: defined territorially, densely populated and divided into neighbourhoods, or *rukun* (harmony).[30]

---

26 Hoey 2003.

27 Antlöv 2005; Pemberton 1994.

28 Dove 1985.

29 Utomo 1967.

30 Antlöv 2005.

In northern Lampung's transmigration areas, this has contrasted markedly with surrounding Lampungese administrative systems which, despite the efforts of the local state, had until recently remained largely genealogy-based and to some extent non-territorial. 'Javaneseness' finds its material expression in the architecture of official buildings such as village halls and meeting places, which have been constructed along the lines of a 'Javanese' *pendopo*, a building comprising a raised platform and a roof supported by pillars, but without enclosing walls. According to Shelly Errington, this pillared pavilion form was traditionally used by 'Javanese' persons of status to receive visitors. It is symbolically representative of other signs of Javanese-Indic kingship such as the banyan tree, the royal umbrella and the sacred mountain.[31] The rhythm of village life is marked not only by sawah cultivation (in contrast to the tree crops and swidden cultivation that has historically existed among local Lampung communities), but also by officially-sanctioned 'traditions' which take place in the transmigration settlement, and which are refracted through a 'Javanese' lens. These include 'traditional' community labour practices (such as *gotong royong* or mutual assistance), imposed across the country to secure free labour for public infrastructure projects,[32] and 'Javanese' ritual feasts (*slametan*), which are the staple of local government ceremonial activities.

A 'Javanese' agro-ecological imaginary underpinned the planning blue-prints on which the transmigration settlement was devised. This shaped the land allocation for transmigrants (a combination of rice field and home garden), the kinds of assistance available to them (for example, seeds and fertiliser), and the activities of agricultural extension workers. Together, these elements promoted sedentary food-crop agriculture, including sawah cultivation (albeit without the necessary investment in irrigation technology,) contrasting with the cultivation of swamp rice (as a staple), and the shifting cultivation and traditional agroforestry systems among neighbouring local Lampung populations. As Patrice Levang has suggested, underlying efforts to promote these kinds of agriculture in Lampung has been a

---

31 Errington 1997.

32 Bowen 1986.

sense that 'modern' Javanese agricultural practices would diffuse and replace 'backward' local Lampung farming systems.[33] Effectively, this gave shape to the kinds of livelihood practices people were able to engage in, and configured permissible 'Javanese' farmer identities.

While observations noted here are drawn from research in a transmigration settlement in Lampung, similar versions of Javanese cultural identity were replicated, if not always fully realised, across Indonesia, enforced by local political and administrative structures and absorbed by those who derived benefit from fitting into it. In a politically authoritarian context where resources were hard to come by, Javanese migrants in northern Lampung had largely embraced this version of Javanese identity to enhance their eligibility for the assistance and support associated with the programme, and contrasted themselves with 'backward' Lampungese people. In the words of one prominent Javanese farmer interviewed in the late 1990s: 'The Lampungese are very different from us. Their customs are still very strong and they are not yet "progressive".[34] Through the discourses and policies of the transmigration programme, and the practices of transmigrants within this, an important and powerful Javanese transmigrant identity was being forged – a reactionary diasporic project – that related less to attachments to particular places in rural Java, but, following John Pemberton, more to the New Order state's appropriation of tradition to serve repressive political ends.[35]

While the production of Indonesia's internal Javanese diaspora owes much to the conservative traditionalism that typified the cultural politics of the New Order era through the practice of an exemplary centre and an administrative periphery,[36] Javanese diasporic identities have also been forged through the everyday practices of those resettled. As Andrew Beatty notes, village ideas and practices are not always like those of the centre.[37] Though they may appear similar, other practices persist in their shadow, contradicting, parodying and

---

33 Levang 1989.

34 Field notes, 24 February 1995.

35 Pemberton 1994.

36 Antlöv 2005.

37 Beatty 2012.

complementing the dominant mode. In transmigration, identities are not just formed through the 'disciplinary geopolitics' of transmigration discourses and practices, but through the ways in which these are resisted and reworked by individuals and collectivities, often with unintended (and not necessarily positive) consequences.

In Lampung Javanese transmigrant identities are also reproduced through the discourses and actions of migrants as they encounter their Lampung hosts. Discussions of cultural difference are a great provider of conversation about variations in language, social etiquette and food in Indonesia generally, and this was also the case in the transmigration settlement area where Javanese migrants and local Lampung people compared their customs and practices. However, pressures on livelihood and resources meant that what might otherwise be delight in diversity sometimes manifested itself through metaphors of moral disapproval about the practices of the other group. In transmigration, where Javanese transmigrants and Lampung people were brought together, contestations of meaning and identity were most intense in the space between the two communities, and struggles over land and livelihood were frequently articulated through an idiom of cultural difference. These struggles rarely took on an overt physical or violent form. Rather, by far the most common way in which the two groups interacted and challenged each other's legitimacy was through the hidden and sometimes not so hidden 'transcripts'[38] – gossip and rumour – through which one group represented and resisted the actions and representations of the other.

The transcripts that circulated in each community had an important effect on how people were able to conduct their lives under the eyes of neighbours watching for any sign of transgression. This scrutiny of practices effectively structured behaviour in line with what was deemed to be the proper conduct of individual and collective lives. Fear of ridicule or malicious gossip from neighbours is particularly important in contexts such as this, where extra-household relations are important for maintaining the flow of life. In both transmigrant and local communities, the good regard of neighbours (and relatives) was an important factor of life, as people depended

---

38 Scott 1990.

on others for small loans and lines of patronage governing access to material and non-material resources.

Many of the transcripts concerning appropriate behaviour emerged around discussions of livelihood issues and livelihood practices, particularly around which of these were deemed to be traditional or modern. This particular code owes much to state-level discourses about modernity in Indonesia which, as Mary-Beth Mills has pointed out for Thailand, 'contrast the "modern" institutions and practices located in urban centres of power with the "traditional" ways of rural communities and regional minorities.'[39] Activities and behaviours considered to be 'modern' have a positive ascription, while those regarded as 'traditional' are negative. Between Javanese transmigrants and local Lampung people, phrases such as *'masih di belakang'* (still behind), were contrasted with *'sudah maju'* (already progressive, modern) to describe different ways of life. Interviews and observation suggested that this type of evaluation was important among Javanese transmigrants, perhaps because of its linkage with the New Order state and its Javanese centre, and also its representation of 'development' through transmigration.

One of the thrusts of transmigration policy was to bring progress and 'modern' agriculture to 'backward' regions of Indonesia. Javanese transmigrants, therefore, evaluated their 'modern' behaviour against the 'traditional' behaviours of their Lampung neighbours. According to a prominent member of the farmers' group (*kelompok tani*) in the transmigration settlement: 'The Lampung people are very different from us. Their adat is still very strong and they are not "progressive" (*adat masih kuat sekali, dan belum maju*).'[40]

Transmigrants contrasted themselves with the Lampung people through rice farming practices, which for them included an aspiration to use modern varieties and methods, the use of which would cement their status as 'progressive' (that is not traditional) farmers. By contrast, transmigrants viewed the swidden rice farming of local Lampung people, which at the time of this research was still in evidence, to be backward and culturally anachronistic.

---

39 Mills 1995, 248.

40 Field notes, 5 December 1994.

The hard work of Javanese farmers in their rice fields was considered by local Lampung people to be base and coarse (*kasar*), and their attempts to supplement meagre agricultural incomes with plantation wage labour similarly was labelled in pejorative terms. Uncertain agricultural incomes for local Lampung people were augmented by various business ventures, which in turn were regarded by Javanese migrants as 'base'. As one transmigrant noted: 'They [local Lampung people] are rough, all they think about is money. For myself, religion is more important.'[41] That transmigrants can believe this, but at the same time value modern agriculture (and the pursuit of profit through farming) shows the tensions and paradoxes which are apparent in these representations. In sum, a strong sense of there being 'some things that we do, some things which they do', pervades livelihood discourses in both communities, bringing with it elaborated expressions of a Javanese identity around what constitutes a 'true' farmer, chiming in with Suharto's agrarian fantasies of Javaneseness.

This slippage is evident in the ways Javanese identity is expressed by women transmigrants as they compare themselves with a local Lampung 'other'. In discussing the contrasts between themselves and Lampungese women, Javanese transmigrant women often allude to notions of 'strength' (*kekuatan*), which they compare with the 'weakness' of the Lampungese women. This notion of 'strength' is very different from the quiet strength of Indonesia's most famous Javanese female icon, Raden Ayu Kartini[42] – an icon appropriated by the state to foster particular ideas about Indonesian womanhood – and is also dissimilar to the much-noted raucous strength of Javanese market women in their tough trading tactics.[43] Rather, it is an idea of 'strength' that has grown out of this particular group

---

41 Field notes, 10 December 1994.

42 Raden Adjeng Kartini (1879–1904) was the daughter of a Javanese civil service official made famous internationally for the correspondence she exchanged with Dutch friends, and which were later published. Whilst she was an important advocate for girls' education, her own life was shaped by the confinements expected of women born into the Javanese elite, with an expectation of being demure, obedient and passive.

43 Brenner 1995.

of transmigrant women's common experience: first, in coming from Java to Lampung; second, on being forced to join the transmigration programme for resettlement to the newly opened transmigration sites in northern Lampung; and third, as Javanese transmigrants struggling to make a living in the harsh environment of their new home. Their life stories narrate female identities borne out of considerable hardship: family breakdown; running away from parents; hiding from the state authorities; contending with disease, poverty, and persistent crop failure in the transmigration settlement; and exhibiting great feats of physical strength as they struggled to overcome labour shortages and/or desertion by feckless husbands.

Two women's stories illustrate the ways in which a femininity based on strength in adversity is being constructed in ways that contradict dominant constructions of gendered Javanese identity within a 'Javanese' diaspora. Ibu Sita has lived in northern Lampung since the early 1980s, when she was first transmigrated. Since then, poverty has meant her having to take on heavy agricultural tasks on the land given to them by the transmigration authorities, as her husband sought to make ends meet by casual logging and plantation work. They were lucky enough to be allocated land that could be converted into sawah, but labour shortages meant that the only person available to work it was Ibu Sita. This meant her learning to plough the heavy soil herself – a job usually given to a man with a cattle-drawn plough. At first, her efforts attracted ridicule, directed in particular at her husband (a rather small man), as ploughing wet rice fields is almost universally a male task in Indonesia. 'Why should I care?' she said. 'Life is difficult here. We are poor migrants. If a job has to be done, it is done. By me. It is better to be like that than just quiet in the house like a Lampung woman.' Although her husband had initially been embarrassed by his wife's feats of strength, her abilities had attracted some measure of admiration. 'Pak Wagiman's wife can plough like a man!' they would say. Far from being a delicate Javanese princess, Ibu Sita wears her physical strength proudly, in the knowledge that she has the tenacity to cope with the adversities of being a migrant.[44]

Ibu Marni has shown similar 'unfeminine' singularity in dealing with the problems of being a transmigrant, emphasising her strength

---

44 Field notes, 14 December 1994.

to cope with a feckless husband, get rid of him, and find another, more manageable husband to farm alongside. Arriving as a transmigrant in the early 1980s, she had to deal with her husband's drinking. 'He drank away all our money', she said. 'In the end, I thought I might as well drink also, seeing as the money was going to be lost in any case!' With no family to turn to, Ibu Marni set about getting rid of her husband and from then on coped on her own, supporting her three young children without the extended family links that might be available were she not a migrant. She married a recently divorced neighbour: a mild and unassuming man who worked hard on the land and 'gave me no trouble'.[45] In reflecting on her experiences, Ibu Marni contrasted her life with that of her Lampung neighbours, as she frequently visited the Lampung village to sell chillies and other vegetables. 'I feel sorry for them', she said. 'They are very constrained, not free as we are. If their husband is unkind, they have to stay with him. Just follow him. For me, I could never do that, not now. My life has been hard, but I learned to stand alone. Lampung women are too afraid to do that. In my opinion, transmigrant women are better at coping.'[46] In different ways, both of these women exemplify a new kind of gendered Javanese identity within the diaspora, which contrasts not only with Lampung ideas of femininity, but also contests dominant ideas of gendered Javaneseness.

Transmigration has been a state policy applied through the cultural politics of the Suharto era, which have contributed to the fostering of conservative traditionalism and fetishised forms of Javanese identity. However, observations from a transmigration settlement in northern Lampung suggest that the narratives and practices of transmigrants themselves highlight the importance of material contingencies and internal variations, and the possibility of 'other Javas' away from the *kraton* (palace). As Beatty has noted, village ideas and practices – answering, as they do, to quite different structures and needs – are not and probably never have been like those of the centre.[47] He goes on to suggest that these differences are

---

45 Field notes, 15 December 1994.

46 Field notes, 15 December 1994.

47 Beatty 2012.

once again becoming visible since the fall of Suharto's New Order, as political reform (*Reformasi*) and moves towards regional autonomy in Indonesia lessen the cultural power of the country's centre.

Political Reform and Regional Autonomy: A Javanese Transmigrant Diaspora Reimagined

Political reform (*Reformasi*), which began in the late 1990s, is an ongoing and much debated project in Indonesia. Broadly it has encompassed a shift from the centralised authoritarianism to decentralised democracy, relocating powers from central government in Jakarta to the regions, granting greater importance to local offices such as *bupati* (district heads), mayors and local parliaments. This has provided a new context in which to understand both transmigration and the conceptual possibility of a Javanese diaspora in Indonesia. An important consequence of Reformasi, and in particular, the decentralisation of power and authority, has been a renewed emphasis on the role of ethnic or regional cultural identity in underpinning struggles for political authority and access to economic resources. A number of studies have alluded to the district- and province-level campaigns for *putra daerah*, literally, 'sons of the soil', where territorially-defined ethnic groups, invoking notions of a place-based cultural identity, sought to address their perceived political and economic marginalisation within decision-making structures.[48] Transmigration, as emblematic of centralised state power, is seen as problematic in a political sense (as decision-making is devolved to the district level), but also as a somewhat anachronistic cultural project in the context of decentralisation of cultural authority in Indonesia.

As Lesley Potter has noted, despite early suggestions that Reformasi (and in particular, political decentralisation) would spell the end of transmigration as a national-level project, this has not been the case. Rather, the programme has been reinvented, becoming aligned more closely with the development aspirations of districts, particularly in providing labour for agro-industrial development, rather than being heralded as a means to achieve national development

---

48 Robison and Hadiz 2004.

agendas.[49] With a focus more squarely on facilitating transactions between sending and receiving districts, in 2000 the former Ministry of Transmigration and Squatter Resettlement became the Ministry of Manpower and Transmigration. A central focus was on spatial affinity: developing urbanised regional growth centres linked to agro-industrial development, particularly around oil palm, and on lifting people out of poverty in densely populated districts where work opportunities are limited. Sending areas now include districts in Lampung, East Nusa Tenggara and West Nusa Tenggara as well as those located in Java and Bali, and thus to a much greater extent the programme involves the movement of a number of different ethnic groups aside from those that identify as Javanese. Ethnicity has not gone away, however. Potter notes that districts in West and Central Kalimantan refused to take transmigrants from East Java in case Madurese households were involved: an indication that memories of the ethnic violence in the mid-1990s between local Dayak and Madurese transmigrants remain powerful.[50] That said, the implicit cultural politics that gave shape to New Order transmigration and that attracted accusations of it being a vehicle for 'Javanisation' appear to have been played down and indeed have given way to an emphasis on the economic management of *Indonesian* labour supply to fuel natural resource-based economic growth.

For Lampung's Javanese transmigrant diaspora, these debates have played out in interesting ways. Early on in the Reformasi period, the ethnic organisation Lampung Sai made its voice heard in the province's two main urban centres, Bandar Lampung and Metro (a city created out of kolonisatie and transmigration). According to Gerry van Klinken, the argument made was that Javanese (descendants of colonists) had been running the place for too long and local bureaucratic positions and business favours should be reserved for regional sons.[51] Over the course of the New Order, Javanese (and in some cases, Sundanese) held most political positions in Lampung. Following the implementation of Regional Autonomy Laws at the end of the 1990s, ethnicity, and by

---

49 Potter 2012.

50 Potter 2012.

51 Van Klinken 2009.

extension, peoples' region of origin, bacome an important element in the context of direct elections for local positions of political power. By 2010, a locally-born Lampung person had been elected in seven of the province's eleven districts (*kabupaten*), while two district heads were Javanese who had been 'Lampungised' through a *mawori*, an adat ceremony in which a Lampung name is granted to a non-Lampung person.[52] Outside the confines of district- and provincial-level political debate, the frustrations of poor local Lampung people could be vocalised in ways that were not so possible under the repressive New Order, and these generally centred on an idea of transmigrants being favoured by the authorities, enjoying better access to state largesse, with local Lampung people being poor and marginalised.

Responses to this new political and cultural landscape in Lampung reflect in part efforts to signal the multiculturalism of the province, and to include double-headed campaigns for political office, in which a Lampungese candidate (representing 'local' people) runs with a Javanese (or Sundanese) deputy (representing descendants of transmigrants), and vice-versa. However, criticisms of transmigration itself, and the ways in which a transmigrant diaspora is represented, are surprisingly muted, perhaps reflecting, as Isabelle Côté has observed in Riau, an idea that negative views of organised migration are seen as unconstitutional and anti-development.[53] This point is illustrated well by the founding and design of the relatively newly established National Museum of Transmigration, located in Bagelen – the place which hosted the very first colonists from Java back in 1905. While carefully avoiding any suggestion that transmigration could be conflated with 'Javanisation', the explicit purpose of the museum is to showcase the development benefits that transmigration has brought throughout Indonesia.[54] Implicitly, the museum is emblematic of an imagineering of the Javanese transmigrant cultural heritage.

The museum is the realisation of the vision of Professor Dr Muhajir Utomo, former rector of Lampung University (UNILA), as an edu-

---

52 Côté 2014.

53 Côté 2014.

54 Department of Transmigration (n.d.), depnakertrans.lampungprov.go.id// uptd/museum-transmigrasi/.

cational facility to document and explain the history of kolonisatie and transmigration, and to house various artefacts relating to these programmes.[55] It was originally conceived in the early Reformasi period, partly to counter negative representations of transmigration's history and impact, and to reiterate the role it could play in fostering multicultural nation-building and regional development in the future.[56] Its initiation coincided with the centenary of kolonisatie in Lampung, which was marked, somewhat controversially, in 2005, at a time when sensitivities around the perceived economic and political marginalisation of Lampung's original population were being voiced. The museum itself officially opened in 2010.[57]

Reading the museum as a narrative representation of transmigration and the history of Indonesia's internal Javanese diaspora, most striking is the way its design mimics that used for Taman Mini Indonesia Indah (Beautiful Indonesia in Miniature), the theme park on the edge of Jakarta founded by the wife of President Suharto in the 1970s. Taman Mini forms an open air museum containing structures and displays to exemplify the different cultures of Indonesia, principally through costume, architecture and cultural forms. As with Taman Mini, what is interesting in the museum's depiction of transmigration concerns what is privileged and what is ignored.[58] Over a 20-hectare site the museum landscape includes a series of ten pavilions ('traditional' houses), each reflecting the geographical rather than ethnic origins of all of those who have been 'transmigrated': from Bali, Madura, West Nusa Tenggara, West Java, Central Java, East Java, Banten, Yogyakarta, Nusa Tenggara Barat (Lombok), East Nusa Tenggara Timur, Jakarta and Suriname. Ethnicity or any sense of a 'Javanese' flavour to transmigration is disavowed in the basing of 'traditional' buildings on administrative regions. In the main building, these depictions of participation in transmigration are then anchored within narratives of development, progress and

---

55 *Kompas* 2010, regional.kompas.com/read/2010/05/02/15472534/Pemerintah. Dirikan.Museum.Transmigrasi.

56 Utomo 2007.

57 *Berita Lampung* 2010, berita-lampung.blogspot.com/2010/05/museum-transmigrasi-menjadi-landmark.html.

58 Errington 1997.

modernisation through a sequence of displays designed to show the 'colonisation' process, from arrival and forest clearing, through to a somewhat aspirational depiction of the *Kota Terpadu Mandiri* or 'Integrated Self-Sufficient City', noted by Potter as part of the new transmigration paradigm.[59]

It is in the displays of transmigrant material culture and the collected narratives of transmigrant experience that representations of a Javanese diasporic subjectivity seep through: ancient farm implements (including the emblematic *ani-ani*, the finger knife used by Javanese in the rice harvest), miniaturised sawah land-scapes (which are pictured in a march of progress, replacing the dense forest, swidden and hunting grounds of the local Lampung people) and household items that represent the material culture of Lampung's 'little Javas' and the Javanese 'agro-ecological imaginary' on which such landscapes and livelihoods are based. Like Taman Mini, the transmigration museum effectively represents the past as an integral part of the future, and in offering a version of 'one nation' transmigration, it attempts to signal the shared nationhood of all transmigrants and local people (although their experiences, whether in Lampung or in other parts of Indonesia, are not exhibited) in a singular Indonesian progress narrative, a vision that is nevertheless inflected with materialised reminders that transmigration is part and parcel of the forging of a Javanese diaspora in Indonesia.

Conclusion

This chapter began by considering the ways in which the Netherlands Indies government's kolonisatie project and the post-independence Indonesian government's transmigration programme have fostered and reproduced a Javanese diaspora within Indonesia. It has largely focused on the ways in which the cultural politics of Indonesia's internal Javanese diaspora have played out in Lampung province, home to the very first Javanese colonists in the early 20th century. In somewhat different ways, the execution of both kolonisatie and transmigration drew on and elaborated notions of Javanese culture and identity, using material and cultural forms to foster a feeling

---

59 Potter 2012.

of 'home' for newly arrived migrants, which in turn had the effect
of reiterating affective ties to a Javanese 'home', albeit one that was
largely imagined by the colonial and transmigrant authorities. In addition, the inflection of state-led development and nation-building
with notions of Javaneseness during the New Order period, when
transmigration was at its height, contributed to the shape of diasporic identity in important ways, through the built environment,
administration, and socio-political culture of transmigration settlements. Within the programme, Javanese transmigrants were seen
as harbingers of progress, representing the centre in the country's
unruly and non-Javanese margins.

However, this is not a seamless process: the cultural politics of
Indonesia's internal Javanese diaspora are also shaped by the experiences and practices of Javanese settlers, particularly as they deal with
a potentially hostile host population. In this respect, this particular
part of the Javanese diaspora shares many characteristics with
the transnational Javanese diaspora, at times elaborating Javanese
cultural forms, sometimes in unexpected and contradictory ways.
More recently, the cultural politics of a Javanese transmigrant diaspora have taken on a renewed significance in the context of political
reform and an accompanying strengthening of the importance of
place-based identities as decentralised governance takes hold. In
Lampung this has meant a new era for the descendants of Javanese
transmigrants, once seen as privileged in their access to state resources when compared with local Lampung people. Specifically,
the opening up of more freedom of speech has meant that criticisms
of the transmigration programme are heard loudly and clearly. In
the face of the possible threats to peace and harmony that this kind
of reversal of ethnic fortunes could potentially represent, there are
attempts to reclaim transmigration, and by extension the Javanese
transmigrant diaspora, as a tool for national integration, progressive
multiculturalism and regional development, an idea showcased in
Lampung's recently founded National Museum of Transmigration.
In this, a theme has opened up that runs parallel to the Indonesian
government's wider interest in the Javanese diaspora internationally; that is, the role such a phenomenon can play in fostering
economic development and integration within a wider context of
nation-building.

References

Antlöv, H. 2005. 'The Social Construction of Power and Authority in Java'. In *The Java That Never Was: Academic Theories and Political Practices*, ed. H. Antlöv and J. Hellman, 43–66. Münster: LITVERLAG.

Beatty, A. 2012. 'Kala Defanged: Managing Power in Java Away from the Centre', *Bijdragen tot de Taal-, Land- en Volkenkunde* 168(2/3): 173–194.

Bhaba, H. 1994. *The Location of Culture*. London: Routledge.

Bowen, J. R. 1986. 'On the Political Construction of Tradition: Gotong Royong in Indonesia', *The Journal of Asian Studies* 45(3): 545–561.

Brenner, S. 1995. 'Why Women Rule the Roost: Rethinking Javanese Ideologies of Gender and Self-Control'. In *Bewitching Women, Pious Men: Gender and Body Politics in Southeast Asia*, ed. A. Ong and M. Peletz, 19–50. Berkeley: University of California Press.

Clifford, J. 1994. 'Diasporas', *Cultural Anthropology* 9: 302–338.

Côté, I. 2014. 'Internal Migration and the Politics of Place: A Comparative Analysis of China and Indonesia', *Asian Ethnicity* 15(1): 111–129.

Cribb, R. 1993. 'Development Policy in the Early 20th Century'. In *Development and Social Welfare: Indonesia's Experiences under the New Order*, ed. J.-P. Dirkse, F. Hüsken and M. Rutten, 225–245. Leiden: KITLV Press.

Dove, M. 1985. 'The Agroecological Mythology of the Javanese and the Political Economy of Indonesia', *Indonesia* 39: 1–36.

Elmhirst, R. 1999. 'Space, Identity Politics and Resource Control in Indonesia's Transmigration Programme', *Political Geography* 18: 813–835.

Errington, S. 1997. 'The Cosmic Theme Park of the Javanese', *Review of Indonesian and Malaysian Affairs* 31: 7–36.

Fasseur, C. 1994. 'Cornerstone and Stumbling Block: Racial Classification and the Late Colonial state in Indonesia'. In *The Late Colonial State in Indonesia: Political and Economic Foundations of the Netherlands Indies 1880-1942*, ed. R. Cribb, 31–56. Leiden: KITLV Press.

Grasveld, F. 1988. *Tanah Sabrang: Land aan de Overkant: Landbouwkolonisatie en wayang in een film van Mannus Franken*. Amsterdam: Mannus Franken Stichting and Koninklijk Instituut voor de Tropen / Hilversum: Nederlands Film Instituut.

Guinness, P. 1994. 'Local Society and Culture'. In *Indonesia's New Order: The Dynamics of Socio-Economic Transformation*, ed. H. Hill, 267–304. Sydney: Allen and Unwin.

Hardjono, J. 1977. *Transmigration in Indonesia*. Kuala Lumpur: Oxford University Press.

Hoey, B. 2003. 'Nationalism in Indonesia: Building Imagined and Intentional Communities through Transmigration', *Ethnology* 42(2): 109–126.

51

Kingston, J. 1987. 'Agricultural Involution among Lampung's Javanese', *Southeast Asian Studies* 27(4): 485–507.

Levang, P. 1989. 'Farming Systems and Household Incomes'. In *Transmigration and Spontaneous Migrations in Indonesia*, ed. M. Pain, 193–284. Bondy, France: ORSTOM / Jakarta: Department of Transmigration.

Mills, M.-B. 1995. 'Attack of the Widow Ghosts: Gender, Death, and Modernity in Northeast Thailand'. In *Bewitching Women, Pious Men: Gender and Body Politics in Southeast Asia*, ed. A. Ong and M. Peletz, 244–273. Berkeley: University of California Press.

McNicoll, G. 1968. 'Internal Migration in Indonesia: Descriptive Notes', *Indonesia* 5: 29–92.

Pain, M., D. Benoit, P. Levang and O. Sevin, eds 1989. *Transmigration and Spontaneous Migration in Indonesia*. Bondy, France: ORSTOM.

Pelzer, K. 1945. *Pioneer Settlements in the Asiatic Tropics: Studies in Land Untilization and Agricultural Colonization in Southeastern Asia*. Special Publication Series no. 29. New York: American Geographical Society.

Pemberton, J. 1994. *On the Subject of 'Java'*. Ithaca: Cornell University Press.

Potter, L. 2012. 'New Transmigration "Paradigm" in Indonesia: Examples from Kalimantan', *Asia Pacific Viewpoint* 53: 272–287.

Raffles, T. S. 1817. *The History of Java*. Volume I. London: Black, Parbury and Allen.

Robison, R. and V. Hadiz 2004. *Reorganizing Power in Indonesia: The Politics of Oligarchy in an Age of Markets*. London: Routledge.

Scott, J. C. 1990. *Domination and the Arts of Resistance: Hidden Transcripts*. New Haven: Yale University Press.

Tirtosudarmo, R. 1990. *Transmigration Policy and National Development Plans in Indonesia (1969–88)*. Canberra: National Centre for Development Studies / Research School of Pacific Studies, Australian National University.

Tjondronegoro, S. M. P. 1991. 'Colonists and Transmigrants in Agricultural Development: Planned and Sponsored Resettlement in Indonesia'. In *Migrants in Agricultural Development: A Study of Intrarural Migration*, ed. J. A. Mollett, 132–152. London: Macmillan.

Utomo, K. (Sajogyo) 1967. 'Villages of Unplanned Settlers in the Sub-district Kaliredjo, Central Lampung'. In *Villages in Indonesia*, ed. Koentjaraningrat, 281–298. Ithaca: Cornell University Press.

Utomo, M. 2007. 'Transmigrasi: Membangun dan merekatkan Bangsa', *Lampung Post* 12 December. [www.lampungpost.com/cetak/berita.php?id=2007121201193256]

Van Klinken, Gerry 2009. 'Decolonization and the Making of Middle Indonesia', *Urban Geography* 30: 879–897.

Van Royen, J. W. 1930. *Catatan Mengenai Marga-Marga Lampung [Nota over de Lampoengsche Mergas]*. Series B, Number 7. Departement van Binnenlandsch Bestuur. Weltevreden. Translated by R. Rusli. Jakarta: Department of the Interior.

CHAPTER 2

A Shared Sense of Belonging

The Javanese in Southeast Sulawesi

AGUS SUWIGNYO AND WIDARATIH KAMISO[1]

My family and I left Java for a better life. If we did not improve our lives compared to what we had in Java, then we would have returned to Java, no matter what.

(Sumantri, a migrant from Yogyakarta in Kendari, Southeast Sulawesi, interviewed in August 2014)

Introduction

The migration of Javanese people from Java to Southeast Sulawesi is part and parcel of two government policies: *kolonisatie*, a colonial programme by the Netherlands Indies government (1905–1940), and the *transmigrasi* programme by the Republic of Indonesia (1948–1998). These resettlement programmes have been studied extensively, yet very few have explored the socio-cultural dimensions of the migrants' life in their new homes.[2] While resettlement programmes often create intertwined issues arising from questions of land ownership,[3] the long-term socio-cultural dimensions that concern re-formation of identity, space orientation and subjectivity in a hybrid intercultural setting are largely neglected. Moreover, in

---

1   We would like to thank the History Department of Universitas Gadjah Mada for the grant under the RKAT-scheme that enabled us to do field research in Kendari and adjacent transmigration resettlement areas in August 2014. Our thanks also go to Wening Pamujiasih for her assistance in collecting archival and interview data during the field research and to two anonymous reviewers for their insightful feedback.

2   See Elmhirst 1999 and 2000; Warsito and Rahardjo 1984.

3   Kinsey and Binswanger 1993.

the discourse of the Indonesian resettlement programmes in particular, the transmigration of the Javanese to Southeast Sulawesi has been generally overlooked.[4]

Therefore we explore the social mobility and shared sense of belonging of the Javanese community in Southeast Sulawesi. In particular we seek to understand why both social mobility and a shared sense of belonging played a crucial role in the making of the 'emergent identity'[5] of the Javanese migrants in the new home. By 'social mobility' we refer to the perspective and horizon of interaction that the Javanese people have developed from their physical movement from Java to Southeast Sulawesi and from the changes of economic circumstances in the resettlement area. Social mobility includes not only a widening network but also a changing orientation of space that influences the scope of imagination about cultural roots and the state of 'being Javanese'. In this sense, we argue, 'social mobility' echoes Henri Lefebvre's 'code of space', whose production 'implies a process of signification'.[6] Following Lefebvre's theory, we situate the resettlement and physical movement of the Javanese transmigrants in a discourse of the making of a social space by which these people gradually switch their orientation of belonging.[7] Thus, although intuitively the cultural attachment to being Javanese remains strong, yet unconsciously the imagined orientation of cultural space to which such an attachment is forwarded in practice has crossed the boundaries of cultural origins. As Rebecca Elmhirst argues, while creating 'uniformity across different cultural groups' through 'a single model of Indonesian citizenship' and 'a specific and homogenous geographical imaginary', the resettlement programme 'marks a very clear space between Javanese migrants and so-called indigenous people'.[8] Elmhirst uses the term emergent identity to illustrate the

---

4   See Risal 2006 and Mangunrai 1989. Studies that touch upon Javanese resettlement in Southeast Sulawesi include Basri Melamba et al. 2013, Sjamsu 1960, Swasono and Singarimbun 1986 and Velthoen 2002.

5   The term 'emergent identity' is used by Elmhirst 2000, 488.

6   Lefebvre 2007, 17, 25–26.

7   Lefebvre 2007, 25–26.

8   Elmhirst 1999, 815.

hybridity caused by feeling culturally connected to the place of origin and living in the location of resettlement.

Rachel Silvey and Rebecca Elmhirst both argue that the trans-migration resettlement of the Javanese is a form of diaspora that does not necessarily imply a crossing of the political and geographical borders of the nation-state.[9] As Silvey puts it, 'Similar to international diasporas, population mobility within Indonesia is shaped by local and transnational capital, politics and cultural practices.'[10] According to Elmhirst, using the discourse "'diaspora'" provides a useful way of framing identities that refuse the essentialism of "nation" and [...] challenge the idea of ahistorical, indigenous identities that are rooted in a place.'[11]

In this chapter, we first explore the governments' transmigration programmes in order to understand the institutional patterns of the Javanese's space mobility that in turn led them to create a social space and a diasporic shared sense of belonging.[12] We then examine individual testimonies of the Javanese migrants in Kendari and its neighbouring areas in order to highlight the making of their shared sense of belonging as a diasporic group. Jessica Lockrem and Adonia Lugo suggest that studying infrastructure 'creates a conceptual space

9 Elmhirst 2000; Silvey 2000.

10 Silvey 2000, 512.

11 Elmhirst 2000, 488.

12 Swasono and Singarimbun (1986) discuss eighty years of transmigration. The volume includes several articles by colonial and post-colonial government officials who had been involved in the making and implementation of Javanese resettlement policy. Velthoen (2002) deals with the poly-centric polities and socio-political landscapes of the region up to the start of the kolonisatie programme in 1905. It provides a useful background about Southeast Sulawesi in the 19th century, although it is not directly related to the 20th-century migration of the Javanese to the region. Our primary sources are the colonial archives of *Binnenlandsch Bestuur* (BB, Netherlands Indies Department of Internal Affairs) deposited at the Arsip Nasional Republik Indonesia (ANRI, National Archives) in Jakarta and the reports and documents of the Indonesian government, especially of the New Order's Departments of Transmigration and of Social Affairs. We traced the latter in the then regional office of transmigration and in the local branch of the Badan Pusat Statistik (BPS, Central Statistics Agency), both in Kendari.

to examine the shifting boundaries between material and immaterial structures, and the shifting networks between assemblages of human and nonhuman actors.'[13] The transmigration programmes led to the physical mobility of the Javanese, as they left their homeland in Java to a designated locality in Southeast Sulawesi. The process of their resettlement in the designated locality required both physical and non-physical spaces, which the government deliberately constructed to stimulate the migrants' attachment to their new homes. Both physical and socio-cultural infrastructures were crucial preconditions for the re-creation of a home similar to what these Javanese had enjoyed in Java. The migrants' sense of belonging developed in a hybrid way. They were factually embedded in a new physical space, namely the resettlement locality. Yet, they lived and grew with the cultural and social realm of their origin, hence remained imaginatively attached to Java. Thus the studying of the infrastructural settings of the transmigration locality reveals a more subtle aspect of the issue, such as the migrants' shifting senses of belonging and identity.

The making of this hybrid sense of belonging, however, only became consolidated when it took place parallel with socio-economic upward mobility. Although the government resettlement programmes in Southeast Sulawesi had relocated the Javanese in physical and socio-cultural settings which were made similar to those in the transmigrants' place of origin, from the transmigrants' perspective the whole process of resettlement was only completed by the improved economic and social conditions of their family. As the quotation at the beginning of this chapter states, many, if not all, of the Javanese who joined the transmigration programmes expected to improve their lives compared to when they lived in Java. This meant not only that a progressive improvement in the family economy was crucial, but also that such progress be achieved through the kind of jobs that gave social prestige. In the case of Southeast Sulawesi, the migrants' jobs that were both economically and socially lucrative were not agricultural but 'white-collar'. To secure a dependable income the migrants tended to work hard from the first days in the resettlement locality. They also made the availability of basic infrastructure, such as schools and health

---

13 See Lokrem and Lugo, culanth.org/curated_collections/11-infrastructure, accessed 12 September 2017.

centres, a top priority because they understood that this infrastructure was key to the future economic and social well-being of their children. In discussing the sense of belonging of the Javanese in Southeast Sulawesi, we therefore analyse the transmigration programmes using the frame of socio-economic mobility.

We use interviews with several Javanese people in Kendari and adjacent transmigration localities such as Tanea, Sindang Kasih, Pondidaha, Konawe Selatan and Lahumbuti. The people we interviewed were transmigrants and former officials of the Kendari Transmigration Local Office, who mostly left Java for Southeast Sulawesi in the 1970s.[14] Utilising the data we gathered through interviews and field observation, we manage to combine both historical and anthropological perspectives to obtain an integrated answer to our research problems. For this we shall, first, deal with the topic of social mobility, which relies mainly upon written archives, and then with the topic of a shared sense of belonging based on interview and observation data.

We argue that the way the Javanese in Southeast Sulawesi developed their horizons and shared senses of belonging and cultural attachment depended as much on the economic resources they could enjoy as on their social network, which was necessarily family-based or family-like, and which they had successfully built in their new place. Gradually 'feeling home while away', these Javanese people continued to see themselves as Javanese in terms of worldview and macro-cosmic principles of life. By way of daily practices, for example in terms of language code-switching, inter-ethnic marriage and space orientation, however, they showed a mixed cultural attachment.

Transmigration

Bill H. Kinsey and Hans P. Binswanger state that different governments across the world tend to manage the resettlement programmes of their people by means of a centralised model rather than in a way

---

14 Not all of the interviewees still lived in Southeast Sulawesi at the time of the interview. One former official and his family returned to Java in 1992 after completing his official duties in Kendari and Makassar. Interviews with transmigrants in Southeast Sulawesi were recorded in late August 2014.

that supports spontaneous local participation and responsibility.[15] Indeed, the ethnic Javanese people who reside in Kendari, Sindang Kasih, Tanea, Pondidaha and Lahumbuti today mostly came to these regions on account of official resettlement programmes rather than by spontaneous collective dispersal from Java. However, as Thomas R. Leinbach suggests, in Indonesia the resettlement of the Javanese occurred often in the form of spontaneous migration (*transmigrasi swakarsa*) with the support of small private enterprises.[16] Consequently, in Indonesia, more Javanese migrated spontaneously than in government-controlled programmes.[17] The resettlement of Javanese migrants involved thus a more complex process than analysed by Kinsey and Biswanger. We identify some patterns showing the process (Table 2.1, see next page). Some of these patterns, we argue, played a crucial role in creating the path of social mobility that the migrants would follow in their new home because they were related to a family or family-like networks of communities.

We briefly review the Javanese resettlement history by discussing the most relevant aspects. As written by a former official of the Indonesian Department of Transmigration, Slamet Purboadiwidjojo, the Javanese resettlement programme began in 1905 when a group of people from the regencies of Karanganyar, Kebumen, Purworejo and Kedu in Central Java resettled to the Gedong Tataan sub-district of Lampung in southern Sumatra. The programme was called kolonisatie and was run by the Department of Internal Affairs (Binnenlandsch Bestuur) of the Netherlands Indies government. These migrants were mostly Javanese-speaking people from Central and East Java, although the programme also included Sundanese-speaking people from West Java, Betawi people from Batavia, and individuals from Madura and Bali. Most of them were small-scale and seasonal farmers who did not own land. They cultivated other people's land for a portion of the agricultural products harvested from the land they worked on. In the place of

---

15 Kinsey and Binswanger 1993.

16 Leinbach 1989.

17 Wirosardjono 1986.

Table 2.1. Patterns of the Javanese resettlement programmes, 1900–2013

Resettlement pattern	Description
Familie-kolonisatie	Transmigration of members of an extended family, following the ones who had resettled earlier
Bawon system	Harvesting season transmigration for the labourers who would work in the farms for a particular proportion of the harvested agricultural products (*bawon*)
Kolonisatie in marga-verband	The dispersal of Javanese people to a Java-style village in the resettlement area, which administratively fell under the authority of ethnic local/*adat* government (*marga*). The Javanese people, who had been socially and culturally prepared, were accepted as members of the marga and had to pay taxes to the marga head
Marga kolonisatie	Immediate dispersal of Javanese to the adat kampong, with no prior social/cultural preparation and no special Java-style village structure
Rand kolonisatie	Temporary relocation of Javanese migrants to work on plantations
Transmigrasi spontan/ swakarsa	Spontaneous, mostly individual transmigration
Bedol desa	Whole village transmigration
Transmigrasi Corps Cadangan Nasional (CTN)	Transmigration of former war combatants, veterans, and army retirees
Transmigrasi Biro Rekonstruksi Nasional (BRN)	Transmigration for social reconstruction, including mostly married, unemployed adults
Transmigrasi umum	General transmigration resettlement programme
Pengerahan tenaga sukarela / Transmigration of professional volunteers	Contract mobilisation of lower- and middle-level professionals, especially school teachers and medical personnel

Sources: Purboadiwidjojo 1986, 12–26; Dinas Tenaga Kerja dan Transmigrasi 2014, 8–17.

resettlement they were expected to become full-time farmers who cultivated their own land.[18]

According to Sri-Edi Swasono, in the course of the first three decades of the 20th century the places of destination of resettlement had covered almost the whole of Sumatra and Borneo and part of Papua.[19] Sulawesi, however, which had been on the government's list of kolonisatie since the beginning of the programme, only became a destination in the 1930s. The first attempts to resettle Javanese in southeast Sulawesi were not successful because land conditions and infrastructure were poor. Moreover, a lack of farming tools and of basic sanitation ensured that the migrants missed the living standards that they had enjoyed in Java. These early migrants were not as a 'happy' as their counterparts from Sumatra.[20] Not only the migrants, but the government itself was not satisfied with the expensive programme which did not live up to expectations. In 1927 the government suspended the programme, but relaunched it in 1932.[21]

A former colonial official of the Department of Economic and Social Affairs, Egbert de Vries, noted that a land survey conducted on Sulawesi in the late 1920s showed that the soil of Sulawesi was not as fertile for agriculture as in Sumatra, Kalimantan or even Papua. In addition, unlike Sumatra and Kalimantan where modest mainland transportation routes had existed, Sulawesi in general still needed major works for road and water system construction to ensure that a relatively large number of migrants could settle. The survey also spotted that the area of northern Sulawesi was the most appropriate area for resettlement. However, as De Vries wrote, it was there that the local population, especially the Minahasan people, resented the founding of a Javanese community.[22]

---

18 Purboadiwidjojo 1986, 9.

19 Swasono 1986, 70–71.

20 ANRI, Binnenlands Bestuur (BB) 2731, Emigratie en landbouwkolonisatie van Javanen naar en in de Buitengewesten van Nederlandsch-Indië door Mr. C. C. J. Maassen.

21 Purboadiwidjojo 1986, 15–17.

22 De Vries 1986, 1–2; ANRI, Binnenlands Bestuur (BB) 2731, Emigratie en landbouwkolonisatie van Javanen naar en in de Buitengewesten van Nederlandsch-Indië door Mr. C. C. J. Maassen.

Figure 2.1. A resettlement area in Konawe Selatan, *c*. 1939 ('Arsip Foto KIT Sulawesi' No. 315/22, ANRI)

It was only in 1938 that Sulawesi, and Southeast Sulawesi specifically, actually began to receive Javanese settlers under the kolonisatie programme.[23] To solve the problems identified earlier, the colonial government sent seven low-ranking officials, thirteen village heads and seven farmers from different localities in Central Java to Sulawesi and the nearby islands (*Onderhoorigheden*).[24] The purpose of this trip, called a *propagandareis* (propaganda trip) was to provide these officials and farmers with an opportunity to gather first-hand information, knowledge and impressions about the resettlement areas in Sulawesi. It was expected that upon returning from their

23 ANRI, BB 2713, Letter of the director of internal affairs (Binnenlandsch Bestuur) to the Resident of Makassar No. A.I.25/5/3, 3 March 1938.

24 These officials were the regent, the district head, and the heads of the Kemrajen and the Cilongkok sub-districts, all of Banyumas; the assistant resident and the Gombong district head of Kebumen; and the district head of Belik in Pekalongan. The group included five lurahs (village heads) from Banyumas, six from Kebumen and two from Pekalongan. The farmers were from Banyumas, Kebumen and Pekalongan.

trip these people would spread 'positive' stories that would attract more Javanese migrants to Sulawesi.[25]

Also in 1938, the Department of Economic Affairs in Batavia sent sets of farming tools to the Javanese migrants in South and Southeast Sulawesi (Table 2.2). The types of tools indicate the variety of work that needed to be done to create a habitable space. But these tools also give an indication of the habits of the migrants in their place of origin, which were to be re-created in the new place of settlement (see below).[26]

After Indonesia's independence in 1945, the government remodelled the resettlement programme; now it was called *transmigrasi*, and included the migration of Javanese to other islands.[27] In 1950 the programme restarted with the sending of people from Java to, mostly, Sumatra. In the following fifteen years more people were sent out to resettlement areas not only in Sumatra but also in Kalimantan, Sulawesi, the Moluccas and Papua. However it was only in late 1969 that Southeast Sulawesi became a destination for this transmigration programme.[28] No official documents explain this, but in a 2008 interview Soekarno Samadi, who headed the provincial branch office of the Department of Transmigration in Kendari from 1972 to 1985, implied that the lack of basic infrastructure in Southeast Sulawesi was one of the reasons for the 'late' dispersal of the Javanese

---

25 ANRI, BB 2713, Letter of the secretary of the commission for emigration and kolonisatie of the indigenous people, Maassen, to the governor of Central Java No. 1022, 10 Nov. 1938.

26 It is also interesting to note that in the same year the Department approved the acquisition of wood cleavers (*golok*) in large quantities. An explanation is lacking, but our assumption is that this large number of *golok* was meant to ease the process of opening up woods for resettlement areas. Perhaps because of the large quantity and for practicality, these *golok* were shipped to the heads of local Sulawesi governments before they were distributed to the Javanese migrants. This included 300, 200, 500 and 1,000 pieces of *golok* respectively sent to the heads of the local administration of Raha, Pare-Pare, Polewali and Malili in South and Southeast Sulawesi. ANRI, BB 2713, Letter of adviser for agricultural affairs, Maassen, to head of consultation bureau, No. A.I.25/10/2, 21 February 1938.

27 Purboadiwidjojo 1986, 19.

28 Jones 1986, 234–36.

Table 2.2: Farming tools sent to the Javanese migrants in Sulawesi, 1938

No	Tool	Quantity
1	*Patjolvork, met 4 ronde tanden* (gardening fork with 4 grinders)	300 pieces
2	*Dissel, grootte 1* (pole, size 1)	68 pieces
3	*Hamer* (hammer)	68 pieces
4	*Nijptang, lengte 8 duim* (pincers, length 8 inches)	68 pieces
5	*Kraanzaag* (crane-saw)	68 pieces
6	*Kraanzaagijzers* (crane-saw irons)	68 pieces
7	*Draadnagels, 3 duim* (nails, 3 inches)	20 barrels
8	*Draadnagels, 5 duim* (nails, 5 inches)	20 barrels
9	*Vrouwenpatjol* (women's gardening fork)	700 pieces
10	*Wiedarit* (large sickle)	2,000 pieces
11	*Golok* (wood cleaver)	50 pieces

Source: ANRI, BB 2713, Letter of adviser for agriculture affairs, Maassen, to head of consultation bureau, No. A.I.25/10/2, 21 February 1938

to the region. This notion of bad infrastructure echoed the colonial government's picture of Southeast Sulawesi. However, this language about the lack of infrastructure can also be read more positively: the arrival of the Javanese brought 'development benefits'[29] and local progress. But it implies that the government's construction of public infrastructure in Southeast Sulawesi was solely for the benefit of the Javanese, thus ignoring the position of the local population.

In addition to the lack of adequate infrastructure, the late dispersal of the Javanese in Southeast Sulawesi was politically motivated. The government had to deal with, as Soekarno Samadi put it, many other problems of independence including the extended effect of the 1965 tragedy.[30] Following a failed coup on 30 September 1965, large-scale killings and captivity occurred over many months, targeting

29 Elmhirst, this volume.

30 Interview with Soekarno Samadi (then 68 years of age, died November 2008), former head of provincial transmigration office of Kendari, interview held Yogyakarta, May 2008.

Figure 2.2: Newly built houses for Javanese migrants in Pondidaha, *c.* 1988 (Collection of Kantor Dinas Transmigrasi Kendari)

communists and alleged leftists, often at the instigation of the armed forces and government. In the 1970s and up to early 1980s, a number of these political prisoners who had been released by the government were sent on a transmigration programme to Southeast Sulawesi. According to Soekarno Samadi, this required a special preparation of the physical setting of the resettlement destination. The government's policy was that the ex-prisoners' resettlement area had to be surrounded by the resettlement areas of retired army and medical personnel and (religious) teachers. The last two groups were relocated from Java respectively under Transmigrasi Corps Cadangan Nasional (CTN, Transmigration Programme for National Reserve Corps) and Pengerahan Tenaga Sukarela (Transmigration Programme for Professional Volunteers, see Table 2.1).

As in colonial times, the post-independence transmigration pro-gramme also included people from the Sundanese-speaking areas in West Java as well as Balinese and Madurese. However, most of the people who were sent to Southeast Sulawesi were Javanese-speaking. They came from villages in Yogyakarta and Central and East Java. The first group consisted of approximately 500 people from East

Java, followed by 491 settlers from Central Java in 1973 and 191 people from Yogyakarta in 1974. They were sent to the South Konawe district of Rambu-Rambu Jaya, the Kolaka area of Towua and the Kendari district of Uepai respectively. The resettlement programmes of the Javanese to Southeast Sulawesi continued until recently. In 2013 a last group of 35 people from Yogyakarta were moved to the Padalere Utama area of North Konawe Regency.[31]

In the end, the government's (post)-colonial resettlement programmes did not bring much relief in the population pressure in Java, as was their original goal. In the period 1905 to 1941, the kolonisatie programme succeeded in dispersing only 257,313 people from Java, instead of one million as was intially planned by the government.[32] Between 1950 and 1976, the number of Javanese who voluntarily joined the government resettlement programme comprised an average of only 2.7 per cent of the total population growth of Java at the time. The highest number in the resettlement history was reached in 1974, when the programme involved 6.8 per cent of the total population growth in Java.[33] Out of this figure, some 1.5 per cent (9,011 people) were dispersed in Southeast Sulawesi in 1974.[34]

Shared Sense of Belonging

Since colonial times policy makers have realised that it is important for Javanese migrants to relate to a particular community structure in the place of destination. When the initial effort to assimilate the Javanese into the local community, either through the cultural patterns of kolonisatie in *marga-verband* and *marga kolonisatie* or through the economic patterns of the *bawon system* and *rand kolonisatie*, did not work out because of cultural constraints with the locals,[35] a new approach was taken by consciously designing a social atmosphere that represented the Javanese place of origin. As

---

31 Dinas Tenaga Kerja dan Transmigrasi 2014, 3–17.

32 Swasono 1986, 82.

33 Wirosardjono 1986, 299–300.

34 Jones 1986, 236.

35 See table 1, Jones 1986, 244, Mubyarto 1986, 308–311.

we have stated above, the farming tools that the colonial government provided indicate not only the variety of work necessary to be done to create a habitable space for the migrants, but also imply the sort of living habits of the migrants in their old place of origin, which were to be re-created in the new place of settlement. According to Slamet Purboadiwidjojo, the resettlement villages were designed to resemble the villages in Java. The social and political system of *lurah* (village head) and assistant *wedana* (assistant district head) in Java was copied and remade in the resettlement areas as a social and political enclave in a local cultural setting.[36]

During our visit to the resettlement areas we noticed that, while the location of houses and roads was designed as blocks and thus more structured than in Java, the infrastructure facilities looked much like those in Java. Following the government's plans, a compound of a Javanese resettlement in Southeast Sulawesi consisted, besides residential houses, of a school building, a health centre, a village head office (*kantor kepala desa*), a village cooperative office (*Koperasi Unit Desa*, KUD), a post office, a cemetery, and religious buildings like mosques, churches and temples.[37] Not all these planned facilities, for example school buildings, had been ready at the time the migrants were dispersed to the areas. Some of them were constructed in a later time, sometimes by the transmigrants themselves, as we shall discuss below. Regardless of this, the physical and social situation in the resettlement areas such as Sindang Kasih, Tanea, Konawe Selatan and Pondidaha, to us, looked very similar to that in the villages in Java. We also noticed several concrete signposts with Javanese names of villages on it, like 'Sido Dadi' (literally, 'it happened'), to mark the borders between two villages. All these obviously indicate that resettlement required not only a physical mobility but also a constructed physical space that was meant to be able to convey, stimulate and nurture the atmosphere and the migrants' imagination about the original home culture.

However, there was a lot more required than a physical space for these Javanese migrants to re-create a home similar to that which

---

36 Purboadiwidjojo 1986, 10.

37 Direktorat Jenderal Penyiapan Pemukiman n.d., 23.

they had enjoyed in Java. This especially concerned a social system that suited the worldview with which they had grown up in Java. One of the factors that bolstered the making of an agreeable social and cultural atmosphere for these Javanese migrants was family or family-like relationships among them. Javanese society is widely known for its kinship system of extended families. The social system in the villages in 20th-century Java showed characteristics of family relations in which a harmonious communal structure became the foundation and purpose of social interaction.[38] This is also reflected in the proverb '*mangan ora mangan, sing penting kumpul*', which implies that even if there is only little food to share, it is always important to keep being together in harmony. In the resettlement areas, the migrants themselves managed to re-create among them such a social atmosphere and family or family-like relationships.

It was often the case that new transmigrants could not be deployed directly to the resettlement sites because their houses-to-be were not yet ready. In that case, these people were lodged in a so-called *transito* (transit house) for a particular period. Endang Sri Utami, the wife of the aforementioned Soekarno Samadi, said that the house her family lived in, which was big enough given her husband's position as head of the provincial transmigration office, was also used as the transit house for the new migrants from Java who were waiting for deployment. It could happen, Utami said, that those people stayed until their departure to the resettlement site and immediately another group arrived. Because of her husband's position, Utami was responsible for preparing the daily meals and lodging during the transit period. 'I had barely known any of those people before, but as we were all Javanese, some even coming from Yogyakarta like me, it was quite easy to prepare things together in *gotong royong* [a voluntarily cooperative way].' Endang set up a public kitchen and made a schedule for the female adult migrants to take turns in preparing meals for everyone. Her husband's office paid the costs.[39]

---

38 Geertz 1961; Koentjaraningat 1957; Mulder 1978.

39 Interview with Endang Sri Utami (60 years old), former coordinator of the transit house in Kendari and wife of Soekarno Samadi, now a retiree living in Yogyakarta, running a student dormitory, interview held in Yogyakarta, August 2014.

Figure 2.3: A transit house (Collection of Kantor Dinas Transmigrasi Kendari)

Endang Sri Utami was not alone in organizing the jobs. Her husband, Soekarno Samadi, had several male assistants, who helped them with different sorts of jobs for the migrants in transit. One of the former assistants, Jumali, recounted:

> During the transit period, the migrants came to know each other and became close to each other. Although some of them might have come from the same district or village in Java, they had not always known each other until they joined the resettlement programme. So, the period of transit created an opportunity to build a family-like tie among the migrants.[40]

The relationship between the Soekarnos and their assistants was itself a story of family-relation making. Jumali was twenty years old when he joined the transmigration programme and left his village of origin in Yogyakarta for Kendari in 1982. He was still single and knew no one in the group that departed from Java. During the transit period, Soekarno noticed Jumali as a young man with a lot of potential. Soekarno deliberately asked Jumali if he wanted to assist

---

40 Interview with Jumali (52), interview held in Kendari, August 2014.

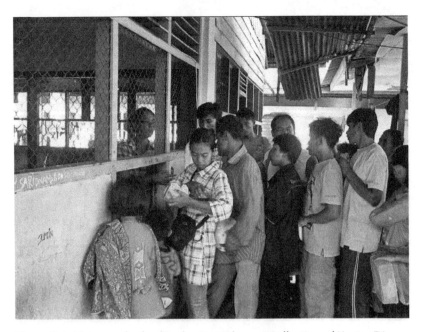

Figure 2.4: Lining up for food in the transit house (Collection of Kantor Dinas Transmigrasi Kendari)

him for some time before dispersing to the resettlement site. 'He had actually wanted me to be a teacher for the transmigrants' children', Jumali recalled. In Java Jumali had earned only a high-school leaving certificate. So, after about a year working in the transit house, Jumali was sent to a training centre in Kendari and gained a teaching certificate. Then he moved to the resettlement site, served as a teacher and became a transmigrant himself as he had intended all along. 'Now I always miss the family-like atmosphere in the transit house. It sort of replaced the family I had left in Java', added Jumali, who, at the time we interviewed him, held the headmaster position at a public primary school in Lahumbuti while also finishing his master thesis at Haluoleo University.[41]

Unlike Jumali, who helped the Soekarnos with domestic jobs, Sumantri and Syahrir assisted Soekarno in organising the male transmigrants to prepare the resettlement sites. Sumantri had come to Kendari with a two-year bachelor degree from Yogyakarta in 1978.

---

41 Interview with Jumali, Kendari, August 2014.

Syahrir was from Jeneponto in South Sulawesi and had moved to Kendari, also in 1978, with a high-school leaving certificate. Syahir explained that:

> We organised the male transmigrants on finishing constructing their wooden houses, paving roads and building other infrastructure in the resettlement sites until they were all ready to be inhabited [. . .]. It was a hard time as there were very limited resources, but we supported each other to work out the problems until they were all done. As a non-Javanese myself, I am still very impressed about how this family-like co-operation took place among us.[42]

'Once in a while it happened that we ran out of food while working in the resettlement sites', Sumantri told us.

> We sought throughout the forest for some food and we found cassava in uncultivated land, so we called it 'wild' cassava. Because we found nothing else in the woods to eat, we uprooted the cassava, put them on a fire, and shared them with all the other men. In Java we had been used to eating cassava, but not wild ones.[43]

When Soekarno Samadi had to leave Kendari for another position in Makassar in 1985, Sumantri replaced him as head of the provincial transmigration office. Syahrir, meanwhile, was appointed head of the resettlement bureau. Jumali, Sumantri and Syahrir continue to live in Southeast Sulawesi until today. They keep a close relationship with Soekarno's family, even though the latter have been back in Yogyakarta for many years now.

In addition to issues relating to settlement, the lack of children's education was another concern for the transmigrants. The story of Syamsul and his family is informative. Syamsul moved from Jember in East Java to Pondidaha in Southeast Sulawesi in 1976, having joined the army retiree transmigration programme. Together with

---

42 Interview with Syahrir (58), former head of the resettlement bureau, now a retiree running a twelve-room inn, interview held in Kendari, August 2014.

43 Interview with Sumantri (60), former head of Kendari provincial transmigration office, now a retiree running a travel business, interview held in Kendari, August 2014.

his wife and two children of eight and ten years old, Syamsul moved to the area, which was largely composed of swampland. 'There was no road except for a footpath as the swampland made it difficult for road construction', Syamsul said. 'But what we immediately missed most was a school for our children. There was no school here in Pondidaha or nearby areas.' Syamsul said that their children had been attending a primary school in Java before they moved to Pondidaha. 'In the first months I truly wanted to go back to Java because I worried so much about the future of my children's education', *Ibu* Syamsul added.[44] More than one year later, Syamsul decided to establish a school himself. 'I saw not only my children but also more and more children of the transmigrants just staying at home with no education', Syamsul said. So he organised the people in Pondidaha to construct a school building of wooden blocks. 'It happened that at that time there was a new transmigrant who had graduated from a *pesantren* [Islamic boarding school] in Gontor, East Java. I asked him if he wanted to become a teacher in our school and he agreed. So the school began only with one teacher for all pupils', Syamsul recalled. The people in Pondidaha paid this teacher's salary with agricultural products instead of money. Syamsul added that the school itself had not been intended to become an Islamic school. 'Only because the only teacher we had at the start was a pesantren graduate, the school developed into a Madrasah or Islamic primary school', he explained. A couple of years before our interview the government had acquired the school and made it public in order to improve it further, using government funds.[45]

Syamsul's story about establishing a school shows that the availability of education was crucial in keeping the Javanese migrants in the resettlement areas and in gradually switching and localising their orientation of 'Java as a home'. The stories of two other transmigrants, Supandi and Syambudiono, underline the strategic position of education in the changing orientation of the Javanese migrants.

---

44 Interview with Ibu Syamsul (50), a farmer, transmigrant and wife of Syamsul, held in Pondidaha, August 2014.

45 Interview with Syamsul (52), a farmer, transmigrant of the Transmigrasi Corps Cadangan Nasional Programme of Pondidaha, held in Pondidaha, August 2014.

Figure 2.5: Mr. Supandi (centre), a religious teacher under the Pengerahan Tenaga Sukarela Programme, and his wife (left), photographed in their home in Tanea (photo by authors)

Supandi joined the so-called *pengerahan tenaga sukarela* programme (volunteer professional mobilisation) as a religion teacher under a two-year contract with the Department of Transmigration. Originally from Yogyakarta, Supandi with his family was sent to Konawe Selatan in 1980. Initially he thought his stay would be only temporary and that after his contract ended he and his family would return to Java. Yet, after the contract ended, Supandi decided to stay in Southeast Sulawesi and moved to another area, Tanea. 'My family has settled here. We have our own land and my children can still go to school', he explained. In Tanea Supandi continued teaching while he also cultivated his land for tropical crops and vegetables. His wife sold the agricultural products from their land to neighbouring villages.[46]

Syambudiono, like Jumali, was about twenty years old when he departed from Yogyakarta in 1982 to join some five hundred other

---

46 Interview with Supandi (58), a farmer and religous teacher, transmigrant of the Pengerahan Tenaga Sukarela Programme of Konawe Selatan, held in Konawe Selatan, August 2014.

people in the resettlement programme in Southeast Sulawesi. He was deployed to Konawe Selatan and found no school there. Although he had initially focused on cultivating his land, Syambudiono then decided to give lessons to the children of other transmigrants, who had so far received no schooling in the resettlement area. Syambudiono had earned a leaving certificate from a Sekolah Pendidikan Guru (SPG, Teacher Training High School) in Yogyakarta and his resolve to become a teacher became even stronger when he met the daughter of one of the transmigrant families, who had also come from Yogyakarta with an SPG leaving certificate. They got married and together set up a school and taught there. 'After I switched to teaching, and even more after I got married to my wife and together we became teachers here, I became more convinced of staying in Southeast Sulawesi rather than returning to Java.'[47] 'I was already grown up and was about to have my own life in Java when my parents decided to move here', Mrs. Syambudiono added. 'It was hard to leave Java, but well, I found my new life here.'[48] Both Syambudiono and his wife were headmasters of two different public primary schools in Konawe Selatan at the time of our interview in August 2014.

These individual testimonies confirm the key position of school education both as a 'guard' for the future life of the migrants' second generation and as a profession for some migrants that diverted them from the agricultural setting of the resettlement programme. Syamsul and his wife had not felt at home in Pondidaha and had wanted to return to Java, until their children finally went to school again. For the Syambudionos, on the other hand, the education world in their case, teaching – provided them with an alternative to escape from the hardship of land cultivation. So it was for Jumali. Teaching and schooling created for these migrants an economic and social security that somehow enlarged their attachment to the localities they

---

47 Interview with Syambudiono (49), transmigrant, married to Ibu Syambudionoas, both Java-born, having grown up in a resettlement locality in Konawe Selatan. Now Syambudiono is a headmaster, just like his wife. Interview was held in Konawe Selatan, August 2014.

48 Interview with Mrs. Syambudiono (47), transmigrant and wife of Syambudiono, interview held in Konawe Selatan, August 2014.

presently lived in and, at the same time, reduced their orientation to Java. Education thus became a key in making these Javanese, while remaining culturally Javanese, turn their horizon of space and belonging from geographical Java to their present geographical locality. In other words, through education there emerged a change in the migrants' sense of attachment, from Java as a physical space to Java as a cultural space of orientation.

The experience of Supandi and his family is an interesting case. During their first two years in Southeast Sulawesi, Supandi and his family had been thinking that their stay would only be temporary, namely for that limited contract period. It implies that their orientation and horizon during the first two years had remained Java as a physical space. Yet, in the span of two years Supandi also developed a different horizon and feeling of attachment, which was stimulated mostly by the improving socio-economic welfare of his family. When he finally decided to remain in Southeast Sulawesi when his official contract ended, Supandi's perception of and his (family's) attachment to Java had clearly changed. He said that he did not have to return to Java to enjoy a better life, socially and economically.

Hence the change in orientation and belonging was a process that resulted from the changes in socio-economic conditions. The migrants' orientation to geographical Java remained strong as long as their imagination about an improvement in their socio-economic life in the migration locality failed to meet their expectations. Sumantri's testimony might explain this further. He remarked:

> I do not want to return to Java. There we had to split a small piece of land we had inherited from our parents with many of my brothers and sisters. Even if you have a good education, it is very difficult to find a good job in Java as there are many well-educated people and competition is very stiff.

In Kendari Sumantri and his family live in a relatively nice house with a garden and two brand new Japanese cars. Next to the entrance gate of his house is a small room from where one of his sons runs the family's travel business. 'Had your life not been like what it is now economically, would you have considered returning to Java?' we asked him. 'Definitely', he answered. 'My family and I left Java for a better life. If we did not improve our lives compared to what we had in Java, then we would have returned to Java, no matter what.'[49]

It should be noted that none of the Javanese we interviewed in Southeast Sulawesi relied primarily upon agriculture as their main source of income. All our informants did own a piece of land and did make some money out of it. Jumali owned a pepper plantation, Supandi had tropical crops and a vegetable farm, Syamsul became the only person in Pondidaha to develop fresh-water fishery. Yet, all of them had non-farming professions as their primary source of income: teaching, small-scale business, transportation. The second generation of these migrants also tended to choose a non-farming profession. Syamsul's daughter served the people of Pondidaha as a midwife after she had earned a certificate from a Health Academy in Makassar. So did Sumantri's daughter, who graduated from a nursing college in Kendari. Supandi's daughter, meanwhile, worked as a teacher in a primary school near their house.

This selecting of non-farming jobs by the Javanese transmigrants and their families in Southeast Sulawesi might be common in other resettlement areas for merely economic reasons. However, we argue that it also reflects somehow the mindset that Javanese people had developed in Java about the dismal lives of peasants. In 20th-century Java, peasants were generally depicted as socially and economically deprived. With the spread of Western education and the accompanying modernisation, better-educated people in Java sought non-labour-intensive jobs in the Western economic sphere. Thus in early 20th-century Java emerged a new social class of a bureaucratic elite and a middle class, who, although coming from an rural society, quickly moved towards a non-agricultural trajectory of social mobility in order to embrace cultural modernity.[50] We argue that not only economic reasons motivated the Javanese transmigrants we interviewed to pursue jobs in non-agricultural sectors. The 'priyayi mentality' (bureaucratic elite) also played a crucial role in their decision for not choosing labour-intensive jobs and for entering the white-collar middle-class professional sector. It seems

---

49 Interview with Sumantri, Kendari, August 2014.

50 Schulte Nordholt 2011, Sutherland 1979, Van Niel 1960.

that these Javanese carried with them the dream of vertical social mobility they, or their parents, had long dreamt of but had not otherwise been able to achieve in fast-changing 20th-century Java. Therefore, although some researchers believe that the transmigration resettlement programme was originally designed to re-create 'a peasant Javanese society' outside of Java by the very fact of large-scale land allocation for agricultural cultivation,[51] we conclude that in the case of Southeast Sulawesi the making of diasporic subjects and a new middle-class society among the Javanese migrants took place in non-agricultural settings.

Another question is whether the switch of orientation and sense of belonging from geographical Java to the Java-like physical space in the resettlement areas also meant a change in the migrants' orientation and sense of belonging from cultural Java to a locally situated cultural identity. Our informants confirmed that they felt that they remained culturally Javanese. They kept performing some rituals of festivities like engagement, wedding and baby birth according to the Javanese tradition they had acquired in Java. They also performed a thanksgiving ceremony (*slametan*) for special occasions, for example, to celebrate a child's graduation and to commemorate the dead.

However, we also noticed that our informants performed inflection many times during our conversations. Unlike the first generation of the Javanese people in Lampung who could still use both the Indonesian and Javanese languages without inflection, even if the Javanese language they spoke was of the lowest level (*ngoko*), our informants, who were also first-generation Javanese migrants in Southeast Sulawesi, switched codes between Indonesian and local dialects, such as adding the expression '*mi*' all the end of all their sentences. They preferred to use Indonesian to Javanese, although we prompted to converse in Javanese. 'We now speak a broken Javanese and I feel rather ashamed about it', Syambudiono told us.[52] Their children lived in a mixed cultural setting with the locals and other ethnic groups from South Sulawesi. Everyday Syambudiono and

---

51 For example, Clauss, Evers and Gerke, 1988; Elmhirst, this volume.

52 Interview with Syambudiono, Konawe Selatan, August 2014.

Jumali had to teach not only the children of the Javanese families but also many other children of different local ethnic backgrounds who spoke their mother tongues at home. Sumantri's daughter was even married to an ethnic Tolaki man, while the son of Supandi had married a local woman.

All this confirmed that despite the self-perception and the Javanese rituals these Javanese migrants still held, their cultural identity had changed along with their changing orientation of the physical space. Although these Javanese migrants might not have lost their sense of belonging to cultural Java completely, their imagination about it has obviously been deconstructed. Here the physical spaces of both the resettlement area and Java served as a bridge in the changing imagination about the geographical and cultural Java of the migrants. Augmented by the Javanese social system and an enlarging economic capital, their physical mobility, which into social mobility that in turn switched their shared sense of attachment. This notwithstanding, it is simply fallacious to say that these migrants have become culturally local. To us, their cultural identity looked more like a hybrid, swinging between cultural Java and cultural local, than like a unitary one. They did not orient themselves towards Java so strongly any more. Yet they, although socio-economically inclined towards the present locality, were not culturally localised completely. A new identity was emerging; it was one in between being Javanese and being local. It was a diasporic identity.

Conclusion

By way of various patterns of resettlement across the 20th century, a number of Javanese people moved to Southeast Sulawesi. This physical mobility required a re-construction of a physical space, which was primarily meant to make the resettlement areas habitable, but which also implied a remaking of the social and psychological atmosphere of a Javanese society in Java. This atmosphere in turn created the migrants' feeling of being at home in the new locality. However, the process to re-present a Java-like society was only effective for switching the orientation and sense of belonging of the Javanese if some other conditions were met. Firstly, in the resettlement community there should be a social system that the

Javanese migrants had been acquainted with when they were in Java, namely a family or family-patterned social relationship. Secondly, an economic improvement of the migrants played a crucial role in strengthening their attachment to their new place of living. In this case education, in addition to small-scale trading, fishery, health and service businesses, were among the most important employment sectors that bolstered the economic improvement of the migrants and their children. Thus the remaking of a Java-like physical space in the resettlement areas did not work out as changing the migrants' orientation and attachment to a geographical and cultural Java. A Javanese social system and an economic improvement of the migrants were the conditions that switched their orientation and sense of belonging from geographical Java to the new space. In this new space they developed a diasporic identity that oriented them to the new socio-economic reality of their current place of residence, while they remained in touch with their cultural Javanese roots.

References

Clauss, W., H.-D. Evers and S. Gerke 1988. 'The Formation of a Peasant Society: Javanese Transmigrants in East Kalimantan', *Indonesia* 46: 78–90.

Dinas Tenaga Kerja dan Transmigrasi 2014. 'Data realisasi penempatan transmigrasi per daerah asal di Sulawesi Tenggara sejak pra-Pelita s.d. tahun 2013'. Unpublished report.

Direktorat Jenderal Penyiapan Pemukiman n.d. 'Laporan pengukuran, pemetaan dan final desain tata letak bangunan pemukiman: *Final report* di Kendari'.

—— 1999. 'Space, Identity Politics and Resource Control in Indonesia's Transmigration Program', *Political Geography* 18: 813–835.

Elmhirst, R. 2000. 'A Javanese Diaspora? Gender and Identity Politics in Indonesia's Transmigration Resettlement Program', *Women Studies International Forum* 23(4): 487–500.

Geertz, H. 1961. *The Javanese Family: A Study of Kinship and Socialization*. New York: Free Press.

Jones, G. W. 1986. 'Indonesia: Program transmigrasi dan perencanaan pembangunan'. In *Transmigrasi di Indonesia 1905–1985*, ed. S. E. Swasono and M. Singarumbun, 232–253. Jakarta: UI Press.

Kinsey, B. H. and H. P. Binswanger 1993. 'Characteristics and Performance of Resettlement Programs: A Review', *World Development* 21 (9): 1477–1494.

Koentjaraningrat, R. M. 1957. *A Preliminary Description of the Javanese Kinship System*. New Haven: Yale University Press.

Lefebvre, H. 2007. *The Production of Space*. Translated by Donald Nicholson-Smith. Oxford: Blackwell Publishing.

Leinbach, T. R. 1989. 'The Transmigration Program in Indonesian National Development Strategy: Current Status and Future Requirements', *Habitat International* 13 (3): 81–93.

Lockrem, J. and A. Lugo, 'Infrastructure', culanth.org/curated_collections/11-infrastructure.

Mangunrai, H. 1989. 'Keadaan sosial ekonomi transmigran spontan/swakarsa di daerah transmigrasi Mamuju, Sulawesi Selatan'. Unpublished research report.

Melamba, B. 2013. *Tolaki: Sejarah, identitas dan kebudayaan*. Yogyakarta: Lukita.

Mubyarto 1986. 'Prospek dan masalah transmigrasi pola PIR – BUN'. In *Transmigrasi di Indonesia 1905–1985*, ed. S. E. Swasono and M. Singarumbun, 303–315. Jakarta: UI Press.

Mulder, M. 1978. *Mysticism and Everyday Life in Contemporary Java: Cultural Persistence and Change*. Singapore: NUS Press.

Purboadiwidjojo, S. 1986. 'Mencari suatu sistem untuk melaksanakan pemindahan penduduk secara besar-besaran'. In *Transmigrasi di Indonesia 1905–1985*, ed. S. E. Swasono and M. Singarumbun, 8–30. Jakarta: UI Press.

Risal 2006. 'Sejarah transmigrasi di Kabupaten Kendari'. BA thesis, Universitas Haluoelo.

Schulte Nordholt, H. 2011. 'Modernity and Cultural Citizenship in the Netherlands Indies: An Illustrated Hypothesis', *Journal of Southeast Asian Studies* 42 (3): 435–457.

Sutherland, H. 1979. *The Making of a Bureaucratic Elite: The Transformation of the Javanese Priyayi*. Singapore: Heineman.

Silvey, R. M. 2000. 'Diasporic Subjects: Gender and Mobility in South Sulawesi', *Women Studies International Forum* 23 (4): 501–515.

Sjamsu, M. A. 1960. *Dari kolonisasi ke transmigrasi 1905–1955*. Jakarta: Djambatan.

Swasono, S. E. 1986. 'Kependudukan, kolonisasi dan transmigrasi'. In *Transmigrasi di Indonesia 1905–1985*, ed. S. E. Swasono and M. Singarumbun, 70–85. Jakarta: UI Press.

Swasono, S. E. and M. Singarimbun 1986. *Transmigrasi di Indonesia 1905–1985*. Jakarta: UI Press.

Van Niel, R. 1960. *The Emergence of the Modern Indonesian Elite*. Chicago: Quadrangle Books.

Velthoen, E. J. 2002. 'Contested Coastline: Diasporas, Trade and Colonial Expansion in Eastern Sulawesi 1680-1905'. PhD. diss., Murdoch University.

Vries, E. de 1986. 'Kolonisasi dan Kemajuan dalam Dasawarsa 1930an'. In *Transmigrasi di Indonesia 1905-1985*, ed. S E. Swasono and M. Singarumbun, 1-7. Jakarta: UI Press.

Warsito, R. and B. Rahardjo 1984. *Transmigrasi: Dari daerah asal sampai benturan budaya di pemukiman.* Jakarta: CV Rajawali.

Wirosardjono, S. 1986. 'Transmigrasi swakarsa di Indonesia'. In *Transmigrasi di Indonesia 1905-1985*, ed. S. E. Swasono and M. Singarumbun, 298-302. Jakarta: UI Press.

CHAPTER 3

The Javanese of New Caledonia

PAMELA ALLEN

Introduction

The story of how almost 20,000 Javanese were taken to New Caledonia between 1896 and 1949 on five-year labour contracts is a little-known part of the colonial history of the Southeast Asian region. Among other things it is a story of the tension between the cultural hybridity that results when populations move, or are moved, and adapt to new surroundings, and notions of ethnic cohesion in the diaspora.

This chapter draws on ethnographic data obtained through my fieldwork in New Caledonia in May 2010, during which time I conducted interviews with New Caledonian Javanese currently living in the capital Noumea. I also visited the Tiebaghi mine. Jean-Luc Maurer's ethnographic work in New Caledonia was a key secondary source for this chapter.

I begin the chapter by providing an overview of the historical circumstances leading to the existence of what may be termed an Indonesian (predominantly Javanese) diaspora in New Caledonia. I then examine some of the cultural markers of the New Caledonian Javanese, using Barth's idea of boundary maintenance to suggest that those markers are not 'definitional characteristics' of the ethnic group. I follow this with a case study of the Tiebaghi mine, which illustrates both the potential for cultural pluralism in an emerging colony and the destructive impact of the indentured labour system. I then discuss some of the individuals and organisations that keep cultural markers alive in 21st-century New Caledonia.

Background

In 1854 Napoleon III established a penal colony in New Caledonia. Most of the convicts transported there were political prisoners from the Paris Commune.[1] Nickel was discovered in New Caledonia in 1870, and European convicts provided the first labour force. The mining industry was largely controlled by one firm, Société Le Nickel (SLN). Towards the end of the 19th century European immigrants began establishing smallholdings and estates, mainly growing coffee. They preferred imported labour – the Melanesian population was considered 'wholly unreliable' because of their tendency towards rebellion against the colonial government.[2] In 1889, 166 Chinese labourers arrived on five-year contracts, followed in 1892 by six hundred Japanese. The Japanese proved to be insufficiently 'docile' and were subsequently repatriated.[3] Vietnam proved a useful source of labour; in 1891, 768 Vietnamese were recruited, and the use of Vietnamese labour continued until World War II.

In 1894, the French Governor of New Caledonia, Paul Feillet, abolished penal immigration and Asian immigrants replaced prison labour. By 1902 the mining officials had begun to turn to sources other than Indochina, and a contingent of six hundred Indian Hindus from Pondicherry and the first group of Javanese had arrived in New Caledonia. Because it was too costly to import Indians in large numbers, Java and Vietnam became the chief source of labour.[4] After recruiters from New Caledonia negotiated an arrangement with the Netherlands East Indies government, recruiting began in 1902 and the 'first wave' of Javanese emigrants to New Caledonia comprised 170 contract labourers. They would subsequently be classified as *wong kontrak* (contract labourers).[5]

The number of Javanese immigrants to New Caledonia was significantly lower than those going to Malaya or Suriname but

---

1   The Paris Commune briefly ruled Paris from 18 March to 28 May 1871. It was hailed by both the anarchists and the Marxists as the first assumption of power by the working class in Western civilisation. The conditions in which the Commune was formed, and its violent end, resulted in it being a very significant political episode of the time.

2   Lockard 1971, 47.

3   Despite this, another thousand Japanese were brought in in 1900, many of whom escaped and some of whom went on strike.

4   Lockard 1971, 47.

5   Maurer 2006, 192.

there was a more important economic role to be played in New Caledonia than in Malaya. A smaller labour force was required in New Caledonia and conditions were apparently considerably worse than in Malaya or Suriname. Dutch officials were aware of this, and restricted the importation of Javanese.[6] As Craig Lockard sums it up, 'The French system in New Caledonia left much to be desired.'[7]

Lockard describes how Javanese emigration to New Caledonia was inextricably tied in with the indentured labour system and the development of large-scale plantation and mining industries.[8] The indentured labour system operated largely through exploitation and coercion, and this shaped the nature of Overseas Javanese society – in New Caledonia and elsewhere.

There was a 'push' factor to emigration from Java, too. By the late 19th century living conditions in rural Java had become difficult enough to impel people to emigrate, either temporarily or permanently, in search of a better life. Maurer's first chapter is tellingly entitled 'La grande misère de Java à la fin du XIXe siècle'.[9] Furthermore, with the growth of European-owned states in Java and Sumatra in the late 19th century, Javanese had become accustomed to working as wage labourers, so this type of work was not unknown to them. The colonial government used transmigration to alleviate population pressure in Java and to increase the population of other islands in the Netherlands East Indies, but under an 1887 law the local population was refused permission to work outside the Netherlands East Indies, ostensibly because 'it would be powerless to prevent exploitation of the Javanese and that it had insufficient staff to handle emigration'.[10] The British, however, managed to circumvent this law and were able to hire Javanese workers on legal contracts for their plantations and mines in Malaya, Borneo and New Caledonia.

Initially, the Javanese in New Caledonia only worked in agriculture and domestic service. The main hardships for these workers were

---

6   Lockard 1971, 53.

7   Lockard 1971, 54.

8   Lockard 1971, 54.

9   Maurer 2006, 21.

10 Lockard 1971, 43.

the restrictions on their movements and the fact that children – who were not allowed to attend local schools until the late 1930s – were required to work along with their parents. At the expiry of their contracts many Javanese chose to stay on in New Caledonia; some began sharecropping and others were hired by the mines, alongside the Vietnamese, valued on account of their agility and small physical stature, which purportedly made it 'easy' for them to negotiate the underground tunnels.

The number of Javanese living and working in New Caledonia fluctuated significantly in the first half of the 20th century. In 1911 they numbered approximately 1,200. By 1929 this had increased to 7,602, but this number was halved by the end of 1933, when repatriations and death had reduced the Javanese population to 3,541.[11] In the 1930s, the New Caledonian economy faced a chronic labour shortage in the face of a boom in nickel and coffee production, which led to negotiations for a renewal of Javanese immigration and gave rise to the 'second wave' of immigration of Javanese in the years preceding World War II. Between 1933 and 1939 over 7,800 Javanese left Java for Noumea.[12] When they arrived they found employment in agriculture and mining, as well as in the domestic labour sector. Lyons reports that in 1941, 85 per cent of the workforce in the mines was Javanese or Vietnamese.[13] Lewis S. Feuer provides the data in Table 3.1 (next page) concerning Javanese employment in New Caledonia, as of 29 November 1943.

Lockard paints a very unhappy picture of life as a contract labourer in New Caledonia, pointing out that, because contract labour was enforced by penal sanction, an impudent remark to an overseer could be punished by fines and imprisonment.[14] The labourers found it difficult to save any money after paying for food, lodging, medical expenses and repatriation dues. In the mines they had to put up with poor quality food and makeshift housing – two hundred people of

---

11 Thompson and Adloff 1971, 446.

12 Lockard (1971, 57) points out that 'Javanese society as it developed in New Caledonia came increasingly to be centered in an urban milieu.'

13 Lyons 1986.

14 Lockard 1971, 54.

Table 3.1 Javanese employment in New Caledonia, 29 November 1943

Public services	414
Société le Nickel	1696
Industry, commerce, agriculture	3145
Domestic service	1003
Allied forces	18
Free residents	985
Total	7261

Source: Feuer 1946, 265.

both sexes and all ages cramped into one building, with no proper sanitation. The inhumane working conditions in the mines prompted the Dutch consul to protest strongly in 1942 about the conditions for Javanese miners at a nickel smelter near Noumea, where hours and conditions were considered far below international standards. Feuer adds that the chrome mines were devoid of safety measures.[15]

It is perhaps unsurprising, then, that there was widespread labour unrest and that strikes were common. For their part, planters complained that conditions were dangerous, and Feuer quotes one declaring that 'An unfortunate white man who finds himself before fifty or sixty Javanese or Tonkinese risks his skin each time they go on strike.'[16] Feuer reminds us that, while the Javanese in New Caledonia were highly regarded workers, they were also instrumental in bringing to an end sixty years of indentured labour in the territory.[17]

The year 1942 marked the beginning of U.S. occupation of the island. Javanese and Vietnamese workers who began working for the Americans were offered fair wages at the same time as the French government decided to renew expiring indentures. There resulted an exodus of Asians to U.S. camps. Early in 1944, the Vietnamese declared a general strike that spread throughout the island. Hitherto, the Javanese labourers had not been active participants in the labour

15 Feuer 1946, 266.
16 Feuer 1946, 265.
17 Feuer 1946, 264.

movement, influenced perhaps by the Dutch consul who advised them to be patient. Eventually, however, they began to demonstrate at the Netherlands consulate and to threaten action with the Vietnamese. The French authorities eventually capitulated, abolishing indenture on 5 July 1945 and granting free residence to all Asians who desired it.

After the end of the contract labour system, the Javanese who chose to remain in New Caledonia progressively left their jobs in mining and public works for employment in other occupations.[18] Post-war, the Javanese continued to migrate to New Caledonia until 1949, when those arriving on the last boat were classified as *wong anyar*, the Javanese term for 'newcomers'.[19] By 1953 the local-born population, the Caledonians, were becoming resistant to the idea of further immigration to the territory, and it was on that basis that the general council in New Caledonia rejected a Dutch proposal to open New Caledonia's doors to Eurasian immigrants from Indonesia.[20]

The 'third wave' of emigration comprised approximately six hundred Indonesians who moved to New Caledonia at the time of the nickel boom between 1967 and 1972, to work on renewable annual contracts, mainly in the construction industry. These were the *wong baru* – a mixed Javanese/Indonesian term for 'newcomers'.[21] Virginia Thompson and Richard Adloff cite figures of 876 male Javanese wage earners and 173 female Javanese wage earners as of 1 January 1967.[22] Their journey to and arrival in New Caledonia was greatly facilitated by the fact that the large public works company Citra, which was well established in Indonesia, had succeeded in acquiring a number of construction contracts in New Caledonia. Many of the wong baru had worked for Citra on the construction of the Jatiluhur Dam in West Java.[23] The Javanese earned the reputation of being industrious workers, but only a few of those third-wave migrants remain in New Caledonia; the vast majority moved back to Indonesia and some have passed away.

---

18 Thompson and Adloff 1971, 441.

19 Maurer 2006, 192.

20 Thompson and Adloff 1971, 369.

21 Maurer 2006, 192.

22 Thompson and Adloff 1971, 442.

23 Maurer 2006, 192–193.

Time and purpose of migration stratified the Indonesian community in New Caledonia. As well as the categories mentioned above, there are those known as *niaouli*. These are the New Caledonia-born descendants of first- and second-wave Javanese emigrants; their moniker derives from the niaouli tree – a hardy eucalypt that is emblematic of New Caledonia – ostensibly because the Javanese were as resilient and adaptable as the niaouli.[24] In addition, the *wong baleh* (returnees) are those Javanese born in New Caledonia who returned to Indonesia but subsequently came back to New Caledonia, and the *wong jukuan* are those born in Indonesia and brought to New Caledonia by local Indonesians – usually women moving to New Caledonia to get married.[25] Currently 1.6 per cent of the population of New Caledonia are of 'Indonesian' ethnicity.[26]

A Javanese/ Indonesian Diaspora?

While acknowledging the ideological debates surrounding the notion of 'diaspora',[27] I nonetheless find it a useful term to describe groups

---

24 Another explanation is that the name was given because the Javanese mothers working in the coffee plantations had the habit of hanging the sarong in which they cocooned their babies on the branches of niaoulis as they worked.

25 Maurer 2006, 192.

26 267,840 (July 2014 est.) *The World Factbook*. www.cia.gov/library/publications/the-world-factbook/geos/nc.html (accessed 17 April 2014). While New Caledonia was a French colony (1853–1946) the Javanese population was listed in the census as 'Javanese.' The term 'Indonesian' has been used in subsequent censuses.

27 Robin Cohen, in his seminal text *Global Diasporas* (2001) identifies a number of common features of a diaspora: dispersal from an original homeland; collective memory and myth; group consciousness; tolerance for pluralism. It appears, however, that not all groups that fit these characteristics can properly be called a diaspora. Cohen alludes to the fact that the term diaspora is often used 'casually, in an untheorized or undertheorized way' (p. x) but concurs with other scholars such as James Clifford and Barbara Kirschenblatt-Gimblett that it should be possible to recognise models of diaspora that do not fit with the 'normative' model of the Jewish diaspora. Ien Ang (2001, 13) laments the fact that the notion of the 'Chinese diaspora' has the effect of essentialising Chinese identity.

of people who have been moved from their homeland to another place. This in turn gives rise to the notion of establishing an ethnic identity in the new place of residence, a process often accompanied by nostalgia for an ancestral homeland that is frequently imagined rather than actual. James Clifford posed the key question almost thirty years ago: 'What does it mean, at the end of the 20th century, to speak ... of a "native land"?'[28]

Harold Isaacs writes of the idea of the 'ancestral homeland' as being a 'critical ingredient' in understandings of group identity.[29] This can sometimes lead to an intensification, rather than a weakening of cultural and ethnic allegiances. In the case of most of the Javanese in the diasporic community in New Caledonia – certainly those who came on the first and second 'waves' – the 'ancestral homeland' was not Indonesia, but Java. Now incorporated into the nation-state of Indonesia, the idea of Java in the diaspora is both geographically and historically removed from the idea of Java in contemporary Indonesia, meaning that many overseas Javanese have an ethnic and cultural allegiance to something that exists largely in imagination and memory. As Bill Ashcroft puts it, '"Home" is deeply embedded in memories that are not one's own.'[30] The result can be a sort of museumisation of cultural practices.

I am interested to discover whether in New Caledonia the idea of the 'ancestral homeland' had led to 'tradition' becoming what Monisha Das Gupta calls an 'embattled category', because new social institutions in the homeland are not transferred to the immigrant community, where cultural practices may become 'museumised'.[31] Das Gupta found that first-generation Indian immigrants in New York took pride in being 'more Indian than Indians in India'.[32]

Both Patrick Griffin and Len von Morze write of the impact of long-distance migration on a sort of constructed unity in the new diasporic community. In his study of migration to America,

---

28 Clifford 1988, 37.

29 Isaacs 1976, 45.

30 Ashcroft 2001, 197.

31 Das Gupta 1997, 580.

32 Das Gupta 1997, 580.

Griffin notes that 'only in America . . . did men and women who left Scotland become Scots, or migrants from German-speaking regions of Europe discover a semblance of German unity' and Morze comments on the phenomenon of 'invented and cultivated ethnic identification' whereby 'transatlantic migration forged new national unities among émigrés that did not exist before'.[33] The history of the Javanese in New Caledonia does indeed reveal an intensification of ethnic identification, certainly in the early days, although national allegiances and generational change have modified the intensity of that identification.

How might a Javanese living in 21st century New Caledonia describe what makes them Javanese or Indonesian? How might they answer the question, 'What is Javanese/Indonesian about you?' It is a question raised by others studying diasporic cultures, including Das Gupta in her study of second-generation Indian women in America. Her conclusion is that 'What is "Indian" . . . is not automatically what is preserved but what is constructed as preserved.'[34]

Cultural Markers

The Javanese constitute a distinct community in New Caledonia, held together, one might argue, by the cultural markers that include language and ritual. At celebratory events one will witness Javanese music, dance, *wayang* (puppet performance) and the consumption of Javanese food. However, Alice Dewey observed the openness to change of New Caledonian Javanese – especially those in Noumea, where there has been no 'ghettoisation' of the Javanese. Intermarriage with other ethnic groups is not uncommon.[35] How important, then, are those cultural markers in defining what it means to be Javanese in New Caledonia?

My discussion of cultural markers among the New Caledonian Javanese is informed by the work of two scholars in particular. The first is Fredrik Barth's challenge to the view that an ethnic group is a culture-bearing unit. Barth sees the sharing of a culture as a *result*,

---

33 Griffin 2001, 4; Morze 2006, 199.

34 Das Gupta 1997, 580.

35 Dewey 1970.

rather than a *definitional characteristic*, of ethnic group organisation. He argues that harnessing culture to an ethnic group does not allow for the 'ecological circumstances' that result in an ethnic group exhibiting regional diversities in their cultural practice.[36] I have found Barth's thinking to be pertinent to my study of the Javanese in New Caledonia on account of his scrutiny of what it is that defines an ethnic group and in his key concern with 'ethnic groups and their persistence'.[37] Specifically, I am interested in what, if any, key cultural practices could be regarded as 'definitional characteristics' of the Javanese ethnic group in New Caledonia. One might ask whether those who participate in localised forms of the *selamatan* ritual (a ritual meal) in New Caledonia can still rightly be called Javanese, because their cultural practice has been subject to the 'ecological circumstances' of migration. One might also ask whether those Javanese in New Caledonia who do not participate in the selamatan and who speak only French can still rightly be called Javanese because they do not engage with Javanese cultural practices.

The second scholar is the American anthropologist Alice Dewey, one of very few scholars to undertake extensive empirical research on the Javanese in New Caledonia.[38] Dewey's focus on the importance of ritual as a mechanism for embedding social relations is particularly pertinent to my discussion of cultural markers below.

Language

Because *bahasa Indonesia* is the language of modern Indonesia – the 'homeland' of the New Caledonian Javanese – I am interested to examine whether and how that language might function as a cultural marker among the ethnic group.

Much has been written about the links between language and identity. Michael Billig tells us that 'an identity is to be found in the embodied habits of social life . . . includ[ing] those of thinking and

36 Barth 1970, 12.

37 Barth 1970, 9.

38 The American historian Craig Lockard and the French sociologist Jean-Luc Maurer have made very important contributions to their respective fields.

using language.'[39] That purported link between identity and language
is very significant when we recall the circumstances surrounding
the development of bahasa Indonesia as the national language of
Indonesia, in a process that successfully persuaded the population of
the ethnically and linguistically diverse archipelago that 'a particular
outside language should become their own integrative, inter-ethnic,
unifying tongue'.[40]

As Webb Keane observes, bahasa Indonesia is not 'freighted'
with religious and ethnic baggage, nor is it a language of 'ancient
lineage' or 'closely guarded cultural property'.[41] Indeed, it seems
to belong 'to no one in particular'.[42] Arguably, the key function of
bahasa Indonesia, as enunciated by Benedict Anderson in 1966, is as
a 'national unifier'.[43]

For people in New Caledonia, bahasa Indonesia is a foreign language, despite it being the language of the nation of which Java
is a part. New Caledonian Javanese speak French and a version
of Javanese known as New Caledonian Javanese. Most Javanese
children attend French schools with children from all ethnic groups.
Unlike Javanese, bahasa Indonesia is not, and never will be, officially
listed as one of the ethnic languages of New Caledonian immigrant
communities. While official discourse in the Indonesian consulate
in New Caledonia is conducted in bahasa Indonesia, the Javanese
community still use mainly *ngoko* or *krama* Javanese. The 'Languages
of the World' database Ethnologue lists 'New Caledonian Javanese' as
a language spoken by four thousand members of the Javanese ethnic
community in New Caledonia, ranking it seventh in the country in
terms of number of speakers.[44]

Those who do speak and learn bahasa Indonesia in New Caledonia
are geographically and historically removed from the political debates

39 Billig 1997, 8.
40 Fishman 1978: 333. One might ask how Billig's notion of language being
   an 'embodied habit' sits with the sudden and conscious adoption of a new
   language – what Joshua Fishman calls a 'linguistic miracle.'
41 Keane 2003, 504.
42 Keane 2003, 505.
43 Anderson 1966, 105.
44 www.ethnologue.com/language/jas

and alliances that have been a part of its development in Indonesia. They can learn the language without taking on board the social and political baggage that accompanies the language in Indonesia. Many New Caledonian Indonesians travel regularly to Indonesia. Marcel Magi is an example of a high-profile New Caledonian Javanese who felt increasingly embarrassed at being unable to communicate with his aunts, uncles and cousins in Java. A niaouli, Marcel was prompted by that sense of linguistic disconnectedness to try to forge some group and ethnic cohesion among locally born Indonesians. (To this end, he was behind the establishment of the group called Asal Usul, meaning Origins, with the aim of fostering some group and ethnic cohesion among locally born Indonesians.) Marcel began taking lessons in bahasa Indonesia at the Indonesian consulate in Noumea.

For Marcel Magi and other New Caledonian Javanese learning bahasa Indonesia, the language inevitably has a different meaning than it does for those who live in Indonesia. It is a cultural marker in New Caledonia, a language associated with a particular ethnic group. As more New Caledonian Javanese learn the language it may increasingly be a unifier of that ethnic group. But it is not a definitional characteristic of the New Caledonian Javanese – because one does not have to speak bahasa Indonesia in order to claim membership of the ethnic group. In Barth's terms, it is a result, rather than a characteristic, of ethnic group organisation.

Selamatan

Central to the Javanese worldview is the notion of correct thought and action, involving the 'matching of inner and outer, thought or word with action leading to the state of *slamet*'.[45] Andrew Beatty's informant Pak Saleh describes the state of *slamet* as 'when you go to bed at night, get up in the morning and you are still there; nothing has happened. Slamet is not being bothered by demons.'[46]

Central to the achievement of slamet is the ritual meal *selamatan* comprising offerings, symbolic food and prayer. While there is still

---

45 Beatty 1999, 163.

46 Beatty 1999, 118.

debate over the origins of the selamatan – Mark Woodward regarding it as a Sufi-inspired Islamic custom, Clifford Geertz describing it as 'a kind of social universal joint' with origins in animist traditions, and Thomas Gibson pointing out that selamatan rituals 'parallel similar practices found throughout the Islamic world' – all agree that it occupies a central place in Javanese religion and culture.[47]

Alice Dewey conducted research in New Caledonia to ascertain whether the selamatan was resilient and flexible enough to survive the displacement inherent in the diaspora. She concluded that 'its continued survival . . . in the foreign urban setting of Noumea indicates that the flexibility of the ritual has been underestimated.'[48] As indicated above, and as reiterated by Dewey, the selametan is not an intrinsic part of Islam, so its continued observance in immigrant communities is not because of Islamic religious observance. It can thus be understood as a cultural, rather than a purely religious marker.

In New Caledonia, as in other diasporic Javanese communities, the selamatan has been adapted, so that it both adapts to local cultural circumstances, and continues its role as a cultural unifier among the diaspora. Dewey points out that this has been done in New Caledonia by merging the selamatan with the secular feast known as *djagongan*.[49] To what extent, then, is the selamatan a definitional characteristic of the Javanese in New Caledonia? It is clear from Dewey's early work, and supported by my observations in New Caledonia in 2010, that what the New Caledonian Javanese term a selamatan is somewhat different than how it is understood by their relatives in Java. Because the New Caledonian Javanese version of the selamatan has incorporated elements of the djagongan, whole families are included (not just male representatives). Rather than taking food home, as is the practice in Java, people tend to linger and socialise longer. There is also more interaction between the guests in New Caledonia, because people do not come together as often as they do in Java. Narrowly defined, then, the selamatan is not a definitional characteristic of the New Caledonian Javanese. An adapted and modified form of the selamatan is, however, a cultural

---

47 Woodward 1989, 85; Geertz 1960, 11; Gibson 2000, 56.

48 Dewey 1970: 438.

49 Dewey 1970, 446.

marker, one that has resulted from ethnic group organisation in this diasporic community.

Neighbourhood and Kinship Ties

While in Java a strongly developed sense of neighbourhood strengthens ethnic cohesion, in New Caledonia the neighbourhood is less important in this respect. Dewey attributes this to a number of factors. Because of a strong economy and mobility in employment, people readily and frequently move for work and, unlike the situation in rural Java in particular, are not dependent on each other for exchange labour in the fields. Dewey concludes that cliques ('friends and friendly kinsmen, united by ties of personal liking and common interest in such things as leisure activities'), rather than the neighbourhood, are the most important groups for the Noumean Javanese.[50]

Dewey adds that notions of kinship are also different, because most Javanese families in New Caledonia have few kin beyond the nuclear family unit. Perhaps of more significance than kinship is the notion of *kawane*. While meaning 'friend', the word has a more profound significance in the New Caledonian context, alluding as it does to the people with whom one shared a boat on the voyage from the homeland to the new settlement. Maurer's respondent Marie-Jo Siban reports that the first question the contracted labourers would ask each other in New Caledonia was not about family but rather about *kawane*: '*Sampean nomer pinten, kapal nomor pinten?*' ('What was your number, what boat were you on?') The kawane, Siban suggests, became a kind of substitute family and those ties are still recognised and honoured in successive generations.[51]

Among New Caledonia Javanese, then, kinship and neighbourhood ties are important cultural markers. However, the 'ecological circumstances' of the New Caledonian Javanese mean that both 'kinship' and 'neighbourhood' are understood differently there than in Java. One's 'kin' can be one's shipmate and one's 'neighbour'

---

50 Dewey 1970, 444.

51 Maurer 2006, 291. Similarly in Suriname the term *djadji* was used to describe a group of people who had arrived on the same boat, and the djadji often became a family substitute, continuing through subsequent generations.

can be a kinsman from a different neighbourhood with whom one shares a particular interest. As with the selamatan, an evolved form of kinship and neighbourliness has thus developed, and has become a key cultural marker of the Javanese in New Caledonia, but it is not the same notion of kinship and neighbourliness that one might find in a rural village in Java.

The above brief analysis of cultural markers reveals a slippage that is not always evident, between definitional characteristics of an ethnic group and practices that have evolved as a result of group cohesion – and that have on occasion become ritualised. From the inside, perhaps, both types of cultural markers are a sort of glue – the stuff that binds the group together. From a Barthian perspective, however, it is notable that the things we might *think* are cultural markers that define an ethnic group may in fact be practices that have resulted from migration, adaptation to a new homeland, and concerted efforts at group cohesion, and which are markedly differ- ent from the 'characteristic' cultural markers of the ethnic group in other locations.

Preserving the Cultural Markers: The Tiebaghi Mine

That participating in cultural practices and rituals – be they 'defi- nitional', learned or constructed – is important for group cohesion is nowhere more evident than at the abandoned Tiebaghi mining village (founded in 1875 and abandoned in 1964), home now to a museum that commemorates both the technical aspects of the mine and its cultural legacy. This compelling contemporary relic of the first and second waves of contract workers in New Caledonia is in the remote mountainous region near Koumac in the north. It was the destination for many Javanese contract labourers (both new immigrants and locally born) between 1896 and 1949. In Tiebaghi, the Javanese worked underground in the lucrative chrome mine, alongside Vietnamese and Japanese.

The mine site and the relics of the mining village harbour a wealth of information about life in the multicultural mining community which, as well as housing the Asian labourers, was home to Italian, American, French, Caledonian, Wallisian and Melanesian miners and their families.

While language was a barrier, preventing non-French speaking Javanese from mixing with the other ethnic groups, they were united by sport, music and theatre. As well as playing soccer for the Tiebaghi team, the Chromes, photographs abound of the Javanese miners playing a variety of musical instruments, including guitar and accordion, and performing *wayang wong* (a classical Javanese theatrical performance) in the Tiebaghi Club. While most were Muslim, there was no mosque in Tiebaghi, so prayers were conducted at home. A former Javanese resident of Tiebaghi recalls the difficulty of observing the fasting month of Ramadan and the fact that most Javanese did their best nonetheless to fulfil their religious obligation. She also notes the understanding and tolerance displayed by members of the other ethnic groups.

Of great interest to geologists on account of its extraordinarily rich chrome and nickel deposits, the Tiebaghi mine and former miners' village at first glance seems an unlikely place to go looking for traces of Javanese culture. However, having made the journey by road to the abandoned mine site and having undertaken the rather arduous trek to the top of the mountain, one is in for a surprise. The multicultural village, home to the miners and their families, now eerily empty yet replete with relics of the past, was divided into quarters based on race. The Italians, the Melanesians and the Wallisians had their own quarters. So too did the Vietnamese and the Javanese. Both the mine and the village are currently being restored by The North Caledonian Society for the Preservation of Mining and Historical Heritage (Association Pour La Sauvegarde du Patrimoine Minier et Historique du Nord Caledonien), which has secured and preserved the mine as it was on the day operations ceased, and restored some of the old buildings.

The relics and documents collected by the Society include notes and memos attesting to the character of the Javanese who lived in Tiebaghi: 'gentle, helpful and loyal' (*doux, serviables et fidèles*), wrote one; 'calm, quiet, hard-working' (*calme, tranquille, travaille*) wrote another. There is a photograph in the museum in Tiebaghi depicting celebrations held in Tiebaghi village to mark Indonesian independence.

A 21st-century visitor to the mine with an interest in Indonesia is struck by poignant reminders of the lives of the miners there – familiar objects in an unfamiliar setting. There is a photograph of three young Javanese miners' wives, dressed in European clothes but bearing platters of sate (satay) for a Javanese selamatan thanksgiving feast. Another photograph depicts a troupe of wayang wong performers, their costumes and masks evocative of their homeland, but the context slightly out of kilter as they pose in front of one of the Vietnamese houses. On the register of arrivals one finds names that are clearly Javanese – Kartodimoedjo, Hassan, Sanadi – and also those that reveal the intermarriage that took place: André Kesman, Henri Midjan. The list of clothing rations reveals that while the clothing issued was almost uniformly European – cotton shirt, pants and hat for the men – the Javanese women were also issued with a sarong.

Keeping it All Together: Javanese/Indonesians in a Plural Society

As Lockard has pointed out, and as indicated in the above scenario of the Tiebaghi mine, over time the Javanese became one segment of what was a socially and culturally plural society.[52] Despite the scenes of conviviality in evidence at the Tiebaghi mine site, however, that plural society was not always a happy and harmonious one. Myriam Dornoy cites the views of a prominent citizen, Louis Forrest, who did not hide his feelings about multiculturalism:

> Noumea is being invaded by yellow hordes, Javanese, Tonkinese, who live in debauched conditions of laziness, prostitution and theft. The scandal is worst when they take over European houses to the detriment of French people . . . Noumea must be rid of these undesirables who do anything but work . . . All Asiatics who are in irregular situations must be deported.[53]

Perhaps because, as Dornoy suggests, they 'consider themselves French and not a minority', or perhaps because of their 'adaptability', Indonesians are fairly well integrated into Caledonian society.[54] The descendants of the Javanese families at Tiebaghi are now dispersed throughout New Caledonia. While many of them have stronger links to France than they do to Indonesia, emotional ties with Indonesia

---

52 Lockard 1971, 43.

53 *Bulletin du Commerce* 5 May 1948 cited in Dornoy 1984, 45.

54 Dornoy 1984, 79, 65.

are keenly felt, especially as many Javanese New Caledonians still have family in Indonesia. Below I give a snapshot of some contemporary New Caledonian Indonesians.

Djintar Tambunan was born on Lake Toba, North Sumatra, in 1945. Tambunan (as he prefers to be called) moved to New Caledonia during the mining boom in 1970, as part of the 'third wave' of migration. He came to work for the big construction company Citra, and still works as an engineer in Noumea. Djintar Tambunan is one of very few Indonesians in New Caledonia who speak fluent Indonesian. His Javanese wife Soetina does not. Nor do his two adult children. Like most of their Indonesian friends, their preferred language is French.

Suminah (who calls herself Evelyne when she goes to metropolitan France) is an example of a wong baleh. She was born of Javanese parents in New Caledonia, moved to Indonesia with her mother in 1953, and then four years later moved back to New Caledonia because her mother was unhappy in Indonesia. Suminah is married to André Vaquijot, whose father came to New Caledonia from Java in 1902. Unlike his wife, who speaks good Indonesian, André cannot speak bahasa Indonesia (but can understand it). Both Suminah and André are active members of the Indonesian Association of New Caledonia; André is on the Executive. Proficiency in bahasa Indonesia, while a cultural marker of the Indonesian community in New Caledonia, is thus clearly not a definitional characteristic.

Shirly Timan is a wong jukuan. She teaches bahasa Indonesia at the Indonesian Consulate in Noumea. She came to Noumea twenty years ago to marry her niaouli husband. She spoke no French when she arrived and earned her living as a singer, an occupation she still follows. Now, however, she is sufficiently fluent in French to be able to use it to teach Indonesian. Mention has already been made of some of the cultural organisations that help preserve and perpetuate the cultural markers that have been discussed in this chapter. The various branches of the Indonesian Association of New Caledonia and organisations such as Club Jeunesse Indonesienne (Indonesian Youth Club) regularly organise events and celebrations designed to reinforce a sense of Indonesian identity. Since 1996, for example, a commemoration has been held to honour the arrival of the first Indonesians in New Caledonia. The official description of such events, in the press and on the Consulate website, is couched in rhetoric about the importance of the Indonesians feeling 'equal' to their 'Caledonian brothers' and being 'up to par' relative to other ethnic groups. The Consulate General of the Republic of Indonesia in Noumea (established in 1951) plays an important role in supporting and promoting Indonesian culture. The Consulate runs dance, gamelan and *pencak silat* (martial art) classes, which attract both Indonesians and those from other ethnic groups.

As I have discussed elsewhere, the 'exhibitionary' nature of the cultural activities and projects supported by the Indonesian consulate reflects its mission of promoting 'national' Indonesian culture, but a significant proportion of those cultural activities that ostensibly 'typify' Indonesian culture are in fact Javanese.[55] The hegemony of the Javanese, an ongoing source of tension in Indonesia, is thus subtly, and probably unintentionally, reinforced.

Concluding Remarks

It must be acknowledged that it is erroneous to think of 'Javanese culture' as 'one culture'; regional variations mean that a diversity of practices and customs can be regarded as 'Javanese' and none can legitimately make claims for 'truth' or 'authenticity'. Koentjaraningrat points out that Javanese culture does not comprise 'homogeneous unity' and that regional diversity 'extends over [the] Central and East Javanese homeland'.[56] It could be argued, then, that what we find in New Caledonia are varieties of Javanese culture that contribute to the diversity highlighted by Koentjaraningrat.

The tension between cultural hybridity and ethnic cohesion, something that is at the heart of the migrant experience, is evident among the Indonesians in New Caledonia. It is a tension that was faced by those early agricultural coolies and mine labourers, who had to learn to speak French and eat bread rather than rice, but who remained Muslim and loved to watch wayang wong. It is a tension experienced by contemporary Indonesians who, while holding French passports, speak Javanese at home and are enthusiastic

---

55 Allen 2011.

56 Koentjaraningrat 1985, 21.

participants in events organised by the Indonesian Association of New Caledonia. It is a tension articulated by Marcel Magi who is married to a Spanish woman and who is perhaps more at home in Europe than in Asia, but who is driven by a yearning to learn bahasa Indonesia so that he can connect with his own family in Java.

References

Allen, P. 2011. 'Javanese Cultural Traditions in Suriname'. *Review of Indonesian and Malaysian Affairs* 45(1&2): 199–223.

Ang, I. 2001. *On not Speaking Chinese: Living Between Asia and the West.* London: Routledge.

Anderson, B. 1966. 'The Languages of Indonesian Politics'. *Indonesia* 1: 89–116.

Ashcroft, B. 2016. *Post-Colonial Transformation.* London: Routledge.

Barth, F. 1970. *Ethnic Groups and Boundaries: The Social Organization of Culture Difference.* Bergen: Universitetsforlaget.

Beatty, A. 1999. *Varieties of Javanese Religion: An Anthropological Account.* Cambridge: Cambridge University Press.

Billig, M. 1997. *Banal Nationalism.* London: Sage.

Clifford, J. 1988. *The Predicament of Culture: Twentieth-Century Ethnography, Literature, and Art.* Cambridge, Mass.: Harvard University Press.

Cohen, R. 2001. *Global Diasporas: An Introduction.* Abingdon, Oxon: Routledge.

Dewey, A. G. 1970. 'Ritual as a Mechanism for Urban Adaptation'. *Man* 5(3): 438–448.

Dornoy, M. 1984. *Politics in New Caledonia.* Sydney: Sydney University Press.

Feuer, L. S. 1946. 'End of Coolie Labor in New Caledonia'. *Far Eastern Survey* 15–17 (28 August): 264–267.

Fishman, J. A. 1978. 'The Indonesian Language Planning Experience: What Does it Teach Us?' In *Spectrum: Essays Presented to Sutan Takdir Alisjahbana on his Seventieth Birthday*, ed. S. Udin, 333–339. Jakarta: Dian Rakyat.

Geertz, C. 1960. *The Religion of Java.* Glencoe: The Free Press.

Gibson, T. 2000. 'Islam and the Spirit Cults in New Order Indonesia: Global Flows vs Local Knowledge'. *Indonesia* 69: 41–70.

Griffin, P. 2001. *The People with No Name: Ireland's Ulster Scots, America's Scots Irish, and the Creation of a British Atlantic World, 1689-1764.* Princeton: Princeton University Press.

Gupta, M. Das 1997. "'What Is Indian about You?'": A Gendered, Transnational Approach to Ethnicity'. *Gender and Society* 11(5): 572–596.

Isaacs, H. R. 1976. 'Basic Group Identity: The Idols of the Tribe'. In *Ethnicity: Theory and Experience*, ed. N. Glazer and D. P. Moynihan, 29–52. Cambridge, Mass.: Harvard University Press.

Keane, W. 2003. 'Public Speaking: On Indonesian as the Language of the Nation'. *Public Culture* 15(3): 503–550.

Koentjaraningrat 1985. *Javanese Culture*. Singapore: Oxford University Press.

Lockard, C. 1971. 'The Javanese as Emigrant: Observations on the Development of Javanese Settlements Overseas'. *Indonesia* 11: 41–62.

Lyons, M. 1986. *The Totem and the Tricolour: A Short History of New Caledonia since 1774*. Kensington: New South Wales University Press.

Maurer, J-L. 2006. *Les Javanais du Caillou: Des affres de l'exil aux aléas de l'intégration*. Paris: Association Archipel.

Morze, L. von 2006. 'Republican Centaurs: Crises of American Legitimacy and the Naming of a Mobile Nation'. *Early American Studies* 4(1): 192–232.

Thompson, V. and R. Adloff 1971. *The French Pacific Islands: French Polynesia and New Caledonia*. Berkeley: University of California Press.

Woodward, M. R. 1989. *Islam in Java: Normative Piety and Mysticism in the Sultanate of Yogyakarta*. Tucson: University of Arizona Press.

CHAPTER 4

Javanese in Malaysia

Labour Migration, Settlement and Diaspora

AMARJIT KAUR

Javanese labour migration to Malaya in the late 19th century was the third most important migration movement after Chinese and Indian labour migration. It correlated with the increased demand for raw materials in industrialising Europe and labour shortages that necessitated the importation of cheap foreign workers. Javanese migrants were hired mostly for employment on rubber plantations and their subsequent settlement in the country laid the foundation for an incipient Javanese diaspora. Following Malayan independence in 1957, the government halted the recruitment of less-skilled foreign labour and expelled non-citizens from the country. In the 1970s Malaysia instigated an export-oriented industrialisation strategy. With the Malays primarily engaged in agriculture, the government espoused federal land development schemes (FELDA) and plantations rather than small farms in the countryside and promoted oil palm cultivation. Concurrently, the government embraced labour-intensive manufacturing production. Apart from increased employment opportunities on the land development programmes, Malaysia also became an important location for foreign manufacturing production. The changing economic structures and Malaysian women's greater participation in the formal sectors created a niche for mainly Indonesian domestic workers. For this reason the Malaysian government re-instated the recruitment of less-skilled Javanese workers chiefly for agricultural development schemes and the construction, manufacturing and domestic work sectors.

Although the Malaysian government originally regarded Javanese (and Indonesians) as the ideal/preferred foreign workers, the influx of large numbers of undocumented Indonesians prompted the government to implement policy changes relating to Javanese/Indonesian labour recruitment. Javanese/Indonesians were thereby seen as 'unwelcome' guests and hence had to meet additional immigration regulations. Crucially, while foreign skilled migrants were allowed to move freely in the country, the less-skilled, temporary Javanese/Indonesian workers became more segregated by occupational status and income, and were also subjected to regular mass expulsions. Accordingly, most Javanese/Indonesian labour migration continued to be mired in the ongoing debates about the downside of letting in less-skilled migrants and Malaysia's inability to devise a coherent policy to deter irregular migration.

This chapter contributes to the literature on Javanese labour migration and settlement in Malaysia since the 1870s. It provides important insights into Malaysia's shifting foreign labour policies and the nexus between the state's evolving strategies and governance arrangements for Indonesian migrant workers. Importantly, it elucidates the rationale for the Malaysian state's recent policies for the recruitment of Javanese migrant workers. This is principally because despite developments in global governance systems designed to promote orderly and safe migration, the dual impacts of globalisation and economic restructuring have resulted in greater labour flexibility and employment insecurity for Javanese (and other migrant workers). Finally, the impact of Malaysian policies on Javanese migrant workers' daily life, accommodation strategies, and sense of belonging will be briefly examined.

Introduction: Boundaries, Colonialism and Migration in Southeast Asia

Southeast Asia was integrated into the world trade system between the 15th and 17th centuries in the wider framework of European seaborne empires and gained an expanded role in intra-Asian trade.[1] The Europeans organised their trading activities via chartered companies, the most prominent of which were the English East India Company (EIC) and the Dutch East India Company (VOC). These companies were largely independent of the home governments;

---

1 The following section is based on Kaur 2004.

they had the authority to conclude treaties with local rulers and also built military establishments to defend themselves. There was strong competition among the Europeans for a share in the East Indian spice trade and they sought to dominate trade networks through monopolies by excluding Asian middlemen who had traditionally controlled the pepper and spice trade. In 1682, the VOC expelled the English from their headquarters at Bantam in Java. Subsequently, the EIC established a permanent base at Bengkulu in Sumatra in 1685. The EIC also organised other 'factories' in western Sumatra for pepper cultivation in order to retain their share of the pepper and spice trade.

The EIC established trading settlements at Penang (1786) and Singapore (1819) to gain control of maritime trade routes in the Melaka Strait while the Dutch expanded their influence from Java onto the surrounding islands. In 1824, the British and Dutch governments concluded the Treaty of London to resolve territorial and trade disputes arising from the British occupation of Dutch properties during the Napoleonic Wars and to demarcate their respective spheres of influence in the Malay world. The Dutch transferred Melaka to Britain in exchange for Bengkulu and Britain's validation of Dutch territorial claims south of the Melaka Strait. In the wake of the Industrial Revolution and the demise of the trading companies, the European powers' stake in Southeast Asia shifted to the annexation of overseas territories in order to gain exclusive control over the region's economic resources.

These territorial agreements and emerging colonial ambitions led to important changes in the political arena. The British traders progressively consolidated their authority over the three separate EIC Settlements and formed a larger entity known as the Straits Settlements (SS) in 1826. The British government later took over the administration of the SS in Malaya, following the removal of the Company's monopoly of trade with India and China and the dissolution of the EIC in 1874. Not surprisingly, Britain extended its political influence over the four western 'tin' states, Perak, Selangor, Negeri Sembilan and Pahang. In 1895, these states were merged to form the Federated Malay States (FMS). A British resident general governed the FMS and Britain assumed responsibility over the Malay states' foreign affairs and defence. The other Malayan states, namely,

Map 4.1 Southeast Asia – colonial states and boundaries
Source: Kaur 2004, 28.

Johor, and the northern Malay states (Kedah, Kelantan, Perlis and Terengganu) were administered as discrete British protectorates and did not have shared institutions.

The consolidation of British domination in Asia preceded the introduction of modern bureaucratic systems and the development of road and rail networks by the colonial government. These facilitated the opening up of new areas in Malaya and the expansion of mining and commercial agriculture by European capitalists. Persistent labour shortages and a demand for a regular labour supply began to play a key role in Britain's colonial policy. From the second half of the 19th century, the Malayan economy was marked by increased flows of capital and commodities, and the growth of export-oriented enterprises and labour migration.

Table 4.1 Population growth in Southeast Asia, 1890–1940 (in thousands)

Country	1890	1900	1910	1920	1930	1940
Indonesia	35,081	40,209	46,086	52,823	60,727	70,476
Malaya*	684	985	1,419	2,044	2,945	4,242

*The figures for Malaya exclude Singapore. Source: Kaur 2004, 36.

With the exception of Indonesia (Java), the other major states in Southeast Asia – Burma, Malaya, Indo-China, the Philippines and Thailand (Map 4.1) – had low population growth rates relative to the extent of their cultivable area. Around 1870, the total population was estimated at 55 million and this figure rose to 69 million in 1900. Between 1870 and 1930 the average annual growth rate in the region was calculated at 1.3 per cent. Moreover, the population was distributed very unevenly and population densities were relatively low. European and U.S. colonialism provoked mass migration. In Malaya, in addition to Chinese and Indian workers, Javanese workers formed a third migration stream that corresponded with the growth of the rubber plantation sector.

Demographic change in Malaya and Indonesia between 1890 and 1940 is presented in Table 4.1, indicating that low population growth was an unvarying feature in Malayan demographic history, despite colonial immigration policy. This situation persists to this day. Crucially, population growth in Malaya was largely due to labour immigration by Chinese, Indians and Javanese.

The Growth of the Export Economy and Labour Migration

Historically, Chinese migrants had gone to the SS, and they later extended their commercial activities to the western Malay states, specifically Johor, Perak and Selangor. Chinese capital and labour also largely dominated the tin mining industry in the western Malay states. The Malay rulers of Johor, Perak and Selangor were also attracted to the opportunities presented by the mining and commercial agriculture sectors, but were not keen on additional Chinese immigration. During this period, the practice of debt-bondage was pervasive in these states and indigenous Malay peasants and fishermen were obliged to perform *kerah* or compulsory services for the rulers.

The British colonial establishment and capitalists originally turned to India to overcome labour shortages in Malaya for the commercial development of the country. The process of Indian labour market operational planning for the plantation sector was organised via legislation, recruitment systems and immigration policies that operated to safeguard the interests of western companies and maintain workforce fragmentation. Plantation labour regimes were essentially based on two considerations. The first was the mobilisation of a largely migrant labour force to accelerate the use of economic and extra-economic resources to maintain low wage bills. The second was an ethnic and gender differentiation of labour that would enable the state to manipulate both workers and wages.

Labour costs on Malaysian plantations were divided into two categories: maintenance and renewal. As regards maintenance, the workers received a daily minimum wage calculated on the basis of their dietary and subsistence requirements, and tied to the prevailing price of rubber. The employers also offered some facilities, including basic housing (compound accommodation), subsidised food, and infrequent medical attention through plantation (estate) hospitals.[2] New staffing to fill vacancies arising from deaths, departures or the expansion of the workforce ensured labour force renewal. The Indian workers were recruited under indenture arrangements or via intermediaries. This entailed either the services of recruitment firms in South India or the planters sending agents to openly recruit labourers for the plantations.[3]

The demand for workers continued to outstrip supply and British administrators in the FMS therefore recommended Javanese labour recruitment for agricultural work. The assumption was that the Javanese had similar cultural and religious attributes to the Malays and would find it easier to assimilate into local Malay society. As demand for rubber rose and prices soared, the Malayan colonial authorities ratified legislation on Javanese labour migration in

---

2   Kaur 2004.

3   Kondapi 1951, 8–29.

1908 and 1909 at the request of European planters, and the FMS government consented to the conditions governing Javanese labour migration to Malaya. This legislation was based on the Dutch colonial administration's ruling of 1877 that had prohibited the emigration of skilled and unskilled Javanese workers outside of the Netherlands East Indies, except under special circumstances. The conditions stipulated that Javanese labour recruitment could only be carried out in Java and Madura, the most densly populated islands during this period.[4]

The agreement on Javanese labour recruitment for Malayan plantations was essentially modelled on legislation approved by the British Indian government in 1904. This legislation had stipulated that South Indian workers were to be employed under the indenture contract system rules. The British administrators in Malaya therefore adopted this legislation for Javanese labour recruitment, which remained in force until 1932 without any significant amendments. Thus, in contrast to Indian and Chinese indentured labour, which was banned in 1910 and 1914 respectively, Javanese indentured labour in the Malay States continued into the 1930s. (The colonial authorities in the Netherlands East Indies favoured the retention of indenture because employment contracts could be monitored and excessive abuses avoided.) Furthermore, the numbers involved were small, abuses were rare and, according to J. Norman Parmer, did not raise an outcry among concerned groups.[5]

The British colonial government, however, did not craft specific recruitment procedures to administer Javanese immigration. Planters had to first obtain approval from the Dutch colonial authorities and then utilise the services of private European recruiting firms in Singapore to obtain workers. Due to the high costs involved, the European planters made personal representation to the Dutch governor-general to establish a scheme similar to that set up by the Indian Immigration Commission, including the Tamil Immigration Fund. The Dutch colonial government, however, rejected their proposal, but authorised the planters to establish their own recruitment firms.

---

4   Jackson 1961, 127.

5   Parmer 1960, 108–109.

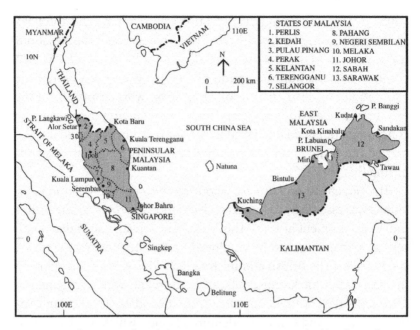

Map 4.2: Malaysia – political divisions/states. Source: Drafted by the author.

Consequently, Javanese workers could only be hired exclusively through the agency of private European firms. Interestingly, this measure was approved because European planters in Malaya had hired licensed professional recruiters to obtain Javanese workers, and the city of Semarang had consequently emerged as the leading hub for the recruitment of Javanese labour. Planters from Sumatra, British North Borneo and Suriname also established recruiting firms in Semarang. The professional recruiters in turn depended on licensed Javanese field recruiters to obtain the workers. Prospective emigrants were required to submit to mandatory medical examinations and their contracts had to be inspected by Dutch officials. The professional recruiters were also obliged to provide accommodation for labour recruits, both at the place of recruitment and port of disembarkation. Recruiters were prohibited from demanding payment from the labour recruits for costs incurred during the journey (including food and medical costs). Planters had to cover all these costs, as well as the recruitment fees.

Javanese workers were also recruited from the 'coolie' depots in Singapore where these workers from Java were housed *en route* for employment on East Sumatran plantations. These workers were obliged to sign indenture contracts in Singapore with the Protector of Chinese in attendance.[6] According to Tungku Shamsul Bahrin, the recruiters, who were paid according to the number of labour recruits hired, often used 'unscrupulous' methods to recruit inexperienced workers, who were often disenchanted and 'unhealthy' as well.[7] Javanese labour migration to Malaya was therefore 'less well organized, though no less regulated'.[8] The employment destinations of the Javanese in Malaya/Malaysia are shown in Map 4.2.

Not all Javanese workers were hired through recruitment/employment firms. According to R. N. Jackson there were four categories or classes of Javanese workers.[9] The first included workers who were 'obtained' directly from Java and hired via permits issued by the Dutch colonial government. The contract period was fixed at between two to four years. No worker could be compelled to stay longer at a place other than that specified in the contract. Employers were not allowed to make any deductions from the worker's wages greater than the cash advance given at the time of recruitment.[10]

The second category comprised workers who signed contracts for fixed periods under the Labour Code regulations. These labourers included persons whose contracts had expired or who were recruited via agencies in Singapore. The main European recruiting agency in Singapore was the Labour Association of Singapore.[11]

The third category included labourers whose contracts had expired and who had become domiciled in Malaya. These workers worked on the plantations on a monthly basis system. Jackson also asserts that there was a large settled Javanese community in the Ulu Langat district of Selangor. It appears that it was common for Javanese migrants to acquire land from Malay landowners, or they 'squatted' on the land upon expiry of their contracts.

---

6   Saw Swee-Hock 1988, 39.

7   Bahrin 1965, 64.

8   Lockard 1971, 52.

9   Jackson 1961.

10 Houben 1999, 39–42.

11 De Silva 2011, 26.

The fourth category consisted of gangs of Javanese and 'Banjarees' (Banjarese) workers who, employed under their own contractors, were hired to undertake tasks such as digging drains and felling trees in the clearing of land for plantations/estates. These gangs were mainly employed in Perak. After 1914, the number of Javanese workers obtained via contracting gangs declined since most planters had their own labourers to develop estates.[12]

Jackson further states that the greatest numbers of Javanese indentured labourers (4,100) were employed on twenty-seven estates in Perak at the end of 1912. Most of them often renewed their contracts for successive periods. In Selangor, the Javanese were recruited locally and worked on monthly contracts. There were comparatively fewer Javanese labourers in Pahang, Negeri Sembilan and other Malaysian states. Chong Yah Lim has noted that 'Indonesians', particularly from Java and Sumatra (classified as Malays in the census), continued to migrate independently to Malaya until the 1920s.[13] Lockard's study confirms that 'free' Javanese immigration to Malaya was 'especially strong in the 1930s'. In 1937, for example, '15,000 Javanese entered Malaya, largely to plant rubber'.[14] Other observers have stated that family members often accompanied the Javanese migrants who went to work in Johor. Moreover, this group of independent Javanese/ Indonesian smallholders played an important role in developing the rubber smallholding sector in Johor and Selangor and contributed to the growth of the Javanese population.

Consequently, although European planters as a rule preferred to hire the more 'docile' Indians, they also employed Javanese workers during periods when it was difficult to recruit Indian workers. Thus the number of Javanese independent migrants increased during periods of Indian labour shortages, such as, for example, just after the abolition of Indian indenture and during World War I. It is also pertinent to point out that Indian nationalists were opposed to Indian labour recruitment in states that were not British protectorates. This explains why the Chartered Company in North Borneo recruited Chinese and Javanese workers.

---

12 Jackson 1961, 129–130.

13 Lim 1967, 186–187.

14 Lockard 1971, 53.

Overall, Javanese labourers comprised a small percentage of the total plantation workforce in Malaya. From forming 10.5 per cent in 1907 this decreased to 1 per cent in 1938. In this period, the Indian and Chinese workers outnumbered the Javanese, and generally accounted for three quarters of the labour pool.[15] Furthermore, the short-term contracts meant that Javanese migrants, like Indian indentured migrants, were essentially 'birds of passage' prior to 1940.[16]

The Dutch administration in Java advocated the retention of the indenture contract system on the grounds that it allowed the authorities to improve foreign workers' employment conditions. A number of researchers, however, have shown that the system sanctioned the Dutch to handle and control employment contracts and keep wages down.[17] Likewise, government-regulated Indian and Javanese labour migration and non-regulated Chinese labour migration in Malaya enabled both the colonial government and European entrepreneurs to manipulate a key factor of production.

Plantation workers were normally categorised into three groups based on their job/skills classification. The main categories were factory workers, rubber tappers and field workers. Factory workers prepared the latex or liquid rubber for initial moulding. Rubber tappers tapped rubber, collected the latex and transported it to collecting stations or the factory. Field workers' duties included various tasks on the estates, but mainly weeding. Of the three categories, tapping was regarded as skilled and thus represented more rumunerative work while field work was considered unskilled, low-paid work.[18] Wage disparities also existed on the basis of gender and race. Indian and Chinese women workers earned lower wages than male workers, typically between 70 to 80 per cent of the male wage. There was also differentiation based on age, with Indian child workers paid between 30 to 40 per cent of an adult male worker's wage. Javanese workers generally earned lower wages than Indian and Chinese workers.

---

15 Adapted from Parmer 1960, 273.

16 Saw Swee-Hock 1988, 41.

17 See, for example, Stoler 1985.

18 Kaur 1998.

Both Indian and Javanese workers lacked a tradition of worker solidarity or collaboration. They consequently had little capability to either organise or bargain for higher wages in the period before World War II. Their labour conditions meant that breaches of employment contracts were judged criminal actions. Importantly, despite differences in plantation recruitment schemes in Malaya and Java, the labour regimes had many parallels in Malaya and Sumatra.[19] Nothwithstanding this, Javanese migrants had the option of planting rubber as smallholders in the FMS, Melaka, Johor and the northern Malay States, and were thus in a better position to improve their economic prospects.

Apart from Javanese labour employment in Malaya on British-, European- and Japanese-owned plantations, Javanese were also hired for railway construction in Johor. The (now defunct) Muar Railway in Johor had the distinction of being the only railway to be built by Malay and Javanese smallholders. The railway, which was constructed between 1888 and 1890, linked Muar Town to Parit Jawa and the main goods transported comprised betel nuts, coconuts, copra and fruit. The Javanese were the main agricultural smallholders and took up commercial agriculture in the Padang district. The Sultan of Johor promoted their economic activities and settlement in the state. The settlers mainly exported their products to Singapore by sea. Javanese settlers in the Muar district also planted rubber, but the onset of World War I affected their trade.[20]

Most Javanese migrants worked and also settled in the western Malay states of Selangor, Perak and Johor, and also in Kelantan, Terengganu and Pahang. Their settlements mostly related to their employment on plantations, in mines, and as smallholders. After World War II, 187,755 persons were classified as Javanese in Malaya. These statistics included 163,040 in Malaya and 24,715 in Singapore. The Javanese comprised 54.6 per cent of the Indonesians in the country (Table 4.2).

The colonial administration continued with the policy of including Javanese and other Indonesians in the 'Malay' category, as shown

19 Houben 1999, Lindblad 1999, Kaur 2004, ch. 4.

20 Kaur 1981.

Table 4.2: Malaya – statistical and associated information relating to Malay and 'Other Malaysian' categories, as enumerated in the 1947 census

Ethnicity	Birthplace	Numbers	Percentage
Malays	Malaya	2,199,598	96.5
Javanese	Java	187,755	54.6
Sundanese	Java	751	0.2
Boyanese	Sumatra	20,429	5.9
Achinese	Sumatra	1,143	0.3
Minangkabau	Sumatra	10,866	3.2
Korinchi	Sumatra	2,412	0.7
Palembangan	Sumatra	1,116	0.3
Djambi	Sumatra	980	0.3
Other Sumatran peoples	Sumatra	9,806	2.9
Bandjarese	Borneo	62,356	18.1
Bugis	Celebes	6,962	2.0
Total *other* Malaysians*		343,971	13.5
Total all Malaysians		2,543,569	100

*Total *other* Malaysians include minor groups not separately enumerated.
Source: Adapted from Fisher 1964, 637.

in the 1957 Census (Table 4.3, see next page). This was intentionally done to preserve the 'Malay' majority in the country and 'safeguard' Malay dominance in Malaya *vis-à-vis* Chinese and Indian immigrants. This policy also strengthened the Malay elite's sovereign position after Malayan independence in 1957.

Javanese in East Malaya/Borneo

In North Borneo (modern Sabah), the British North Borneo Chartered Company had become a significant employer of Javanese labour in the early 20th century. The Company had originally employed Chinese workers on indenture contracts and had hired them mainly through the agency of the Chinese protector in Singapore and also directly from Hong Kong. Chinese were hired for work in the coal mines, on

Table 4.3: British Malaya – distribution of population
by race, 1911–1957 (per cent)

Year	Malays	Chinese	Indians	Others	Total
1911	58.6	29.6	10.2	1.6	100
1921	54.0	29.4	15.1	1.5	100
1931	49.2	33.9	15.1	1.8	100
1947	49.5	38.4	10.8	1.3	100
1957	49.8	37.2	11.1	1.9	100

Source: Adapted from Saw Swee-Hock 1988, 65.

the tobacco and rubber plantations, in timber camps, and for the construction of the North Borneo Railway. The Company's recruitment of Indian workers after the Indian abolition of indentured labour was unsuccessful. The Company consequently decided to recruit Javanese labourers in Singapore. Labour brokers in Singapore organised the recruitment of the Javanese under the state-administered indentured labour system and also on a private basis.

The Singapore agents recruited the first batch of seventy Javanese workers in 1882. Then, in 1903 and 1907, following negotiations between the Company, the Dutch consulate in Singapore and the Netherlands East Indies colonial government, planters were authorised to recruit Javanese labour on two-year indentured labour contracts in Singapore. However, in 1914, the British Colonial Office nullified the arrangements to recruit Javanese indentured labourers in Singapore, following the abolition of indentured labour in 1910.[21] Consequently, the Company commenced recruitment of Javanese workers on two-year contracts directly from Java under the 'Dutch Contract' stipulations. The migrants were mainly recruited from Semarang, shipped to Singapore and thence to British North Borneo. In 1926, the Company was allowed to appoint an official recruiter in Semarang and authorised to hire 2,000 Javanese workers annually on three-year contracts. Two years later the Dutch permitted Javanese workers to be transported from Java directly to North Borneo, to

21 Rai 2006.

forestall desertions in Singapore.[22] Additionally, the colonial government in the Netherlands East Indies periodically sent Dutch labour inspectors to investigate the workers' working conditions there.

The circular labour migration arrangements, which included a special penal clause, operated from 1914 to 1930. Subsequently, in 1932 the Dutch government banned indentured labour recruitment; the final contracts expired two years later. In 1938 an attempt by the Company to recruit 'free' Javanese labour came to naught. Henceforth attempts were made to recruit free Javanese labour via the intercession of Javanese workers resident in Malaya, but this strategy had limited success. The Japanese occupation of Malaya thwarted the colonial administration's and European planters' latest plans to recruit Javanese workers.

Between 1914 and 1932, 9,969 male and female Javanese workers were recruited for work in North Borneo under the 'Dutch Contract'.[23] Interestingly, it was reported that about 1,489 women workers married local residents and settled in the area. With the exception of 725 Javanese who later died in North Borneo, the others were repatriated upon completion of their contracts.[24] This was done in compliance with the Dutch Contract, whereby employers were obliged to offer free repatriation to workers and their families to their homeland upon expiry of their contracts.

Industrial Relations Structures and Labour Organisation

Given that Britain had a central role in the mobilisation of labour, it played a vital role in shaping industrial relations structures. In fact, migrant workers' efforts at organisation and labour solidarity were mostly insignificant for four reasons: the elastic supply of low-skilled labour; the workers' temporary contracts; the geographic and social isolation of migrant workers on the plantations, in mines or in urban labour lines; and the linguistic, cultural, religious and occupational differences between migrant workers. Moreover, employers used

---

22 De Silva 2011, 32.

23 De Silva 2011, 33, Kaur 1998, 109–110, 157.

24 Kaur 1998, 106.

economic and non-economic strategies to maintain low wages and immigration regulations. Disparate recruitment systems and dissimilar government legislation similarly accentuated workforce fragmentation. Concurrently, the indentured labour system bound workers to employers since they were often formally contracted via advance payments. Intermediaries, such as the Indian *kangani* and labour contractors, also fostered a culture of abuse. In the case of the Indians, the labour departments and labour inspectorates generally focused on the supervision of migration, rather than on migrant workers' rights. Crucially, Indian and Javanese workers' poverty precluded solidarity among the workers.

For both Indian and Javanese agricultural labourers, the threat of losing their income and accommodation increased their insecurity and passivity. The Indians were also disadvantaged by language communication problems. Since Chinese workers were hired via their own contractors, who also provided accommodation, they became more vocal in demanding their labour rights. However, workers generally avoided direct and open confrontation against individuals who harassed and exploited them. Invariably, they relied on what James Scott has labelled as 'everyday forms of resistance'.[25] These passive actions required little or no cooperation and were not meant to directly challenge the authority of plantation owners. Essentially, the workers sought to release their frustration, ensure their survival, and also cause some minor destruction.

After World War II and following political transformations in India, Britain decided to improve its image overseas and promoted the development of trade unions in Malaya. This policy was associated with Chinese activism, and resulted in the enactment of additional draconian legislation that essentially destroyed Malayan trade unionism. More Malays also entered the paid labour force and the British abandoned efforts to improve the labour conditions of the other workers. The colonial administration also destroyed the alliance between Chinese, Indian, and Javanese workers. The Malays mostly supported the British administration and a colonial trade union adviser assisted the workers to advance the integration of the various state plantation unions. The unions were also steered

---

25 Scott 1985.

into forming a central union, the National Union of Plantation Workers (NUPW) in 1954. The NUPW was essentially established to cooperate with the government, rather than be confrontational to plantation management.[26]

Ethnicity and the Javanese in Malaya

In 1934 the superintendent of the 1931 Malayan census had sur-mised that 'only a negligible fraction of the Malay population [of the peninsula] consists of descendants of pre-19th century immigrants and (. . .) more than half of [them have] less than 50 years' prescriptive rights to the designation "owners of the soil".[27] Fisher further noted that there were broad dissimilarities in the growth of the Indonesian population in the country and that the superintendent's remarks were relevant primarily for the western Malay states (FMS), where capitalist development of rubber and tin had taken place. In the northern and east coast states, the Malay population had grown mostly through natural increase.[28] As regards the Javanese population in Malaya and North Borneo (Sabah) in the early 1960s, Lockard asserts that the Javanese comprised about 190,000 and 5,400 persons respectively in these territories.[29] Bahrin however maintains that the Indonesian population in Malaya in-creased from 117,600 in 1911 to 342,600 in 1957.[30] The general view was that Javanese comprised about 70 per cent of Indonesian immigrants during this period.

Charles Hirschman further maintains that the British initially developed a 'systematic' classification of the major ethnic categories and the category of 'Malays and Other Natives of the Archipelago' as early as 1891 in the Straits Settlements (SS) census.[31] Subsequently, this classification was also employed in the Federated Malay States

---

26 Ramasamy 1994, ch. 5.

27 Fisher 1964, 636.

28 Fisher 1964, 636.

29 Lockard 1971, 42.

30 Bahrin 1967, 274–275.

31 Hirschman 1987, 563.

(FMS). Then, from 1931 to 1957, the category 'Malaysian' was used as an 'inclusive category for Malays and natives from Borneo and Indonesia'. World War II and its aftermath saw Britain rethinking its possessions east of Suez. In 1946, the British merged the FMS, the SS and the northern Malay States into a Malayan Union with a view to self-government. The Federation of Malaya that replaced it in 1948 achieved independence in 1957. Afterwards, in 1963, Sabah and Sarawak joined the Malayan federation in the larger political alliance known as Malaysia. In other words, Britain's knowledge and understanding of Malay ethnicity, including the Javanese under the category of 'Malays and Other Natives of the Archipelago', was a politically motivated decision and designed to bolster Malay numerical supremacy in Malaya. Britain's definition, and reclassification, of ethnicity in Malaya and the 'fluidity' of the boundaries of Malay ethnicity further demonstrates that the Malay ethnic majority was essentially a colonial construction established to preserve the numerical superiority of the 'Malays' in their 'own' land.[32]

The above classification structure also supports the proposition that the British socially constructed ethnicity since they envisaged the Malayan state as being constructed around the native ethnic majority, that is, the Malays. While the Chinese and Indians were clearly seen as strangers and outsiders, the Javanese benefited from this classification, especially in regard to 'Malay rights'. In addition to being Muslim (as defined in the Federal Constitution), persons of the Malayan or Arab race were considered as fulfilling the eligibility stipulations for acquisition of Malay reservation land. This policy enabled Javanese to meet the 'legally Malay' race prerequisites and qualify for 'Malay' special privileges.[33] The eligibility stipulations also made it possible for former Javanese migrants to take up rubber cultivation as smallholders on Malay reservation land after 1957.

The Malayan government's policy on 'Malayan' citizenship after independence must also be understood from the perspective of political transitions and competing ethnic aspirations in the country. The 1948 Federation of Malaya Agreement granted Malays special

---

32 See also Nagata 1974.

33 See, for example, Choo 2011.

constitutional rights relating to their 'federal' citizenship, whereas Chinese and Indians could only obtain citizenship through fulfilling explicit residential credentials. However, most Chinese and Indians did not possess the documentation required to substantiate their periods of residence and Malayan nationality status, owing to the fact that the British had not provided this documentation to them. Their religious beliefs also set them apart from the Malays. In 1957, the Malayan government instigated new legislation that effectively restricted Chinese and Indians' access to the labour market. Next, the government's Immigration Act of 1959 epitomised new policy procedures that denied citizenship rights to Chinese and Indian residents who were unable to provide documentation relating to their birth/residential status. These residents were then compelled to leave the country.

In 1968, the Malaysian government implemented the Employment Restriction Act that made access to the labour market for non-citizens contingent on possession of work permits or labour contracts. The work-permit system was also intended to ensure that only skilled non-citizens could join the workforce and have the right of entry into Malaysia. The Malaysian government subsequently instigated the process of reconstructing its national, racial, cultural and economic borders, and discontinued less-skilled immigration. In May 1969, race riots led to a leadership change. The new leadership endorsed the supremacy of Malay rights and established clear dividing lines between Malays (citizens) and foreigners. The new prime minister also seized the opportunity to espouse state-led economic growth and launched the New Economic Policy (NEP) in 1971.

Independent Malaysia and Indonesian Labour Migrants

Development Programmes and Labour Force Growth

Malaysia became the largest employer of foreign migrant workers in Southeast Asia in the 1970s. Observers have mostly attributed the labour shortages to the NEP and Malaysia's immigration policies after the May 1969 riots. The NEP had two principal objectives: the reduction and eventual eradication of poverty irrespective of race and the elimination of the identification of race with economic function.

The second objective dictated reducing Malay concentration in subsistence agriculture alongside increasing Malay employment in the modern rural and urban economic sectors. The government thus became highly interventionist and adopted a policy aimed at raising the living standards of the Malays in particular.

The NEP coincided with the espousal of an export-oriented industrialisation strategy and the creation of jobs in the modern rural and urban economic sectors. The Malaysian government commenced poverty reduction and income redistribution schemes and instigated affirmative action policies for Malays. These schemes underlined public sector enlargement and expansion of white-collar occupations for Malays. Concurrently, the government launched vast land development projects under the auspices of the Federal Land Development Authority (FELDA). These projects were intended for Malays, who were allocated blocks of land to grow commercial crops, such as, for example, rubber, cane sugar and oil palm for export. The commodities were to be grown as plantation crops and were to be managed on a cooperative basis. Malay settlers were also allocated housing and other facilities on these rural development projects.[34] This policy of land distribution essentially emphasised agribusiness rather than individual farm holdings and correlated with the government's plans to promote agribusiness and oil palm plantations over the needs of small farmers.

A large-scale population shift to urban areas resulted in labour shortages in key economic areas, specifically the agricultural and plantation sectors. Simultaneously, transport expansion and the construction boom in the urban areas involving the development of factories and housing, further impacted on labour supply. According to the World Bank, 14 million jobs were created in Malaysia between 1987 and 1993, while the domestic labour force grew by only 3.9 per cent.[35] Local labour was either scarce or the working conditions were not attractive for Malaysians. Labour shortages in the rural areas then led to the clandestine hiring of Indonesians either via illegal labour-hiring syndicates or Indonesian-Malaysian residents'

---

34 www.felda.net.my/index.php/en/ (accessed 25 March 2016).

35 World Bank 1995, 58.

informal social networks. Initially the 'new' irregular Indonesian workers were restricted to the rural agricultural land development schemes away from the main urban centres. This situation changed when Malay companies started hiring Indonesians in the expanding construction sector. Additionally, the Malaysian government's policy of hiring more women in civil service jobs also resulted in an exponential growth in the demand for foreign domestic workers. In 1979, the government reported the presence of 12,000 irregular Indonesians; by 1981, this figure had increased to 100,000 in Johor state alone.[36]

Intergovernmental Labour Agreements and Indonesian Migrant Labour

Predictably, the government then turned to Indonesia for its labour needs. As expected, contract work also became the preferred model of temporary employment for the plantation, manufacturing, con- struction and domestic work sectors.[37] Three phases subsequently epitomised Malaysia's shifting labour-importing policies and its management of Indonesian labour migration between 1969 and 1994. These periods generally approximated with Indonesia's Labour Emigration Plans and official targets for exporting migrant workers to West Asia and Southeast Asia (Table 4.4, see next page).

During the first period (1969–1980) Malaysia adopted a fairly flexible policy for the recruitment of Indonesian labour. Thus Malay- sian companies and executives were allowed to covertly employ un- authorised Javanese workers residing in illegal squatter settlements or on Malay reservation land. Some companies afterwards directly recruited Indonesian workers via private labour brokers, mostly for the plantation and construction sectors.

In the second period (from about 1981–1986) Malaysia officially endorsed a foreign labour employment policy and established an authorised channel for the employment of Indonesian and other Southeast Asian workers via bilateral agreements. A Committee

---

36 Kassim 1987, 268.

37 Kaur 2004, ch. 9.

Table 4.4: Indonesia: Labour emigration to West Asia and Southeast
Asia under the National Development Plans, 1969–1994

Destination	Plan I 1969–74	Plan II 1974–79	Plan III 1979–84	Plan IV 1984–89	Plan V 1989–94
West Asia	–	4,752	60,093	226,030	390,556
Saudi Arabia	–	3,817	55,976	223,573	384,822
Southeast Asia	21	3,008	16,461	49,251	215,492
Malaysia	12	536	11,441	37,785	156,312
Singapore	8	2,432	5,007	10,537	48,896

Source: Amjad 1996, 345.

for the Recruitment of Foreign Workers was formed in 1981 and
Malaysia signed a bilateral agreement with Indonesia in 1984. This
agreement, the Medan Agreement, was an intergovernmental accord
and was intended to approve the strategic recruitment of Indonesian
workers for the plantation and domestic work sectors. This was largely in response to the approximately 500,000 irregular Indonesian
workers employed in the plantation sector in both Peninsular and
East Malaysia.[38]

Nevertheless, irregular Indonesian migration continued to expand. Furthermore, there was rising public disquiet in Malaysia due
to worsening economic conditions. The government then implemented a national campaign against irregular (mainly Indonesian)
workers and authorised the Malaysian Task Force on Refugees (or
Task Force VII) to identify the main boat-landing sites or entry
points and apprehend the irregular immigrants.[39] The government
further stationed enforcement units to patrol known landing points
along the Straits of Melaka. Irregular immigrants who were caught
during these raids were confined in detention camps.

Significantly, both the government's and the public's perception
of Indonesians changed. The Indonesians were viewed both as
a security threat and as an annoyance. Malaysian newspapers

38 Kaur 2004.
39 See also Kaur 2004.

repeatedly published unfavourable reports on Indonesians' activities in Malaysia. Most of the accusations included illegal entry and transgressions such as armed robbery, homicide, housebreaks, rape, gangland crimes, larceny and clashes with the police authorities. By the end of October 1983, 12,000 irregular Indonesians had been apprehended and deported to Indonesia. It was also reported that the issue had become a race-based problem due to Malaysia's preferential treatment for Malays (including Indonesians).[40] Malaysian (especially Chinese and Indian) citizens' resentment towards Indonesians and the government's inability to manage the labour issue heralded a new phase in Malaysia's migration policy.

In the third period (1987-early 1995) Malaysia suspended the recruitment of foreign labour and commenced a legalisation programme for irregular migrants. Wong states that Indonesians comprised about 83 per cent of the 442,276 irregular workers who requested registration/legalisation.[41] It was further alleged that since the statistics on irregular workers exceeded the number of registered workers, the overall figure for foreign workers in the country totalled well in excess of one million migrants. Interestingly, the figure for Indonesian migrants was referred to as 'over 500,000' workers.[42] Moreover, there were indications that the treatment of irregular migrants and conditions in the detention camps – where they had been incarcerated pending their deportation – were appalling. A 1995 report by Tenaganita (a Malaysian NGO) further emphasised the 'deplorable' conditions in the detention camps and provided statistics on the deaths in custody.[43]

The above account underscores the complexities faced by the Malaysian state in the management of Indonesian labour migration until 1995. As noted earlier, Indonesian labour migration did not take place accidentally. It came about due to historical linkages, the government's 'Malay indigenisation' policy, and the socio-cultural networks that facilitated migration between the two countries.

---

40 Kassim 1987, 270–272.

41 Wong 2006, 213–227.

42 *Migration News* 1995, www.un.org/popin/popis/journals/migratn/mig9512.html (accessed 25 March 2016).

43 Amnesty International 1996, 218.

According to an article in the *Washington Post*, Malaysia could 'not succeed in keeping Indonesians out' since 'migration from Indonesia to Malaysia [. . . was] less a trend than an industry, creating an entrenched subculture of migrants, labour brokers, prostitutes and corrupt immigration authorities who (. . .) created a massive cross-border network.'[44]

The Asian Financial and Economic Crisis of 1997–1998 and Indonesian Migrant Labour

The Asian financial and economic crisis of 1997–98 signalled the commencement of a new phase in Malaysia's evolving immigration policy. Against the backdrop of declining growth rates, Prime Minister Mahathir Mohamad (1981–2003) instigated an austerity plan that focused on reducing the number of foreign workers to stabilise the economy and reinforce security in the country. He also reviewed Malaysia's immigration legislation and employment statistics to establish the legal status of migrant workers. Amnesties and regularisation programmes were implemented to encourage undocumented workers to turn themselves in to the authorities.

The altered landscape further coincided with the suspension of new labour hires. Employers were advised to recruit undocumented migrants held in detention centres to meet their labour needs. The government also transferred foreign labour recruitment to the Immigration Department's Foreign Workers Division Authority and also amended the Immigration Act in 1997 and 2002 to remove ambiguities and tighten regulations. It became a criminal offence for foreign labourers to work without a work permit or visa, and punitive measures, including caning, were introduced. Documented domestic workers, who had been abused or had run away from their employers, were also classified as irregular workers and detained in detention camps. Errant employers who employed more than five irregular workers were subject to fines, imprisonment, and physical punishment as well.[45]

---

44 Shiner 1998.
45 Sreenevasan 2006.

Mahathir Mohamad then authorised the light infantry arm of the Royal Malaysia Police, the General Operation Force, to carry out raids and arrest irregular migrants in Sabah, Sarawak and Johor. In early 2002, about 700 irregular migrants were detained under a special police operation. These measures, and the detention of sixteen Indonesian textile workers in Negeri Sembilan (who had tested positive for drugs), however, led to a 'violent' protest by the Indonesian labourers. Following their aggressive demonstration, the police arrested approximately 125 Indonesian textile workers, who were deported together with other Indonesian workers at the end of January 2002. The Immigration Department further cancelled the work permits of the remaining 401 Indonesian workers. Three days later, seventy Indonesian workers, armed with machetes, went on a rampage at Cyberjaya (Mahathir's new technology city) to protest against the deportation of Indonesian nationals.

Their actions not only disclosed their hostility towards the Malaysian authorities but also strengthened Indonesian migrant workers' solidarity in the country. Mahathir Mohamad was infuriated by this turn of events and ordered a crackdown on Indonesian migrant workers. He also threatened to deport 10,000 foreigners monthly. Additional security personnel were also deployed and increased patrolling was maintained. The government also banned the hiring of additional Indonesian labour migrants. Nevertheless, two sectors, namely, plantation and domestic service, were exempted from this ruling. This was mainly because Malaysia wanted to retain its position in the world market as the leading exporter of rubber, palm oil and other primary commodities. Indonesian domestic workers continued to be hired because they were regarded as an indispensable workforce and their employment permitted Malaysian women to work (especially in the public sector).

The Malaysian Prime Minister further announced that the government would implement a 'Hire Indonesians Last' policy (also known as 'Indonesians are the last priority'). Additionally, the government decreed that all irregular migrants would be deported immediately upon arrest instead of being incarcerated in detention camps.[46] A

---

46 Said and Mohd 2002; Scalabrini Migration Center 2002, www.smc.org.ph/administrator/uploads/pdf/1373006349.pdf (accessed 25 March 2016);

Table 4.5. Malaysia: Protocols on the country of origin of
foreign workers in designated sectors, 2006/2008

Construction	Philippines (males only), Indonesia, Cambodia, Kazakhstan, Laos, Burma, Nepal, Thailand, Turkmenistan, Uzbekistan, Vietnam, Bangladesh
Manufacturing	Philippines (males only), Indonesia (females only), Cambodia, Kazakhstan, Laos, Burma, Nepal, Thailand, Turkmenistan, Uzbekistan, Vietnam, Bangladesh
Plantation/ Agriculture	Philippines (males only), Indonesia, India, Cambodia, Kazakhstan, Laos, Myanmar, Nepal, Thailand, Turkmenistan, Uzbekistan, Vietnam, Bangladesh
Services	
– Restaurant	All source countries for general worker categories (excepting India – cooks only). Restaurants in major towns in Peninsular Malaysia
– Laundry	All source countries except India
– Cleaning/ Sanitation	All source countries except India
– Caddy	All source countries except India
– Resort Islands	All source countries except India
– Welfare Homes	All source countries except India
– Cargo	All source countries except India
– High Tension Cable	India only
Domestic Workers	Sri Lanka, Indonesia, Thailand, Philippines, Cambodia India, Nepal, Vietnam, Laos
Foreign Nurses	Albania, India, Bangladesh, Philippines, Pakistan, Indonesia, Burma

Source: Kanapathy 2006, revised 2008.

parallel deportation exercise in Sabah resulted in a humanitarian
crisis at one of the evacuation sites on Nunukan (an Indonesian island

Migration News 2002, migration.ucdavis.edu/mn/more_entireissue.php?
idate=2002_03 (accessed 25 March 2016); www.themalaymailonline.com/
malaysia/article/horrible-bosses-taken-to-task-over-abuse-of-foreign-
workers; www.wsj.com/articles/SB10001424052702303448204. . ..

offshore from Sabah), when around eighty Indonesian migrants died due to starvation and poor sanitation. The government requisitioned the services of the Ikatan Relawan Rakyat Malaysia (Peoples' Voluntary Corps, RELA) to arrest irregular migrants (including refugees and asylum seekers). RELA personnel allegedly carried out the systematic caning of undocumented migrants and destroyed the identification cards of legal migrants to justify the raids.[47]

Malaysia further centralised foreign labour recruitment in 2005. Employers wanting to recruit migrant workers had to obtain approval from the Ministry of Home Affairs and The One-Stop (Migrant Recruiting) Centre. This policy was consistent with the Indonesian government's 2004 Overseas Placement and Protection for Indonesian Workers Law (No 39/2004). The legislation subsequently led to the establishment of an Indonesian state company (PT Bijak) and private labour supply companies (PJTKIs) to manage the recruitment, deployment and 'protection' of Indonesian migrant workers abroad. Malaysia also improved its recruitment mechanisms and lifted the ban on private labour agents, conceding that these agents played a vital role in recruitment. Malaysian firms wanting Indonesian workers were permitted to recruit directly via Indonesian agencies or they could utilise the services of local labour/employment agencies. The latter then liaised with the manpower division in the Indonesian embassy to obtain workers via labour exporting companies. In 2013, Malaysia implemented a new policy that effectively transferred all immigration and employment approval charges onto the foreign workers themselves rather than their employers. Malaysian employers were also permitted to retain the workers' passports.

With reference to the country of origin of migrant workers, Indonesians continued to be in the lead in almost all the major economic sectors (Table 4.5).

The Services Sector: Domestic Workers

The employment of foreign domestic workers has allowed Malaysian women to reconcile their participation in the formal workforce with

---

47 Human Rights Watch 2007, 285–286.

Table 4.6 Malaysia: Migrant workers by nationality and sector, November 2007

Nationality	Domestic Workers	Construc- tion	Manu- facturing	Services	Plantation	Agriculture	Total
Indonesia	296,984	210,838	206,898	40,116	267,615	102,629	1,155,080
Banglad.	17	49,289	151,376	26,069	24,552	15,016	266,319
Nepal	30	4,624	178,714	28,764	2,810	8,171	223,113
Burma	30	15,111	79,425	20,617	1,483	6,556	123,222
India	99	7,577	30,803	60,750	23,298	21,631	144,158
Vietnam	10	5,220	106,686	2,826	90	623	115,464
Philipp.	10,397	1,686	2,856	2,765	5,038	2,581	25,323
Thailand	417	1,105	790	15,216	63	555	18,056
Pakistan	1	4,387	3,296	1,829	816	5,080	15,409
Cambodia	6,825	176	2,404	231	201	86	9,923
Others	893	2,508	2,857	3,174	369	248	10,049
Total	315,703	302,440	766,105	202,357	356,335	163,176	2,106,116

Source: Suaram 2008, 155.

their household and child-rearing responsibilities and the provision of elder care in their homes. Domestic workers enable both flexibility and affordability in Malaysian society. They are paid comparatively lower wages than male foreign workers, and moreover, since they are employed in the private home, they are regarded as informal workers by the government. There are neither precise job specifications nor are there explicit educational or skill requirements for the job. Originally, the age category was also not stipulated but this oversight was subsequently rectified in 2005.

Normally, a Malaysian employer wanting to hire a domestic worker was required to firstly approach a licensed Malaysian domestic worker recruitment agency. The agency then initiated a search or instruction/ order with a counterpart agency in the sending country and presented a selection of applicants to the client. After selection, the prospective employer had to pay for all training, visa and travel costs up front. Employers were then allowed to recoup their costs through monthly salary deductions. Furthermore, employers were allowed to retain their domestic workers' passports to thwart the workers' flight from the country, manage their 'surveillance' responsibility, and monitor the domestic workers' freedoms and mobility.[48]

Consequently, domestic workers have had to contend with a range of restrictions due to their exclusion from the broader labour rights enshrined in the Malaysia-Indonesia 2004 Memorandum of Understanding (MOU). Human Rights Watch subsequently exposed the Indonesian and Malaysian governments' lack of concern for this category of migrant.[49] Malaysia then made a few more concessions to domestic workers, but several issues relating to their rights continue to be a source of concern for Indonesia and other sending countries. Domestic workers in Malaysia are predominantly recruited from Indonesia (see Table 4.6).

The inherent unequal gender hierarchies in both countries have also meant that domestic workers have fewer opportunities for redress and are susceptible to abuse by employers. After a series of well-publicised cases of abuse, Malaysia and Indonesia signed a MOU in May 2006 that specified a standard contract for Indonesian domestic workers in Malaysia. Although the pay scale was revised upwards, the practice of withholding salary generally continued and employers retained the domestic workers' passports.[50]

In 2009 there were fresh cases of abuse and deaths of Indonesian domestic workers at the hands of employers. The Indonesian government then imposed a moratorium on the recruitment of domestic workers by Malaysia. After lengthy negotiations on working conditions and under the scrutiny of international and Indonesian NGOs, the Indonesian government lifted the ban on the recruitment of domestic workers by Malaysians in late 2011. A new MOU on domestic worker employment was then signed between the two countries. This MOU included the stipulation of a day off, permitted domestic workers to retain their passports, incorporates a revised pay scale, and obliges employers to bank the domestic workers' salaries in the workers' bank accounts. Significantly, since domestic workers cannot join or form trade unions, they are allowed to

---

48 Kaur 2007.

49 Human Rights Watch 2004.

50 Kaur 2007.

file complaints relating to mistreatment to the Labour Office and seek assistance from enforcement agencies and NGOs. These new arrangements nevertheless have expanded the role of labour brokers and also absolved the Malaysian government from incurring additional costs in the regulation of domestic workers.

In addition to the illicit activities of unscrupulous intermediaries, the evolving border control system has further added to migrant workers' vulnerabilities. An Amnesty International study of migrant workers' human rights violations in Peninsular Malaysia concluded that while individual recruitment agents perpetrated labour trafficking, the government of Malaysia facilitated the abuse with its 'loose regulation of agents, abusive labour laws and policies and the practice of allowing employers to confiscate their workers' passports.'[51]

Restricting the freedom of movement and association of foreign workers is an outright violation of twenty-eight ILO (International Labour Organization) conventions that Malaysia has signed up to. It is also alarming that Malaysia's management of its urban spaces for irregular migrants, whether refugees or trafficked individuals, is judged to be the worst in the region. Malaysia also remains a destination, source and transit country for men, women and children exposed to conditions of forced labour. The protection of low-skilled migrant workers has been included as an objective in the 2009 ASEAN Socio-Cultural Community (ASSC) Blueprint and the 2007 Declaration on the Protection and Promotion of the Rights of Migrants, but implementation of these recommendations has been slow and all migrant workers continue to be discriminated against in Malaysia. Malaysia's current immigration legislation also criminalises migrant workers and the state's systematic 'Operation Nyah' or Operation Expunge aimed at halting irregular migration has not addressed the root causes of irregular migration and the role of migrant brokers in both Malaysia and Indonesia.

Daily life, Accommodation Strategies and Sense of Belonging

Since the late 19th century Javanese workers have left Indonesia and temporarily settled in Malaya/Malaysia to work and earn a living.

---

51 Amnesty International 2010.

The racial, linguistic and religious similarities between the Javanese and the Malay population group in the host country have eased processes of accommodation and contributed to the maintenance of their identity. However, 'kinship' at the level of diplomatic relations between Indonesia and Malaysia and in the context of personal connections between Javanese and Malaysians appears to constitute a complex space of negotiation that determines frequently changing senses of belonging to 'the nation' and 'the family'.[52]

The ethnic propinquity between Indonesia and Malaysia notwithstanding, most Javanese migrant workers tend to keep to themselves and make attempts to observe where possible their customs and values from their native country. These are often related to Javanese village life and associated with social norms, family traditions and power relations that are embedded in *adat* (customary law). In particular, Javanese interactions with Malaysian authorities impact on their daily life. Whether hired as plantation, construction, manufacturing or domestic workers, they are dependent on and regulated by employers who are responsible for their well-being, but who often fail to offer services that are the official norm. Income, housing, sanitary services, recreational facilities and freedom of movement might diverge significantly. Undocumented Javanese workers, who are more vulnerable, generally confront adverse circumstances, are disrespected and/or badly treated. The majority are unable to stand up for themselves.[53]

While most Javanese migrants, particularly domestic workers (in 2017, there have been more than 250,000 registered domestic workers in Malaysia) look forward to returning home to Indonesia after their stint in Malaysia, a growing number would prefer to stay on in Malaysia (and in Singapore).[54] Their sojourn in Malaysia is a conscious choice to improve their standard of living and have a better life. They take pride in working hard and saving money so that they can transfer remittances to their families in Indonesia. These remittances are used mainly to support their families, for example

---

52 Liow 2005; Killias 2014.

53 Kassim 2000.

54 A number of my co-researchers have reported that Javanese domestic workers, whose husbands have married other women in their absence,

133

to provide for the education of their children or to meet their daily expenses, but also to invest in business ventures. Since Jakarta increasingly views remittances as flows of capital that reinforce the Indonesian nation-state, Indonesians progressively consider migrant workers as valuable members of the 'diaspora family'.

References

Amjad, R. 1996. 'Philippines and Indonesia: On the Way to a Migration Transition'. *Asian and Pacific Migration Journal* 5(2–3): 339–366.

Amnesty International 1996. *Annual Report 1996*. [www.amnesty.org/en/documents/pol10/0002/1996/en/]

——— 2010. *Trapped: The Exploitation of Migrant Workers in Malaysia*. [www.amnesty.org/en/documents/ASA28/002/2010/en/]

Bahrin, T. S. 1965. 'Indonesian Labour in Malaya'. *Kajian Ekonomi Malaysia* 2(1): 53–70.

——— 1967. 'The Growth and Distribution of the Indonesian Population in Malaya'. *Bijdragen tot de Taal-, Land- en Volkenkunde* 123(2): 267–286.

Choo, N. 2011. 'Siapa Melayu'. *The Nut Graph* 14 February.

De Silva, M. 2011. 'Javanese Labour Migrants in British North Borneo, 1914–1932: A Historical Perspective'. *Bumantara: Journal of Social and Political Development* 1(1): 23–41.

Fisher, C. A. 1964. *South-East Asia: A Social, Economic and Political Geography*. London: Methuen & Co.

Hirschman, C. 1987. 'The Meaning and Measurement of Ethnicity in Malaysia: An Analysis of Census Classifications'. *Journal of Asian Studies* 46(3): 555–582.

---

would prefer to stay on in Malaysia (and Singapore). These women also remain committed to providing a good education for their children so that they will not have to face job insecurity. www.imi.gov.my/index.php/en/main-services/foreign-workers.html (accessed 25 October 2017). Additionally, Malaysian and Singaporean women have become accustomed to having domestic workers to look after them. In Malaysia for example, the government announced on 27 October 2017 that it would allow Malaysians to recruit domestic workers directly from nine countries without the assistance (and charges) demanded by intermediaries. The nine countries include Indonesia, Thailand, Cambodia, the Philippines, Sri Lanka, India, Vietnam, Laos and Myanmar. www.freemalaysiatoday.com/category/nation/2017/10/27/ngo-lauds-direct-hiring-of-domestic-workers-from-9-countries/ (accessed 25 October 2017).

Houben, V. J. H. 1999. 'Before Departure: Coolie Labour Recruitment in Java, 1900–1942'. In *Coolie Labour in Colonial Indonesia: A Study of Labour Relations in the Outer Islands, c. 1900–1940*, ed. V. J. H. Houben and J. T. Lindblad, 25–42. Wiesbaden: Harrassowitz.

Human Rights Watch 2004. *Help Wanted: Abuses against Female Migrant Domestic Workers in Malaysia*. [www.hrw.org/report/2004/07/21/help-wanted/abuses-against-female-migrant-domestic-workers-indonesia-and-malaysia]

—— 2007. *World Report 2007; Events of 2006*. [www.hrw.org/legacy/wr2k7/wr2007master.pdf]

Jackson, R. N. 1961. *Immigrant Labour and the Development of Malaya, 1786–1920*. Kuala Lumpur: Government Printer.

Kanapathy, V. 2006. 'Migrant Workers in Malaysia: An Overview'. Country Paper Prepared for the Workshop on an East Asian Cooperation Framework for Migrant Labor, Kuala Lumpur, 6–7 December.

Kassim, A. 1987. 'The Unwelcome Guests: Indonesian Immigrants and Malaysian Public Responses'. *Southeast Asian Studies* 25(2): 265–278.

—— 2000. 'Indonesian Immigrant Settlements in Peninsular Malaysia'. *Sojourn* 15(1): 100–122.

Kaur, A. 1981. 'The Muar Railroad 1890–1921'. *Journal of the South Seas Society* 36 (June): 69–78.

—— 1998. *Economic Change in East Malaysia: Sabah and Sarawak since 1850*. Basingstoke: Macmillan / New York: St. Martin's Press.

—— 2004. *Wage Labour in Southeast Asia since 1840: Globalisation, the International Division of Labour and Labour Transformations*. Basingstoke: Palgrave Macmillan.

—— 2007. 'Refugees and Refugee Policy in Malaysia'. *UNEAC Asia Papers* 18: 77–90.

Killias, O. 2014. 'Intimate Encounters: The Ambiguities of Belonging in the Transnational Migration of Indonesian Domestic Workers in Malaysia'. *Citizenship Studies* 18(8): 885–899.

Kondapi, C. 1951. *Indians overseas 1838–1949*. New Delhi: Indian Council of World Affairs.

Lim, C. Y. 1967. *Economic Development Of Modern Malaya*. Kuala Lumpur: Oxford University Press.

Lindblad, J. T. 1999. 'Coolies in Deli: Labour Conditions in Western Enterprises in East Sumatra, 1910–1938'. In *Coolie Labour in Colonial Indonesia: A Study of Labour Relations in the Outer Islands, c. 1900–1940*, ed. V. J. H. Houben and J. T. Lindblad, 43–77. Wiesbaden: Harrassowitz.

Liow, J. C. 2005. *The Politics of Indonesia-Malaysia Relations. One Kin, Two Nations*. London/New York: RoutledgeCurzon.

Lockard, C. A. 1971. 'The Javanese as Emigrant: Observations on the Development of Javanese Settlements Overseas'. *Indonesia* 11 (April): 41–62. [cip.cornell.edu/seap.indo/1107124113]

Nagata, J. 1974. 'What is a Malay? Situational Selection of Ethnic Identity in a Plural Society'. *American Ethnologist* 1(2): 331–350.

Parmer, J. N. 1960. *Colonial Labour Policy and Administration: A History of Labour in the Rubber Plantation Industry in Malaya, c. 1910–1941.* Locust Valley: J. J. Augustin for the Association for Asian Studies.

Rai, R. 2006. 'Singapore' in B. V. Lal (ed.), *The Encyclopedia of the Indian Diaspora*. Singapore: Editions Didier Millet.

Ramasamy, P. 1994. *Plantation Labour, Unions, Capital and the State in Peninsular Malaya*. Kuala Lumpur: Oxford University Press.

Said, R. and A. Mohd 2002. 'PM: Decision to Hire Indon Workers as Last Resort Will Not Sour Ties'. *New Straits Times* 25 January. [www.highbeam.com/doc/1P1-82631156.html]

Saw Swee-Hock, 1988. *The Population of Peninsular Malaysia*. Singapore: Singapore University Press.

Scott, J. C. 1985. *Weapons of the Weak: Everyday Forms of Peasant Resistance*. New Haven: Yale University Press.

Shiner, C. 1998. 'Malaysia Gets Tough on Illegal Immigrants'. *Washington Post* 7 April.

Stoler, A. L. 1985. 'Perceptions of Protest: Defining the Dangerous in Colonial Sumatra'. *American Ethnologist* 12(4): 642–658.

Sreenevasan, A. 2006. 'Obligations of Labour Contractors and Agents'. Paper presented at the LAWASIA Labour Law Conference, Kuala Lumpur, August.

Suaram 2008. *Malaysia Human Rights Report 2007: Civil and Political Rights*. Petaling Jaya: Suaram Kommunikasi.

Wong, D. 2006. 'The Recruitment of Foreign Labour in Malaysia: From Migration System to Guest Worker Regime'. In *Mobility, Labour Migration and Border Controls in Asia,* ed. A. Kaur and I. Metcalfe, 213–227. Basingstoke: Palgrave Macmillan.

World Bank 1995. Malaysia: Meeting Labor Needs, More Workers and Better Skills. Washington, D.C.: World Bank.

CHAPTER 5

Migration Systems and Identity

Javanese Domestic Workers in Hong Kong and Singapore

WAYNE PALMER

In its more than forty years of existence, Indonesia's overseas labour migration programme has recorded almost seven million departures, with Hong Kong and Singapore being popular destination countries in the Asia-Pacific region. These migrants' capacity to integrate into these countries is circumscribed by a migration system that makes their stay temporary and extracts between 30 and 100 per cent of their income during their first and sometimes subsequent periods of employment for payment of fees to migration intermediaries. Like Singapore, post-handover Hong Kong has a legislature that passes employment and immigration laws for application in that territory only. The conditions and experience of Indonesian migrant workers in the city-states are similar in this respect, but they are different from each other in three main ways. In Hong Kong, there is a minimum wage; it is criminal for employers to deny some labour rights; and the state there guarantees migrant workers a wider range of civil and political rights. Each place presents migrant workers with a unique set of opportunities and constraints to negotiate life and work, and the ways Indonesian domestic workers have gone about this have contributed to the formation of stereotypes about their character there.

Comparative approaches such as these have been used to study the behaviour of other large Asian diaspora groups, including the Chinese and Indians.[1] These studies warn against essentialism and so risk drawing conclusions that are in fact generalisable to a much broader

---

1   Oonk 2007, Tan 2004.

segment of the global population.[2] At the same time, they recognise that there are characteristic ways in which certain diaspora groups respond to life and work outside their country of citizenship. To illustrate: a group of migrants that hails from the same village in upland Southeast Asia may share similar practices for resisting unfairness when they find themselves on the weak end of power relationships with employers. In such conditions, they are expected to use 'foot-dragging, dissimulation, false-compliance, pilfering, slander, flight, and so forth' rather than directly challenge those with more power.[3] As a result of the specific ways in which Javanese migrant workers do so in Hong Kong and Singapore, employers and employment agency staff have come to espouse certain stereotypes about the Javanese's behavioural, emotional, mental and personal characteristics.

This chapter demonstrates that the migration system determines the migrant workers' capacity to engage with political, economic and socio-cultural institutions in Hong Kong and Singapore, prompting them to behave in ways that are partly influenced by their ethnic and national identity. The first section introduces the Javanese working in Hong Kong and Singapore, explaining how and why they are mostly temporary labour migrants who do not have the right to settle. The second section shifts the focus to a set of constraints and opportunities that shape the way in which this group of migrants responds to life and work in their host setting. The final section discusses how these circumstances have contributed to the formation of stereotypes about Javanese character and suggests methods to further examine them. In conclusion, this chapter argues that migration systems determine the level of engagement that migrant workers have with their host setting and in the process contribute to the process of stereotype formation about the character of migrants.

Who Are the Javanese Domestic Workers in Hong Kong and Singapore?

Indonesians constitute a significant proportion of the ethnic minority population in Hong Kong and Singapore. In both cities, they are

---

2   See also Ang 2005.

3   Scott 2013, 1.

mostly temporary labour migrants who have been employed by residents to clean their apartments, shop, cook and look after their children.[4] In 2013, there were around 140,000 temporary Indonesian migrants working in Hong Kong while 100,000 or so were employed in Singapore. Indonesian citizens constitute over half the foreign domestic worker population in both cities. Migrant workers from the Philippines make up the other significant proportion, with much smaller numbers of workers from India, Sri Lanka, Thailand, Myanmar and Bangladesh. In Singapore, these migrant workers live and work in a society of four million people who identify with various Chinese (74 per cent), Malay (13 per cent), and Indian (9 per cent) ethnic groups.[5] By contrast, Hong Kong is a distinctly Chinese city, where over 93 per cent of the population speaks a Chinese dialect as their first language.[6] In both cities, Indonesian domestic workers constitute roughly 0.02 per cent of the entire population.

The Javanese make up the majority of the Indonesians there. The Indonesian government recorded that in 2011 and 2012 just over 60 per cent of those who used the overseas labour migration programme were resident in Central and East Java.[7] These statistics record residency at the time of registration. It is common for migrant labour employment companies to recruit citizens in different parts of the country and then have them processed in jurisdictions where they are not normally resident[8] With this in mind, Brebes, Cilacap and Kendal in Central Java were among the top ten local government jurisdictions that reported processing migrant workers in 2011 and 2012. In these years, government data on poverty show that Brebes and Cilacap had the first and third greatest number of residents living below the poverty line.[9] The high number in Kendal

---

4   Huang and Yeoh 1996, Sim 2007.

5   www.indexmundi.com/singapore/demographics_profile.html (accessed 21 March 2016).

6   www.indexmundi.com/hong_kong/ethnic_groups.html (accessed 21 March 2016).

7   www.bnp2tki.go.id/statistik-penempatan/6779-penempatan-berdasar-daerah-asal-kotakabupaten-2011-2012.html (accessed 21 June 2015).

8   Palmer 2012.

9   BPS 2016.

is due less to poverty and more to the fact that the local government has special relationships with the labour recruitment industry that it developed under the leadership of a former official of the Ministry of Manpower in the early 2000s.[10] Following the moratorium on placements to Saudi Arabia in 2011, Malang, Ponorogo and Blitar in East Java were elevated to the top ten local jurisdictions, revealing the greater extent to which residents of Java migrated for work. In 2012, 86 per cent of labour migrants in the top ten local government areas last resided in Central and East Java, with Hong Kong and Singapore being the second and third most popular destinations.

Although Javanese labour migrants constitute a small proportion of the population, the job makes them much more visible than would otherwise be the case. On a day-to-day basis Hong Kong and Singapore residents delegate household tasks to foreign domestic workers in order to free up energy and time for other activities, including gainful employment and relaxation. It is for this reason that Javanese can be seen washing vehicles in carports, shopping for groceries in markets, posting letters on the street, taking children to school and accompanying the elderly to hospital appointments. On Sunday, large numbers of Javanese migrant workers can be found enjoying time off work in public spaces. In Hong Kong, the main meeting points are Causeway Bay, Yuen Long and Tuen Mun, where the labour migrants gather to socialise and organise cultural, religious and other entertainment activities. In Singapore, they frequently meet in and around the Orchard Road area to socialise only, partly because the state does not support migrant groups to associate in public spaces as freely as in Hong Kong. By contrast, employment relations are frequently hidden from the public eye, taking place as they do within the private sphere of employers' homes. Regardless, extreme cases of physical abuse are infrequently picked up by the international mass media, serving to remind observers that Hong Kong and Singaporean residents do far too little to ensure foreign domestic workers' physical safety.

The typical Javanese domestic worker is a woman. The reason for this in both places is largely because of immigration policy and employer demand. The Hong Kong Immigration Department does

10 Palmer 2016.

not specify that foreign domestic workers must be women. The Sex Discrimination Ordinance prevents the Department from doing so. Nonetheless, it recognises that Hong Kong residents normally employ women as domestic workers and so asks prospective employers to make a special case if they want to hire men. Similarly, the Singaporean Ministry of Manpower only allows employers to bring in men for domestic work if they have valid reasons, such as requiring a physically strong worker to help bathe an elderly male. This combination of employer preferences and government policy means that Javanese men employed on foreign domestic helper visas in Hong Kong and Singapore are few and far between. To deal with the risk that the women might give birth in Singapore and then sponsor their babies to stay in the country, the government there requires them to undergo pregnancy tests bi-annually. If the migrant is found pregnant and wants to keep the child, the employment contract is terminated. In Hong Kong, abortion is a subsidised health service. But employers frequently put pressure on the migrants to resign if found to be pregnant, and so avoid providing the migrants with labour entitlements such as maternity leave pay.[11]

Javanese domestic workers have at least a primary school education. Singapore requires foreign domestic workers to have eight years of formal education. In Hong Kong, they should have two years of relevant work experience. In 2004, Indonesia passed a law that required citizens to have nine years of formal education if they wanted overseas domestic work. The education limit was lowered a few years later after migrant labour recruitment companies challenged it in the Constitutional Court, arguing that the law denied all citizens equal access to employment, which was a constitutional right.[12] Privately, recruiters admit that, regardless, they routinely send citizens who fall short of requirements for overseas work because it is no problem to purchase 'real but fake' (*asli tapi palsu* or *aspal*) documents from the Indonesian authorities as a workaround. As a result, large numbers of Indonesians work overseas with *aspal*

---

11 Constable 2014.

12 Constitutional Court decisions 28/PUU-IV/2006 and 029/PUU-IV/2006 dated 11 April 2007. www.mahkamahkonstitusi.go.id (accessed 24 March 2016).

qualifications, with the effect that Indonesian, Hong Kong and Singaporean government data do not accurately reflect the actual education level of migrants.

Javanese domestic workers' personal identity documents are frequently changed before they apply for employment visas. Dates of birth are doctored in order to circumvent the minimum age requirement.[13] In part, this is due to the fact that the law in some respects is aspirational about who should migrate for work. For example, Indonesian law requires citizens to be at least twenty-one years old if they want to work overseas as a domestic worker. Singaporean immigration policy sets the minimum age at twenty-three, and Hong Kong at eighteen. However, migrant labour employment companies lament that it is difficult to meet demand for the kind of people that governments want to migrate for work at the wage level offered by employers. To do so, the companies pay around Rp 5,000,000 (US$ 500) to informal intermediaries for each migrant they recruit. All, part, or none of this fee is disbursed to the migrants in the form of a financial inducement, such as pocket money (*uang saku*).[14] It is at this stage that most migrants' identity documents are altered by changing dates of birth, with the view to making them eligible for an overseas employment visa. To meet Indonesian, Hong Kong and Singaporean eligibility criteria, ages are revised upwards with the effect that the state represents migrants as being older than they really are.

The migrant demographic has changed over time, shifting in response to factors that are beyond the migrants' control. The 1997 Asian financial crisis had the effect of wiping out employment opportunities in Indonesia, eroding real wages for those still in work and making foreign currency much more valuable. This resulted in a spike in demand for overseas work.[15] In Singapore, demand for Indonesian domestic workers rose despite the crisis, partly fuelled by promotion campaigns that advertised 'zero cost' migrants.[16] This business practice effectively transferred all migration costs, including payment of international travel, to the workers. In Hong Kong, demand also rose

---

13 Ford and Lyons 2011.

14 Killias 2010.

15 Athukorala and Manning 1999.

16 Palmer 2016, 50.

as migrant labour employment companies found employers willing to underpay those they hire.[17] The number of Indonesian domestic workers doubled by the end of 1999, and despite significant wage cuts in 2003, the number doubled again, whereas the population of Filipinos declined and other nationality groups remained small. In summary, the Indonesian labour migrant population grew quickly in both cities despite the fact that the cost of migration increased and employers offered poorer employment conditions. This indicates that those who left Indonesia at this time came from families that had fallen on hard times and were willing to make compromises in return for income so as to help make ends meet at home.

In another way, changes to education policy in Indonesia have meant that those going to Hong Kong and Singapore have higher levels of education. In 1984 President Suharto attempted to make six years of basic education free and mandatory for Indonesian citizens following reports that around 1.5 million children had never been to school. In 2003 President Megawati Sukarnoputri worked with the legislature to extend free and mandatory education to nine years. Problems with implementation meant that this schooling was not always free or otherwise accessible, but various interventions since then have resulted in much higher attendance rates of children at primary schools and much greater levels of enrolment at junior high school.[18] Local governments have also made budget allocations to subsidise or pay entirely for senior high school education in line with the national government's ongoing programme to at least make twelve years of schooling free. As this indicates, Indonesians born in 1992 will often have at least nine years of education, while those who are older were only guaranteed to have six. Migrant labour recruitment companies in Indonesia admit that they falsify more education certificates for older migrants because that age bracket regularly falls short of the minimum education requirements for employment visas.

In both places, the geographic distribution of Indonesian domestic workers is largely determined by the social class of employers. They are

---

17 Palmer 2013.

18 Sumintono 2009.

frequently hired by the lower social classes and so are concentrated in certain areas.[19] In Hong Kong, the increasing number of Indonesian migrant workers in the early 2000s is partly attributed to the success of migrant labour recruitment companies in finding employers who were willing to risk paying between 40 and 60 per cent of the minimum wage.[20] Yuen Long is one area where large numbers of employers did so. In Singapore, there is no minimum wage and residents have a much longer history of employing Indonesians as domestic workers, so the distribution is more even. In both cities, employers who want the domestic worker to help educate their children are encouraged by family, friends and migrant labour recruitment companies to employ Filipinas, for the reason that Filipinas generally have a much higher level of formal education than Indonesians, and speak English. As a result, Filipina domestic workers tend to be employed in middle-class areas that put a premium on this kind of assistance. By contrast, migrant labour recruitment companies recommend that employers hire Indonesians to take care of elderly family members, as they have developed a strong reputation for patience and attentiveness to older household members.

In turn, the social class of Indonesian domestic workers distinguishes them from employers, migrant labour recruitment companies, government officials and compatriots. Their lack of knowledge about systems and processes as well as their limited ability to understand rights and obligations enable employers to abuse and otherwise exploit Javanese domestic workers with relatively little fear that law-enforcement authorities will intervene. Individual law-enforcement officers frequently dismiss reports of abuse and exploitation as misunderstandings, which even occurs when an interpreter is hired to facilitate communication, suggesting that language is not the only barrier that prevents Javanese domestic workers from seeking assistance to enforce rights.[21] The relationships between Javanese

---

19 Interviews with migrant labour recruitment companies in Singapore, July 2009; interviews with agencies in Hong Kong, November 2009.

20 Palmer 2013.

21 Interview with a migrant support organisation that provides paralegal assistance to Indonesian domestic workers with immigration, labour and police cases, April 2014.

domestic workers and other Indonesian residents, including consulate staff, international students and expatriates show that social class is a more significant barrier. These other Indonesians frequently complain that the behaviour of Javanese domestic workers has given Indonesians a reputation for not understanding how to behave in middle- and upper-class social settings.[22] The women in particular feel the need to differentiate themselves as a social group, doing so by referring to one another as Ms or Mrs (*ibu*) and domestic workers as Miss (*mbak*) – regardless of other factors such as age and marital status. This form of othering plays out much more subtly in relationships with government authorities, but nevertheless influences the degree to which Javanese domestic workers are assisted.

Javanese domestic workers constitute a large majority of the ethnic minority population in both Hong Kong and Singapore and their presence in both places has much to do with employers' demand for labour migrants, government policy and the profit-driven practices of migration intermediaries. They are a segment of the Indonesian population that has responded to opportunities for gainful employment, which in Singapore paid SG$ 450 (US$ 360) per month in 2015. Hong Kong paid HK$ 4,110 (US$ 530) per month in the same year. These income earnings contribute significantly to consumption expenditure in Indonesia, as migrant workers remit money to family especially, and these remittances constitute the second largest foreign income earner after the export of crude oil and gas. The opportunity for overseas employment helps to compensate for the fact that decent employment prospects are lacking at home. However, it is employers' demand for their labour that has allowed migration intermediaries to make a business out of helping migrants to negotiate the various administrative processes that states require them to go through before they can start work. In their host setting, it is the stance of host governments, employers, and the society there more widely that determines the way in which these migrants negotiate life and work.

---

22 Participant observation at the Indonesian national day celebration in Hong Kong, August 2014.

Migration Systems and their Impact on Life and Work

The 'context of reception' is a kind of 'fait accompli which alters [migrants'] aspirations and plans and can channel individuals of similar background into widely different directions.'[23] In the case of foreign domestic workers in Hong Kong, this context has been defined to include laws that determine legal status, residency rights, and social mobility.[24] The largest part of the host population's direct experience of Javanese is through foreign domestic workers and those migrants' responses to this context. Although there is little that is uniquely Javanese about their responses, this has not prevented the formation and maintenance of stereotypes about Javanese behavioural, emotional, mental and personal characteristics. Javanese domestic workers have developed a reputation for working hard but not demanding employers to respect their labour rights. Nevertheless, employers generally agree that Javanese workers are unable to perform basic tasks without training and that they often lie to get out of work.[25] In order to understand these ideas about Javanese identity, it is worth examining the context in which these characteristics find their expression.

The context of reception is best understood by paying attention to the intention of schemes that admit foreign domestic workers. These schemes are not unique in the sense that they admit migrant workers to help meet employers' demand for labour, for example when the local workforce does not have the requisite skills or is not willing to do the work. In the case of foreign domestic workers, the problem is the latter because employers want full-time domestic workers who live in, who will accept a wage below the market rate for local domestic workers, and will agree to flexible work hours. Policymakers in Hong Kong and Singapore have sensitised the immigration regime to this demand, allowing it to solve the problem that their societies have come to require affordable solutions for childcare, care of the elderly, and help looking after private households. This

---

23 Portes 1989, 14.

24 Sim 2003.

25 Participant observation in Labour Department conciliation meetings and Labour Tribunal hearings, January-November 2014.

solution enables such societies to keep working long hours for what are sometimes modest wages. In Hong Kong, employers and their spouses earning HK$ 15,000 (US$ 1,935) per month can afford to bring in a foreign domestic worker.[26] In Singapore, the Ministry of Manpower considers applications for those with earnings less than SG$ 2,000 (US$ 1,600).[27] As this suggests, a group of employers hire foreign domestic workers out of necessity rather than as a luxury.

Foreign domestic workers in Hong Kong and Singapore have different degrees of labour rights. In Singapore, they are not covered by the Employment Act. In Hong Kong, the Employment Ordinance applies but they are not entitled to the universal minimum wage, as there is a much lower one for their job category. Further, working hours standards do not apply. Policy-makers in both cities argue that it is not practical to regulate the latter because employers find it difficult to calculate overtime, as they choose not to define workers' work and free time. Wages should be paid within seven days of becoming due. In Hong Kong, employers are liable to prosecution, and upon conviction may be imprisoned for up to three years and fined HK$ 350,000 (US$ 45,160). Nevertheless, some employers pay wages irregularly and foreign domestic workers do not report them to the government authority with powers to seek enforcement, especially when they are still in employment.[28] Reasons for this include that foreign domestic workers in Singapore are denied access to the Ministry of Manpower's mechanisms for mediating labour disputes. In Hong Kong, where it is possible, they choose not to do so when they believe they have a 'good' employer.[29] Good employers are people who do not lose their temper too frequently and do not

---

26 www.immd.gov.hk/eng/services/visas/foreign_domestic_helpers.html (accessed 24 March 2016).

27 The Singaporean Ministry of Manpower does not publicise the exact amount of income an employer needs to hire a foreign domestic worker. Migrant labour recruitment agencies claim that the Ministry will normally consider applications where the employer earns at least SG$ 2,000 per month (Interviews, July 2009).

28 For a detailed explanation why this is the case, see Tan 2016.

29 Participant observation of a migrant support organisation helping migrant workers sue their employers, January-November 2014.

make unreasonable demands such as requiring employees to be on duty eighteen hours a day.

The immigration policy that requires foreign domestic workers to live at their workplace further complicates the employment relationship, encouraging employees to compromise on labour rights. The live-in arrangement is the product of three major considerations. First, there is a demand for full-time, live-in domestic workers but most employers cannot afford to hire a local worker to perform the role. Second, the immigration authority recognises that more employers are in a better financial position to pay the wages of a foreign domestic worker if they live in, as it justifies the payment of lower wages in exchange for providing accommodation and food. However, the fact that immigration authorities in Hong Kong and Singapore do not allow employers the option to choose a live-out arrangement indicates that government is equally concerned about the consequences of allowing hundreds of thousands of migrant women to participate more in life outside the workplace. Although the state in Singapore prohibits specific conditions and activities, including being pregnant or getting married during their working sojourn, the live-in arrangement in both Singapore and Hong Kong has the effect that it delegates responsibility to control other forms of social participation to employers.

The collection of migration intermediaries' fees strains the employment relationship between foreign domestic workers and their employers. Indonesian law only permits migrant labour recruitment companies with a licence in Indonesia to provide job-matching services for work overseas. In Hong Kong, furthermore, the Indonesian consulate uses a local immigration policy to force all citizens to use those companies as a condition to apply for a foreign domestic worker visa.[30] These companies typically charge HK$ 13,436 (US$ 1,733) for jobs in Hong Kong and SG$ 1,807 (US$ 1,455) for Singapore. The employment contract period is typically two years but either party can terminate the agreement before its expiration. Both migrant workers and their recruitment companies prefer fees to be collected after employment has commenced.[31] Migrant workers want to see

---

30 Palmer 2013.

31 Palmer 2016.

the job before they pay and the companies find that migrant workers bargain less if they do not have to pay anything upfront. As a result, the lion's share of migrants' wages in Hong Kong and Singapore goes towards settling recruitment debts in the first six months. These systemic practices influence the labour migration experience of most Javanese domestic workers.

Negotiating Life and Work

Wages are higher in Hong Kong, which motivates Javanese labour migrants from other countries in the Asia-Pacific region to try their hand at domestic work there. Singapore is seen as a jumping board for jobs there partly because migrants are told that they should work in Singapore for two years in order to become eligible for a Hong Kong employment visa. Those who follow this advice directly experience two different systems for collecting fees for recruitment services, one in which employers make deductions from wages (Singapore) and one where the migrants make payments to private financiers (Hong Kong). They also know about the better quality of labour rights that foreign domestic workers should have in Hong Kong. But whether those rights are respected depends squarely on employers, who have their own reasons for hiring Javanese workers.[32]

Employers claim that Javanese domestic workers are more compliant because they respect authority figures. Friends and migrant labour recruitment companies are often the first port of call for employers seeking advice on whether to hire a Javanese domestic worker. They warn against candidates who are young, who are not expected to remit money regularly to support their families at home, or who have had too much work experience, as they are more likely to resist employers' directions. In addition, employers are told to avoid hiring domestic workers from East Indonesia, where the population has a reputation

---

32 The following expectations and complaints are based on participant observation of labour dispute resolution processes between December 2013 and November 2014 in Hong Kong. They resonate with interview data collected from employers and labour recruitment companies during PhD fieldwork in 2009 and 2010. The narrative applies to employers in both Hong Kong and Singapore unless otherwise stated.

for being more direct and outspoken. By contrast, domestic workers from Central and East Java are said to be more amenable, especially towards employers who occupy a higher social position based on achieved status, including education, employment and income. Ascribed status, including sex, race or parental social status, is another determining factor. As Indonesian domestic workers typically come from areas of Java where social stratification positions them on the lower tier of the system, employers expect to exercise greater power in their employment relationships, including that the domestic worker will accept unreasonable and even unlawful work conditions.

Employers complain that Javanese domestic workers lie to take annual leave and other paid holidays because they are opportunistic. Javanese domestic workers frequently claim some urgent matter such as an accident, an illness, or a death in the family to take paid and unpaid leave from work, often giving the employer short notice. In Hong Kong, the employment ordinance allows employers to appoint paid leave and rest days after consulting employees. But the government department with responsibility for implementing the law does not define consultation or other caveats such as reasonable excuse for failure to grant leave. At the very least, this legal context gives employers flexibility to determine when employment entitlements are given, with the effect that the power relationship around this matter is further skewed in favour of employers. As a result, employees learn that employers will consider the urgency of the leave request against their own immediate needs. It is partly for this reason that Javanese foreign domestic workers attempt to tip the scale in their favour by claiming a major life event as the purpose for taking leave.

Employers observe that the migrants are less professional than other nationality groups during normal work hours. Specifically, they complain about the frequency with which the migrants use cell phones to communicate with friends and family, and so frequently introduce rules such that the workers may only chat and make calls after work is finished for the day. Typically, a foreign domestic worker's day starts between six and seven o'clock in the morning and concludes by nine or ten at night. They do not always work for the entire period but many employers do expect the migrants to be available for work six days a week. This effectively restricts the migrants' ability to participate in social interactions outside the household from Monday to Saturday. Their use of cell phones helps to compensate for this restriction during rest time but also when they are idle at work. Employers are known not to assign sufficient tasks, which sometimes leaves the migrants with little to do, and so the domestic worker uses their phones to compensate for feelings of boredom with the monotony of daily routines.

In Hong Kong, employers are generally supportive of their workers' participation in social activities outside the workplace on the weekly day off, which punctuates the cycle. Indonesian domestic workers can join a wide range of formal and informal groups which encourage and promote practices from the homeland, including social gatherings that function like a rotating savings association (*arisan*), that discuss religion and worship God (*pengajian*), and that teach dance and music. A wide range of civil society organisations provide avenues for these groups to compete or otherwise interact with one another in a public forum. Hong Kong employers are more cynical about the migrants' involvement in social activism, such as membership in unions and associations that advocate change to immigration and labour policies, which typically benefit employers at the migrants' expense. Employers' wishes in Singapore are similar in this regard but migrants there are denied the opportunity to participate in organisations regardless largely because there are so few organisations concerned with migrant labour rights. Singapore does not support migrants to self-organise for political and other social purposes, and the weekly day off was only introduced in 2013, which prevented them from doing so despite the ban. As a result, the migrants have had much less time to engage in life outside the workplace and so the scale of migrant activities is much smaller than in Hong Kong.

Employers are told that Javanese domestic workers will show little initiative because they expect to receive instructions to perform even simple tasks. For example, employers often complain that if told to vacuum the living room, a newly-hired domestic worker from Java will do so but then hesitate to neaten the employer's possessions lying on the coffee table. Employers claim that Javanese domestic workers do not receive adequate education and training before commencing work. At the same time, Javanese domestic workers also feel like guests in their employers' homes even though immigration policy requires them to live there. They frequently worry that the employer will deduct from their wages the cost of accidentally breaking an item. Furthermore, they are concerned that the employer might accuse them of theft. Migrant labour recruitment companies in Indonesia reinforce these feelings when they tell intending migrants not to make assumptions about what the employer expects, with the result that the migrants decide it is safest to only carry out work that they have explicitly been asked to perform.

Employers agree that Javanese domestic workers lack common sense. Their conclusion is based on direct observation of how the workers perform tasks such as maintaining certain levels of hygiene in the household. In the kitchen, employers complain that Javanese domestic workers wash crockery and cutlery with cold water. In the bathroom, a common complaint is that Javanese domestic workers hang used towels to dry rather than put them in the washing machine, allowing bacteria to proliferate. Employers claim that these are examples which show that Javanese domestic workers lack common sense – understood to be 'the basic human faculty that lets us make elemental judgements about everyday matters based on everyday, real-world experience.'[33] But there are two major reasons why Javanese domestic workers do this. First, their homes in Java rarely have hot water systems. Nor do they have washing machines, which means that clothing, bedsheets and towels are often hung to dry or aired before being washed by hand. Second, although Javanese domestic workers share the wisdom that bacteria can cause disease, education in Indonesia about the kinds of conditions in which bacteria can develop is not as detailed as in Hong Kong. As this suggests, the 'common sense' expected by employers is often based on their own particular experience of life in Hong Kong and is not a basic ability to understand how to live in a hygienic environment.

Employers' perceptions of Javanese domestic workers are the product of myriad factors, including the quality of education that the migrants receive before their departure overseas for work. The expectation that Javanese domestic workers will transition seamlessly into life and work in Hong Kong is often based on the assumption that the migrants share common understandings about how things should be done. The fact that this is not always the case further frustrates

---

33 Rosenfeld 2011, 1.

employers who believe that Javanese domestic workers lack initiative, as those employers feel that they have to give detailed instructions about how to perform simple household chores. However, Javanese domestic workers are often keenly aware of the unequal power relationship that exists between employer and employee, and so try to prevent situations that might give employers grounds to terminate employment contracts such as an allegation of carelessness or theft, by only following explicit instructions. These conditions are not particular to the Javanese, as domestic workers from other regions have very similar experiences, which then raises questions about whether there is anything that is particularly Javanese at all about the migrants' behaviour in this context.

Javanese Identity, Essentialism and the Persistence of Stereotypes

These migrants' responses are not necessarily Javanese, not least because non-Javanese subjects also react in similar ways to the context. Other foreign domestic workers and even local employees are expected to use similar strategies to negotiate life and work when they find themselves on the weak end of power relationships.[34] Employers and employment agencies have adopted stereotypes about the Javanese and the certain ways in which they do things. A way in which to examine the extent to which such stereotypes reflect reality is to pay attention to how they develop. The experience of individuals and their patterns of communication about certain categories of people have strong explanatory power. At the same time, a focus on the social structures that order relations between both groups can reveal details about the process of stereotype formation. This processual approach to examining stereotypes will not only make a contribution to knowledge about the Javanese in Hong Kong and Singapore, but will also offer an alternative starting point to draw comparisons between them and the other nationality groups that live and work under similar conditions.

---

34 Participant observation of labour dispute resolution processes in Hong Kong involving Indonesians, Filipinos, Sri Lankans, Indians and Nepalese, December 2013 – November 2014.

The persistence of stereotypes explains how and why those about the Javanese are confirmed and strengthened, sometimes despite counter-evidence and logical arguments against them. At the same time, it enables the identification of aspects of Javanese identity that are maintained by Javanese individuals and groups outside the home-land. Focusing attention on persistent structures of social order such as stereotypes has potential to reveal examples where behaviour in the diaspora setting is indeed best explained by way of reference to practice in the homeland. This effort may then provide a resource to isolate and refine an understanding of attributes, necessary to ethnic and national identity, which persist despite distance from the home-land. Comparisons between Javanese and non-Javanese behaviour in the diaspora context subject the beliefs and thoughts about the Javanese to critical analysis. But this approach also enables analyses of the form and function of Javanese practices that persist beyond the homeland, providing another basis from which to examine how and why individuals and groups within the diaspora retain or rein-vent aspects of their homeland identity outside that context.

The capacity of the Javanese to integrate into Asian host societies is severely circumscribed by temporary labour migration regimes that prevent settlement. Policy-makers in Hong Kong and Singapore explain that foreign domestic workers are issued temporary employ-ment visas for a very specific purpose, namely to help provide the good life for residents. Singaporean authorities have gone as far as to proscribe pregnancy and marriage in the host setting, but both states have set up immigration regimes that prevent the Javanese and other foreign domestic workers from making applications for permanent residence. This effectively prevents settlement for most, which in the minds of Javanese labour migrants reinforces the idea that the working sojourn is only temporary. Labour migrants may aspire to remain for as long as possible, but know that the host state's administrative systems compel them to leave when their employment visas expire. Surveys of Indonesian domestic workers reveal that this system orients many to the homeland as the place where they can return with social and economic capital acquired while overseas.[35]

---

35 ATKI-HK 2007.

Yet the working sojourn certainly influences processes that result in both cultural loss and cultural gain among the Javanese. Employment agencies in Indonesia and Hong Kong especially encourage Javanese migrant workers to refrain from practices that are unfamiliar in their host country.[36] Employers in Hong Kong, for example, usually will not allow Muslim employees to take time away from the job to pray five times a day, three to four of which would fall within normal work hours. Chinese employers usually object to the use of white cloth, which is customary for Muslim women to wear at the time of prayer, because they associate it with ghosts. This and other requirements such as that foreign domestic workers should adapt to the diet and cuisine of their employers, for example by cooking and eating pork, have put pressure on Muslim Javanese workers to reprioritise the importance of practices that are widely accepted in the homeland. In other words, the migrants frequently compromise and dispense with practices that can and do frustrate relationships with their employers, partly in response to the fact that the migrants live and spend the majority of their time abroad in their employers' homes.

At the same time, the Indonesian government discourages the migrants from adopting liberal behaviours that it deems are incompatible with conservative beliefs about social norms at home. The Indonesian consulate in Hong Kong, for example, recommends new arrivals in its mandatory Welcoming Programme – which is not always attended – to keep their heads down and do what they came to do: work and earn money rather than develop lifestyles that are not easily replicated at home.[37] In particular, migrants are warned against consumerism, lesbianism, immodest dressing and atheism. The consulate engages with migrant support groups, including Dompet Duafa Hong Kong, an Indonesian civil society organisation that promotes Islamic values, to reach longer-term migrants. In Singapore, the embassy is less concerned with these matters largely because the state prevents the large-scale visibility of liberal behaviour as a consequence of denying migrants a weekly day off before 2013.

---

36 Interviews with migrant labour recruitment companies in Hong Kong, November 2009 and Indonesia, December 2010.

37 Participant observation at the Indonesian consulate's bi-weekly Welcoming Program for newly arrived migrants, November 2009.

Social conservatism in the city stifles public displays of affection by same-sex couples. By contrast to Hong Kong, where the context of reception is more conducive to these things, officials in Indonesia's diplomatic mission in Singapore are not as strongly motivated to influence aspects of migrants' private lives.[38]

The Indonesian government encourages migrant workers before they leave home to learn and adopt Hong Kong and Singaporean ways of life, arguing that the practices are responsible for those societies' capacity to modernise and maintain a relatively high standard of living.[39] Specifically, Indonesian authorities encourage intending migrants to observe their host society's approach to raising children and using public space. They condemn the practice of Javanese mothers overindulging their children with the result that young adults are not trained to be more independent and responsible members of society. Pride in the maintenance of clean public spaces, such as roads, sidewalks and parks, is another value that authorities want migrant workers to develop outside Indonesia. Of course these are institutional objectives that the government of the day also wants to achieve at home. Nonetheless, the expectation is that the migrants will adopt these practices during their working sojourn overseas and transfer them to their place of origin after they return home, where they are then also expected to re-adopt cultural and religious practices abandoned while working in their employers homes, such as exhibiting liberal behaviours that are thought to be incompatible with life and work in the homeland.

Conclusion

This chapter argues that migration systems determine the level of engagement that Javanese domestic workers have with their host setting and that they contribute to the formation of stereotypes about Javanese character. As a result of the host immigration regimes in Hong Kong and Singapore, contemporary labour migrants from Java arrive with little expectation that they will integrate into the

---

38 Interview with Labour Attaché, July 2009.

39 Participant observation at mandatory Pre-Departure Training in Surabaya, September 2009.

host society and so behave accordingly. The migrants know that they will live with their employers, who will use their greater power in the relationship to enforce rules about when the migrants can interact with people or participate in group activities outside the workplace. But the migrants are not always emotionally prepared for the reality of what this means, in part because it is a secondary concern to most who sign up for labour migration. The primary concern is the income that the employment offers. A minority of migrants leave their jobs and go underground in search of greater freedoms, such as those with boyfriends or who become pregnant and want to live with the baby and perhaps the baby's father. The majority, however, remain in employment, where they negotiate life and work with their employers for the whole time that they spend in the host society.

During their temporary working sojourn abroad, this group of labour migrants remains oriented towards the homeland, where they will ultimately be forced to return. Even many of those who go underground do not intend to settle in the host society. The greater freedoms and income often provide a temporary fix, as the migrants can pursue short- and medium-term goals, such as establishing a family in the host society and earning more money to save or remit home. They may want to remain but know that life can be very difficult, constantly living in fear of detection by the authorities. Settling in this way also effectively prevents them from leaving the host society to return home through authorised immigration check points without first reporting to the authorities, being punished and then deported. For this group, Java is not only a place where they have friends and family, it is also a place where they have the right to remain. In the minds of many of these migrants, then, settlement in the host society is not a long-term option. Rather, the stay is inevitably temporary with very few exceptions.

Nevertheless, the experience provides a limited encounter between the Javanese and the host society, which serves as a basis for individuals and groups in that society to form thoughts and beliefs about Javanese identity. In fact, these encounters offer the host society a snapshot of Javanese character and always one that is a product of the migrants' response to their particular context of life and work in the host society. The experiences of migrants from Java who have permanently settled, including ethnic Chinese who emigrated between

1996 and 1998 in response to mass violence that victimised Chinese Indonesians, may in part be the same or quite different. A study that examines these experiences and maps the ways and purposes of these settled migrants' interaction with the temporary migrant group from Java will help identify experiences that are unique or generalisable to migrants from Java and the host population as a whole. As a starting point, this chapter presents some detail on the formation of stereo-types about the temporary migrants from Java and offers a useful schema against which to locate accepted assumptions about the form and function of practices that in the homeland are considered to be necessarily Javanese.

References

Ang, I. 2005. *On Not Speaking Chinese: Living Between Asia and the West*. London: Routledge.

Athukorala, P. and C. Manning 1999. *Structural Change and International Migration in East Asia: Adjusting to Labour Scarcity*. Melbourne: Oxford University Press.

ATKI-HK (Asosiasi Tenaga Kerja Indonesia Hong Kong) 2007. *The Truth Behind Illegal Salary Deductions to Indonesian Migrant Workers in Hong Kong*. Hong Kong: ATKI-HK in collaboration with AMCB (Asian Migrants Coordinating Body).

BPS (Badan Pusat Statistik Propinsi Jawa Tengah). 2016. 'Penduduk Miskin Menurut Kabupaten/Kota di Jawa Tengah Tahun 2010, 2011 dan 2012'. [jateng.bps.go.id/linkTabelStatis/view/id/793]

Constable, N. 2014. *Born Out of Place: Migrant Mothers and the Politics of International Labor*. Hong Kong: Hong Kong University Press.

Ford, M. and L. Lyons 2011. 'Travelling the Aspal Route: "Grey" Labour Migration Through an Indonesian Border Town'. In *The State and Illegality in Indonesia*, ed. E. Aspinall and G. van Klinken, 107–122. Leiden: KITLV Press.

Huang, S. and B. Yeoh 1996. 'Ties That Bind: State Policy and Migrant Female Domestic Helpers in Singapore'. *Geoforum* 27(4): 479–493.

Killias, O. 2010. '"Illegal" Migration as Resistance: Legality, Morality and Coercion in Indonesian Domestic Worker Migration to Malaysia'. *Asian Journal of Social Science* 38(6): 897–914.

Oonk, G. 2007. *Global Diasporas: Exploring Trajectories of Migration and Theory*. Amsterdam: Amsterdam University Press.

Palmer, W. 2012. 'Discretion and the Trafficking-like Practices of the Indonesian State'. In *Labour Migration and Human Trafficking in Southeast*

Asia: Critical Perspectives, ed. M. Ford, L. Lyons and W. van Schendel, 149–166. London: Routledge.

Palmer, W. 2013. 'Public-Private Partnerships in the Administration and Control of Indonesian Migrant Labour in Hong Kong'. *Political Geography* 34: 1–9.

—— 2016. *Indonesia's Overseas Labour Migration Programme, 1969–2010*. Leiden and Boston: Brill.

Portes, A. 1989. 'Contemporary Immigration: Theoretical Perspectives on its Determinants and Modes of Incorporation'. *International Migration Review* 23(3): 606–630.

Rosenfeld, S. 2011. *Common Sense: A Political History*. Cambridge, Massachusetts: Harvard University Press.

Scott, J. 2013. 'Introduction'. In *Everyday Forms of Peasant Resistance in Southeast Asia*, ed. J. Scott and B. Kerkvliet, 1–4. New York: Routledge.

Sim, A. 2003. 'Organising Discontent: NGOs for Southeast Asian Migrant Workers in Hong Kong'. *Asian Journal of Social Science* 31(3): 478–510.

—— 2007. 'Women in Transition: Indonesian Domestic Workers in Hong Kong'. PhD diss., University of Hong Kong.

Sumintono, B. 2009. 'School-based Management Policy and its Practices at a District Level in the Post New Order Indonesia'. *Journal of Indonesian Social Sciences and Humanities* 2: 41–67.

Tan, C. 2016. 'Enforcing Socioeconomic Rights: Everyday Resistance and Community Resources among Indonesian Migrant Domestic Workers in Hong Kong'. In *The Everyday Political Economy of Southeast Asia*, ed. J. Elias and L. Rethel, 218–235. Cambridge: Cambridge University Press.

Tan, C.-B. 2004. *Chinese Overseas: Comparative Cultural Issues*. Hong Kong: Hong Kong University Press.

CHAPTER 6

'No to Racial Discrimination'

Javanese Guest Workers' Experiences of Racism
in Taiwan and their Stratagems of Resistance

ROBERT TIERNEY

Introduction

In the post-World War II period, Taiwan gradually became one
of the most affluent countries, by Asian standards,[1] from a poor
economic base, as reflected in the historical data on per capita GDP.
In 1952 the island had a per capita gross national product of US$
170, endowing upon it the status of one of Asia's poorest countries.
By 2013, however, per capita GDP, adjusted for purchasing power
parity, had soared to US$ 39,600, somewhat comparable to those of
prosperous Western economies.[2]

Taiwan's economic rise has corresponded with the development
of severe labour shortfalls, as local employees no longer brook 3D
(dirty, dangerous and demeaning) jobs.[3] Successive governments
and employers have experienced rapidly escalating fiscal pressures

---

1 Pressman 2007, 185–186.

2 Taiwan's economy has undergone a number of distinct phases since the
   early 1950s, characterised by the development of rural and subsequently
   manufacturing import-substitution industries, followed by the ruling
   party's (Guomindang) aggressive promotion of export-oriented manufacturing. In the so-called fourth phase since 1981, national and provincial
   governments have prioritised the expansion of high technology, export-
   focused manufacturing, particularly in the fields of petrochemicals and
   semiconductors. In the first decades after 1960, the island's gross domestic
   product grew impressively by 8 to 10 per cent per annum; the national
   product subsequently fell to about 6.4 per cent yearly in the first half of the
   1990s, although this was still high by world standards.

3 Tierney 2007, 207–211.

and labour costs, emanating from an occasionally restive workforce, who ratchet up demands for higher real incomes and improved social wages.

Taiwan's guest worker programme began in the early 1990s, roughly a decade following its rise to membership of the Asian club of newly industrialised 'tiger economies', along with South Korea, Hong Kong and Singapore. Since this time, temporary migrants have been locked into the island country's minimum wage system. Transnationals make up a large portion of the minimum wage cohort and are typically ghettoised in the worst jobs, which locals disdain and shun.

Indonesians constitute the largest national group within Taiwan's migrant population. They dominate jobs at the most exploitative end of the county's wage spectrum, including female caregivers and male fishers. Indonesians are also concentrated in the cohort of undocumented migrant workers – those who break their labour contracts by fleeing their workplaces.

Although the demographic record of Taiwan's Indonesian migrants is far from complete, there can be little doubt that the vast majority are Javanese, from rural and fishing villages. This chapter accordingly examines the economic and social backgrounds of those from Java – the villages in which they lived and worked prior to temporary emigration. It also considers the means by which the legislative framework maximises the exploitation and repression of Javanese and other migrant workers on the island.

The working and living conditions experienced within Taiwan's racialised labour market give rise to inter-ethnic tensions between local Taiwanese and Javanese as well as between Javanese and other migrant nationalities. This chapter examines the ways in which these conditions, together with the tensions arising from them, have been contested by Javanese caregivers and fishers, by domestic helpers and fishers from the Philippines, and by local Taiwanese organisations which are sympathetic to the island's guest workers.

Javanese guest workers celebrate their cultural heritage through song, dance and drama, as do other migrant nationalities, and are prepared to stage them in halls, parks and on the street. The chapter analyses the political dimensions of cultural performances when protest is taken to the streets. These challenge oppressive identities that have long been imposed on Indonesians, specifically identities based on the presumption of docility and voicelessness. In the course of politicised cultural performance, the Javanese have built activism-based coalitions with other migrant communities, weakening ethnic divisions in the process.

Data for this chapter are derived from statistical publications by the Taiwanese Ministry of Labor and personal information from social workers or staff members of NGOs that run migrant organisations and shelters in Taiwan.

Documented and Undocumented Temporary Immigration

In response to upward pressures on labour costs, emanating largely from unrelenting labour shortfalls, Taiwan's Council of Labor Affairs (hereafter referred to as the Ministry of Labor, which replaced the Council in February 2014) promulgated the Employment Services Law 1992. This enabled temporary immigration, allocating guest workers exclusively to 3D work in factories, on building sites and on deep-sea trawling vessels, as well as to domestic help and care of the aged.[4] Between 2002 and June 2017, the population of documented migrants more than doubled, from 303,684 to 653,804 people. In June 2017, documented migrants represented 5.5 per cent of the aggregate workforce of some 11.8 million people. They are drawn from four countries. Indonesians constituted 38.7 per cent of the documented aggregate in June 2017. The others comprised people from Vietnam (29.9 per cent), the Philippines (22.1 per cent) and Thailand (9.3 per cent).[5]

The Ministry of Labor has administered temporary immigration to recompose Taiwan's working class and to racialise the labour market, as reflected in migrants' allocation to pre-specified industries. In June 2017, just over six in ten temporary migrants were employed in factories, while 37 per cent were engaged in the so-called 'human

---

4   Three-year contracts gradually became the norm. As a consequence of persistent labour shortages, the Legislative Yuan amended the Employment Services Law in 2004, allowing applications for additional visas. Reverend Peter O'Neill, letter to the author, 23 February 2015.

5   Ministry of Labor 2016b.

health and social work' sector, comprising domestic maids and aged-care workers. Some 77 per cent of the female-only domestic help and aged-care employees were Indonesians, with Filipinas and Vietnamese constituting the remainder.[6]

Indonesian men occupied 67 per cent of documented temporary migrants in the deep sea trawling industry in mid-2017; Filipinos and Vietnamese constituted the bulk of the remainder: 16 per cent and 17 per cent respectively. Thai men have long been heavily concentrated in migrant jobs in the building and construction sector, but this has fallen considerably over the past seven years, from an average of 85 per cent in 2010 to just under 50 per cent in mid-2017. Indonesians and Vietnamese make up the remainder. This has always been an industry which men from the Philippines have shunned and disdained. All four nationalities were represented in manufacturing, with the Vietnamese most heavily concentrated in this sector.[7]

The 'racial' categorisation of jobs extends to manufacturing employment internally. In January 2016, migrant production workers in the most labour intensive, tedious and dangerous spheres of the factory work process were largely Indonesians, Vietnamese and Thai. Indonesian men represented 14.6 per cent of the aggregate of migrants in the factories. However, their concentration in the declining and technologically backward 'paper and paper products' factories of Taiwan, where jobs were more dangerous than the manufacturing average, partly because of the high risk of exposure to asbestos, organochlorins and heavy metals, amounted to nearly twice this rate, at 24.7 per cent.[8] The only sector of manufacturing in which one nationality made up more than half of the guest workforce of that sector was 'electronic parts and components'. Filipino men controlled most of the migrant jobs in Taiwan's technologically sophisticated and relatively clean sectors, courtesy of their English language dexterity and greater experience as skilled and semi-skilled factory hands back home.

The gendering of Taiwan's migrant labour market has intensified slightly over the past decade and a half. In 2002, women averaged

---

6   Ministry of Labor 2016b.

7   Ministry of Labor 2017b.

8   Ministry of Labor 2017b.

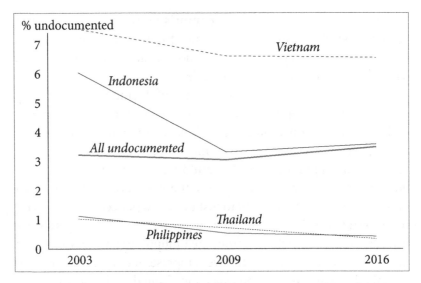

Figure 6.1. Percentage of undocumented migrants as a proportion of aggregate documented migrants by nationality in selected years, 2003, 2009 and 2016 Sources: Adapted from Ministry of Labor 2017c and 2017d (accessed 27 July 2017).

55.8 per cent of the aggregate documented migrant workforce; this proportion has remained quite steady for a decade and a half: 55.6 per cent in June 2017.[9] Migrants in the 'human health and social work' industry are engaged in caregiving and domestic help. The latter is dominated by Filipina women. Indonesian women are almost exclusively aged-care givers, although in recent years many Taiwanese families have shown a preference for hiring Vietnamese.

As is the case with all receiving countries, Taiwan's guest worker programme has long experienced the 'runaway problem', as a result of migrants deserting their workplaces and becoming undocumented. In December 2016, the aggregate undocumented migrant population amounted to 21,708, that is 3.6 per cent of the aggregate documented cohort. Indonesians accounted for just over 44 per cent of undocumented workers,[10] as one might expect considering their relatively large presence in the migrant pool. Comparing undocumented workers by country of origin over a longitudinal timeframe,

9   Ministry of Labor 2017c.

10   Ministry of Labor, 2017d.

however, provides a more precise means of measuring Indonesian representation in the undocumented population. As figure 6.1 illustrates in three selected years since 2003, the number of 'runaways', as a proportion of aggregate documented migrant populations, has been substantially higher for Indonesians and in particular for Vietnamese than for guest workers from the Philippines and Thailand.

Desperation has always been the key factor underpinning the 'runaway problem'. Making oneself undocumented reflects a profound sense of isolation, of help being beyond reach. Escaping unbearable workplaces, however, can also be an expression of defiance,[11] and only Vietnamese factory workers have been able to express such resistance on a scale surpassing that of Indonesian caregivers.

Migrants' motives for becoming undocumented vary between the Indonesians and Vietnamese. Sister Anne, a Vietnamese Catholic nun and social worker at the Hsinchu shelter, points out that Vietnamese 'runaways' seek to better their economic prospects by fleeing to other factories, where they desperately hope the burden of brokers' fees is either weaker or non-existent, while fully realising that future employers may well expect them to accept wage packets even further below the standard minimum. Indonesian care workers take flight not only because of the desire to escape brokers' fees but also because of the psychological need to find 'racially' tolerant, dignified and non-continuous work environments, which respect the right to at least a modicum of leisure and rest.[12] Indonesian caregivers are the most highly represented among those routinely subjected to continuous labour, commonly amounting to 17 hours per day and without any leisure; in other words, few week-ends, no public holidays and certainly no recreation leave. Running away, however, tends to lead to greater despair for the island's transnationals because their new employers and brokers tend to take even greater advantage of their vulnerability and because it can culminate in incarceration. The vast majority of migrants and their supporters caution against becoming undocumented, urging instead that legal help be sought.

Indonesian men dominate the documented migrant fisher population, and anecdotal evidence points to a large presence of

---

11 Lovebrand 2004, 345, see also Killas 2010, 908–911.

12 Sister Anne, telephone interview, 24 June 2013.

undocumented Indonesian fishers. Like caregivers, these fishers seek to escape exploitative brokers as well as employers who expect relentless labour and servitude. However, the Indonesian fishers are not the largest ethnic group in the category of undocumented fishers; Mainland Chinese dominate this category, with significant consequences, as will be discussed below.

The Preponderance of the Javanese

Temporary emigration to Taiwan is important to the Indonesian economy not only because Indonesians constitute the largest migrant workforce in Taiwan but also because Taiwan is Indonesia's fourth largest source of migrant remittances. In 2009 this amounted to US$ 425 million which was equivalent to 6.5 per cent of the aggregate of US$ 6.6 billion.[13]

Indonesians constitute the dominant presence in the island's overall migrant workforce. But from which Indonesian islands and provinces do they emigrate? Government-sourced data about the temporary migrants' regions, towns and villages of origin, prior to departure, are elusive.[14] Fortunately, databases that have been developed by other organisations and persons are of some use despite their small samples sizes. This evidence points to the dominant presence of the Javanese.

All of the eighteen Indonesian women whom Jason Kennedy interviewed for his study of caregivers in Taipei originated from small rural villages in Java; the occupation of their parents was overwhelmingly farming.[15] Most were women in their twenties, and all but one were mothers.[16] None had lived and worked in Java's cities.[17]

---

13 International Organization for Migration 2010, 23.

14 The Indonesian Economic and Trade Office has repeatedly ignored this author's requests for assistance in this matter.

15 Kennedy 2012.

16 Initially, Kennedy intended to interview seventy Indonesian caregivers in depth, but time constraints made this target impracticable. Informal discussions with the other fifty-two caregivers in the study's early stages demonstrated that they, too, were previously surplus farm labour in Javanese villages, although a handful came from Javanese towns.

17 Jason Kennedy, email correspondence with the author, 27 June 2014.

Sister Lenny, a nun and social worker at the Catholic Hope Workers' Centers of Chungli and more recently Hsinchu, has developed a data base on all Indonesian caregivers requesting legal and social counselling from the Hsinchu Center over the past five years. Her records show that the clear majority were derived from rural villages in Java, surrounding the cities of Indramayu, Cirebon, Subang, Bekasi, Brebes, Karangayan, Magetan, Tulungagung, Ponogoro, Grobagan, Bayuwangi, Bondowoso, Banjarnegara, Wonosobo and Tegal. A small minority were Sumatran women, from the villages of Sukadana and Cakung in southern Lampung province.[18]

The limited data indicate that Indonesian fishers in Taiwan are also previously Javanese villagers. The Stella Maris Seafarers' Center, a Catholic NGO sheltering migrant fishers at Kaohsiung Harbour, has kept a record over many years on fishers who have sought help from the shelter. According to its director, Reverend Ranulfo Salise, most of the migrant fishers at the shelter have been Javanese men, from a wide range of coastal villages that depend on the fishing industry for their survival, including those in the Indramayu and Karawang regencies of West Java and the Megalang and Demak regencies of north Java. Some of these sheltered fishers, however, had formerly resided in agricultural villages in central Java, such as those around Sukoharjo, and in the Megalang Regency.[19]

The Politico-Legal Bases of Migrant Exploitation and Compliance

The Indonesian authorities responsible for labour export rarely register complaints in Taiwan over the poor treatment of Indonesians. Instead, they extol Taiwan's employers and government officials.[20] This undeserved flattery operates amidst overwhelming evidence of rights' violations of transnationals, a problem arising in large part from legislation regulating temporary immigration into Taiwan.

---

18 Sister Lenny, email correspondence with the author, 17 June 2014.

19 Reverend Ranulfo Salise, letter to the author, 17 December 2014.

20 'Taiwan Praised for Good Treatment of Indonesians'. *Taipei Times*, 7 March 2014, 3.

The most active people in Taiwan providing evidence of systematic rights breaches are representatives of organisations lobbying on behalf of transnationals, with the objectives of bringing about fundamental change in guest worker legislation and of aiding transnationals' protests against injustice. There are at least several scores of migrant supporters on the island, comprising some far-left activists within academia and human rights groups, together with at least a similar number of people in some key industry unions. The clear majority of the unions, unfortunately, refuse to support transnationals at migrant rallies and in the halls of political lobbying because of the perception that migrants rob locals of jobs. The evidence is overwhelmingly to the contrary – despite growing unemployment the citizen population have always refused to enter those occupations in which migrants are heavily concentrated.[21]

The most effective organisation supporting migrant workers is the Taiwan International Workers' Association, an NGO of labour rights and human rights protagonists, established in 1998. Various religious groups have also acquitted themselves admirably, such as the network of seven Catholic support centres in the major industrial cities. The longest-serving and most influential representative of these centres is the Reverend Peter O'Neill, an Australian priest of the Columban Missionary order. He has been heavily involved since arriving in Taiwan in mid-1990. Reverend O'Neill was appointed the Director of the Hsinchu Catholic Diocese Migrants and Immigrants Service Center in 2007; he himself lives at the shelter.

These activists concur that the most repressive dimension of migrant regulation is the failure of the aforementioned Employment Services Law to penalise employers from imposing abject workplace entrapment. The experiences of one caregiver, in Hsinchu, illustrate the immensity of the problem. Ponirah is a married woman, aged forty-four, with a husband and two children living and working on the farm of her parents-in-law, located in a village named Kintangan, in Ponorogo Regency, East Java. She arrived in Taiwan in mid-2013, after undertaking to care for an eighty-nine-year-old woman in Hsinchu. In early 2014, the elderly woman passed away, forcing Ponirah to seek new employment. She found work in

---

21 Tierney 2008, 484–485.

caring for a ninety-three-year-old man who had almost no mobility whatsoever. Ponirah's working day now began at 6 a.m. and finished at 11.30 p.m., seven days per week. Throughout the seven months that she worked in this household, she did not get a solitary day off work. At one stage, she visited the local hospital, complaining of exhaustion, depression, anxiety and dizziness. In November 2014, she could cope no longer, fleeing to the Hsinchu migrant shelter.[22]

Caregivers are expected to be domestics, simultaneously. But this multi-skilling does not end there because employers often insist on tasks outside the household, for instance as servants or cooks in the families' restaurants. Employers thus violate the provisions of Section 57 of the Employment Services Law, stipulating a single workplace in the labour contract. They do so with impunity because transgression penalties are weak and rarely enforced. Migrants are disinclined to report Section 57 violations for fear of dismissal and repatriation; this particularly applies to those working under initial visas and to undocumented workers.

Neither caregivers nor domestic workers are entitled to the legal minimum wage. In consequence, a dual wage system operates. As from 1 July 2015, the majority of migrants earn the standard and regular (without penalty rates or overtime) rate of NT$ 20,008 per month, approximately US$ 610, which amounts to 51 per cent of the average regular monthly wage of NT$ 38,869.[23] The state has repeatedly resisted demands to extend the standard regular minimum rate to domestics and caregivers, who consequently earn the same rate as that which existed when the guest worker programme first came into being on the island in 1990, namely NT$ 15,840 per month. This amounts to 82 per cent of the standard migrant minimum rate and to 42 per cent of the average regular monthly wage. The caregivers' and domestics' real minimum wage has fallen significantly more than the real wage declines of all other migrants.

While the state regulates wages, it neglects to promulgate legislation to control brokers' fees.[24] These are mandatory for most placements,

---

22 Ponirah, telephone interview, 10 February 2015, questions and answers translated by Sister Lenny.

23 For data on average regular monthly earnings in July 2015, see Ministry of Labor 2017a.

24 Tierney 2007.

although the financial burdens vary between nationalities. Migrants from the Philippines pay differentiated placement rates; domestic helpers pay no fee for placement whatsoever, whereas the remainder fork out US$ 480. Migrants from Indonesia, on the other hand, pay US$ 3000, irrespective of gender and occupation.[25]

Governments and financial institutions in the countries of origin can intensify the exploitation of their citizens abroad; none more so than those of Indonesia. The Ministry of Manpower and Transmigration in Jakarta refuses to process applications for working abroad until each aspiring emigrant borrows US$ 2,600 from a local bank at the fixed interest rate of 18 per cent per annum, to be repaid over ten months. Aggregate repayment amounts to US$ 3000.[26] Fees are then paid directly to the brokers who take their cut. Guest workers from the Philippines thus live and labour in environments of debt bondage that are less severe than those confronting Indonesian workers.

Brokers' fees and clandestine kickbacks engender economic and political benefits to employers; they reduce the cost of labour while pushing out the frontier of control. The immigrant's compliance is in direct proportion to the fear of retrenchment and deportation before debts are cleared. Broker companies are also a source of political control; they monitor migrants closely in order to diminish their capacity for political organisation. Indeed, as an institution of surveillance, the brokers are more powerful and more unforgiving than are the police and employers.

The divergent burdens of broker fees impose significant effects on the comparative political dimensions of employer–migrant relations. As Reverend O'Neill states, the sooner that transnationals escape debt bondage, the more their fears and anxieties diminish of workplace dismissal, and consequently the greater their confidence grows in negotiating the length of the working day and week.[27] Variable debt bondage engenders disparate degrees of confidence in their powers of struggle for free Sundays, and all guest workers in Taiwan are acutely aware of this.

25 O'Neill, email correspondence with the author, 23 February 2015.

26 O'Neill, telephone interview, 29 November 2014.

27 O'Neill, telephone interview, 4 December 2014.

In 2011, migrant support bodies successfully lobbied the Executive Yuan and Legislative Yuan to amend the Labor Union Law 1929 which forbade migrants to form their own unions. In May 2013, eighty-nine fishers from the Philippines unionised in Yilan County, in the northeast part of the island. No other migrant fishers have since succeeded in establishing a union.

Occupational health and safety laws are ineffectual and unjust to the victims of accidents, illnesses and diseases, especially to migrants. This emanates partly from the unwillingness of the police and Ministry of Labor to enforce legislation and from the weak penalties imposed by the courts for failure of compliance. The Labor Insurance Law 1959, responsible for providing compensation, did not cover workplaces of five or fewer employees until the Legislative Yuan amended the statute in 2002. Undocumented migrants have always been the most vulnerable to unsafe work practices. In the construction sector, it is common practice for bidders to privilege the recruitment of undocumented workers, Indonesians and Thais alike, as a means of pushing down labour costs. This applies to Government contracts as much as to those in the private sector, as the lowest bidders are typically the most successful. Documented migrants are always readily recruitable. The problem, however, has been that an untold number of employers, especially in building and construction, have found the recruitment of illegals irresistible, not only because the lower costs facilitate successful bidding but also because employers can evade culpability in the event of injuries and fatalities.[28]

Typecasting Caregivers

The state, brokers and the mass of families engaged in the employment of migrant domestics and caregivers portray the latter according to divergent essentialist stereotypes. According to Shu-Ju Ada Cheng, they regard domestics from the Philippines as 'aggressive, disobedient, and militant yet better educated',[29] and much the same applies to their perspectives on Filipino men in the manufacturing sector.[30]

---

28 O'Neill, telephone interview, 14 December 2014.

29 Shu-Ju Ada Cheng 2006, 57.

30 Tierney 2008, 487.

As is the case with the Filipinos, Filipina domestics are well educated in spoken and written English. Taiwan's domestic employers value this asset because it enables free, informal language classes at home for their school-children, who grapple with English as a compulsory discipline. Many Filipinas are prepared to tolerate such exploitation because it provides them with a bargaining chip over the length of the working week.[31]

Employers value Indonesian caregivers less highly, partly because of the Indonesians' inferior English language skills, which make them less useful as home-based educators, and partly because of racist perceptions of 'docility'.[32] In her study of Indonesians in Taiwan, Anne Lovebrand contends that:

> According to the 'common truth', Indonesian women are best suited as carers of the chronically ill, the paralysed and elderly patients, because they are more 'caring' and 'loyal' and they can cope with the repetition of washing, cleaning of people, clothes and households more easily than the cleverer Filipinas who tended to argue about their rights and precise job specifications. Indonesians are also supposedly more accepting because, as one employer suggested to me, 'they are Muslim'.[33]

Assumptions of diligence and quiescence have often culminated in a racist disrespect for Indonesian religious practices, including employers' attempts to insist on the care of dogs as pets, which Islamic traditions regard as unclean. Moreover, many employers pressure their Indonesian workers to eat pork, defending their actions by falsely asserting that pork builds strength and productivity.[34] Tiwi, an Indonesian Muslim caregiver, claimed in late 2010 that all three Taiwanese families who had employed her over seven years insisted on pork in her diet. Tiwi's claim that this coercion had little to do with considerations of health and productivity and much to do with a racist disrespect for her religion was no doubt accurate. Employers

---

31 Reverend Ngyuyen Van Hung, Director, Vietnamese Migrant Workers' and Brides' Office, Taoyuan, interview, 24 November 2011.

32 Cheng 2006, 57.

33 Lovebrand 2004, 339–340.

34 Huang 2010, 2.

Figure 6.2. Protest against the forced eating of pork, 24 October 2010. Source: Taiwan International Workers' Association. Photo Albums. IMG0109. [www. flickr.com/photos/tiwa1999/5120167514/in/set-72157625251310224] (downloaded 22 December 2014)

who force Indonesians to eat pork are driven by the desire to violate and degrade Islam, partly because its followers are deemed to be more compliant and deferential.

Taiwan's migrants themselves sometimes typecast other migrant nationalities. Filipino workers in the manufacturing sector once joined the Taiwanese in labelling Thais as 'buffalo', on the basis of their heavy concentration in the unsafe construction sector and in the worst factory jobs offered.[35] This was one of several factors contributing to the outbreak of mass violence between male workers from Thailand and the Philippines at the Formosa Plastics plant in September 1999.[36] Racist tensions have also plagued relations between Indonesian caregivers and Filipina domestic helpers. As stated earlier, the dissimilar rates by which domestics and caregivers can clear themselves of placement debt have profound implications for the length of the working week. Filipinas are far more structurally advantaged in this sense. Moreover, they are inclined to exploit

---

35 Tierney 2011, 293.

36 Tierney 2011, 300–301.

their English teaching skills to enhance their working conditions. The latter factor can generate political discord between domestics and caregivers because the latter often complain about the Filipinas' penchant for labelling them as 'stupid' on the basis of their relatively poor English.[37] The Indonesians have at times perceived Filipinas to be unsympathetic to the caregivers' more severe circumstances of economic and psychological hardship and vulnerability, emanating from workplace entrapment.

Stratagems of Resistance: Caregivers and Domestic Helpers

A significant proportion of migrants are on their second, third and fourth visas, facilitating the development of Mandarin skills while making them more adept at coping with cultural differences. This also enables them to build confidence in their capacity to contest exploitation and marginalisation. Many Indonesian women under return visas have been no less capable of developing stratagems of defiance and resistance than the people of other nationalities.

Those under second or subsequent visas are more likely to attend Sunday gatherings at and around Taipei Main Rail Station, despite surveillance and harassment by police[38] and rail authorities, together with racist disparagement springing from the lips of some citizen commuters. The six-storey station, together with the small dilapidated area within a distance of one hundred metres to the southeast of it, has long been a territory over which the Indonesians feel a sense of belonging. Indeed, this tiny district is known, by locals as well as the Indonesians themselves, as 'Little Indonesia'.[39] Indonesian restaurants and grocery stores amplify the sense of being part of 'Little Indonesia'. But it is the station lobby area which is most important because they have defiantly turned it into 'their home floors', reproducing some Indonesian ways of life as a means of surmounting social and cultural alienation.[40] This physical space is every bit as culturally and politically

---

37 Lovebrand 2004, 340.

38 Chen 2013, 280.

39 Chen 2013.

40 Lan 2006, 188.

important to the Indonesians as 'Little Manila' (the area surrounding Saint Christopher's Church and the Catholic Hope Workers' Center in Chungli) is to the Filipinas and Filipinos.

While there have been tensions between caregivers and domestics, these women have been at the forefront of struggles which are expressions of inter-ethnic unity. Various support organisations have played a prominent part in the emergence and perpetuation of these struggles. In 2000, former Indonesian guest workers established an organisation, based in Jakarta, to assist current Indonesian guest workers across the globe, entitled Asosiasi Tenaga Kerja Indonesia (ATKI, Association of Indonesian Migrant Workers). A branch emerged in Taiwan in February 2003 under two interconnected appellations: ATKI-Taiwan and Ikatan Pekerja Indonesia Taiwan (IPIT). For the sake of convenience this chapter will refer to it as IPIT. The Taiwan International Workers' Association (TIWA) has given IPIT its support from the outset, partly by recruiting politically active Indonesians on a full-time or part-time basis. In mid-2014, IPIT's membership, amounting to approximately ninety, was composed almost entirely of caregivers. With the help of TIWA, IPIT aims to lift membership well beyond this figure. But several factors hinder this aspiration. The main obstacle is the ever-frustrating burden of the seven-day working week. Fear has also played a part, as indicated by the relatively small presence of caregivers on initial visas.

IPIT provides a Facebook page through which Indonesians can keep in touch with one another, making their deep sense of isolation a little more tolerable. IPIT and TIWA cooperate in helping to dissolve Taiwanese racism against migrants in general by encouraging the latter, irrespective of nationality, to participate in cultural events that are treasured by the Taiwanese, such as the annual Dragon Boat Festival in June. They provide advice on ways to access legal counsel in the event of workplace bullying and other rights' violations. They organise social events at designated locations, where the Indonesians can indulge in their own cultural practices, such as singing and dancing, often in traditional costume.

Taiwan's migrants regard home songs and dances as their own national cultural treasures, generating some of the most enriching means of remembering the past, which for the vast majority represent happier times. As is the case with transnational and even

Figure 6.3 Indonesians entertaining one another, 24 October 2010. Source: Taiwan International Workers' Association. Photo Albums. IMG0032. [www.flickr.com/photos/tiwa1999/5120163250/in/set-72157625251310224] (downloaded 22 December 2014)

permanent immigrants, communal singing and traditional dancing exist for 'keeping up one's spirits on the long journey'.[41]

The two organisations also provide a means of political mobilisation, even though IPIT's membership is limited. This is illustrated by the rallies which corresponded with IPIT's formative development and by subsequent effective protests that IPIT and TIWA have helped to build.

A crucial event in IPIT's emergence was the 1500-strong migrant 'Anti-Slavery' protest in Taipei on 12 December 2005, the first migrant anti-human trafficking protest of its kind in Taiwan.[42] This was deemed a successful protest, partly because of the impressive turn-out overall, in spite of heavy rainfall, and partly because several caregivers participated, with or without their employers' permission. This and subsequent 'Anti-Slavery' rallies allowed IPIT to consolidate political ties with its Philippines' counterpart organisations in Taiwan, namely Migrante Internationale and Kapulungan ng Samahang

---

41 Coplan 2006, 226, 239.

42 Tierney 2011, 308.

Figure 6.4. Indonesians dancing in traditional dress, Hsinchu Migrant Shelter, June 2013; courtesy of Sister Lenny (private collection)

Pilipino (KaSaPi). The latter is a self-help organisation that was also founded in 2003, largely by Filipina domestic helpers.

The robustness of social and political links between migrants from Indonesia and the Philippines became clear for everyone to witness in February 2011, after the Ministry of Labor applied a temporary ban on hiring Filipinas and Filipinos, in opposition to the Philippine Government's deportation of ten Chinese and fourteen Taiwanese men to China for alleged racketeering, in accordance with its extradition treaty with Beijing. The Filipinas, Filipinos and Indonesians rallied at the Ministry of Labor's headquarters in Taipei on 6 March, fearing the prohibition could whip up racist hatred against migrants from the Philippines. Realising that Manila was unlikely to express regret diplomatically, the protestors themselves decided to apologise, insisting that guest workers from the Philippines were innocent and vulnerable.[43] Such rallies reveal how cultural performances in protest can create opportunities to make new identities and to dismantle demeaning ones. Lai has demonstrated the extent to which public performances of traditional and contemporary song, mimetic dance and drama have contributed to the formation of incipient transnational political

---

43 Huang 2011, 3.

Figure 6.5. Caregivers dancing in quasi-traditional dress, Taipei, May 2006. Source: Taiwan Indonesian Workers' Association (Indonesian wing of the Taiwan International Workers' Association) [www.flickr.com/photos/tiwa1999/4577759434/in/set-72157623988822132] (downloaded 12 February 2015)

communities in Hong Kong.[44] During these performances, witnessed by curious citizen onlookers and the media, transnationals communicate their grievances, build political self-confidence, and attract erstwhile unaffiliated migrants to the common cause.[45] When cultural performances are combined with protest, the political aesthetic strengthens the capacity of transnational groups to dissolve divisions between themselves, jettisoning prejudicial images of docility in the process. This was certainly true for the dancing Javanese, Filipinas and Filipinos at the anti-Philippines ban rally in Taipei.

Migrants' protests frequently conclude with rehearsed dramas at the places of destination, which very often are near the steps of the Head and Provincial offices of the Ministry of Labor in all of the main cities, and outside the Presidential Office in Taipei. These

---

44 Lai 2010a, 502.

45 Lai 2010a, 504; see also Lai 2010b.

Figure 6.6. Indonesian dance performers at a social function in Hsinchu, organised by IPIT, circa 2014. Courtesy of Sister Lenny, Hsinchu Migrant Shelter (private collection)

dramas tend to focus on the issue of 'slavery', performed at the Anti-Slavery rallies held in December every year. Slavery, as Kevin Bales emphasises, contains three key elements: super-exploitation, control by violence or by the threat of violence, and the expropriation of free will.[46] Taiwan's guest workers believe that they are enslaved in precisely these ways: their wages are far lower than those earned by Taiwanese citizens, especially after the interventions of the broker firms; their lives are almost entirely controlled by the employers and brokers to the extent that they are denied leisure and recreation; and they often work and live under conditions of abject subjugation, to the extent that all forms of free will vanish. It is little wonder that the dramas that have been created, rehearsed and performed by Taiwan's guest workers often portray life in chains, especially for those who become undocumented.

Although the aforementioned protests tend to be dominated by guest workers from Indonesia and the Philippines, it has become clear that Vietnamese and Thai workers are prepared to extend solidarity.

---

46 Bales 2007, 10–11.

Figure 6.7. Migrants from the Philippines and Indonesia, formation dancing at the anti-Philippine ban protest. Source: Taiwan International Workers' Association, photographic collection [www.flickr.com/photos/tiwa1999/5514234825/in/set-72157626111452193] (downloaded 12 February 2015)

This was evidenced in protests at the Taipei Main Station between 2011 and 2014, triggered by the public transport bureaucracy's efforts to frustrate Indonesian migrants' efforts to establish a public space for celebrating Eid al-Fitr, the Feast of Breaking the Fast, the world-wide Islamic event signifying the end of Ramadan.

Irrespective of the cities in which they resided, those managing to obtain a day of leisure on the Sunday immediately following Eid al-Fitr journeyed directly to Da-an Forest, opposite the Taipei Grand Mosque. This witnessed the largest Eid al-Fitr celebration since the inception of Taiwan's migrant programme; participants amounted to 'thousands'.[47] From Da-an, they ventured on foot to their own exceptional space, the Taipei Main Railway Station. There, they continued performing religious rituals, including dances and other performances.

Celebrating Eid al-Fitr was threatened in the aftermath of the 2011 celebrations, when the station-master announced new regulations proscribing mass gatherings on the basis that they marred the 'aesthetic of the area' and inconvenienced passengers. He cordoned off

47 Loa 2008, 2.

much of the lobby and forbade people to rest, eat or drink anywhere in its vicinity.[48] Indonesians and their supporters, on the other hand, were convinced that the new regulations were racist, particularly considering the timing of their implementation. This transformed a specifically religious event into one catalysing a united migrant political voice. Moreover, Taiwanese labour and human rights activists joined the struggle. Initially, they comprised a tiny portion of a small but highly emotional rally. Thereafter, they constituted the majority in a relatively large protest.

On the eve of Eid al-Fitr in September 2012, between twenty and thirty Indonesians, together with four or five Taiwanese labour activists, gathered at the Station, carrying signs written in Chinese, English and Indonesian which stated: 'No to racial discrimination', 'We need a place to stay' and 'What's wrong with holiday celebrations?'[49] Subsequently, Prosecutor Huang Chao-kuei, of the Taiwan High Prosecuting Office in Tainan, commented on his Facebook page that 'tens of thousands' of guest workers, mostly Indonesians, had 'taken over' the Main Station. Migrants and their supporters regarded the Prosecutor's remark as repugnant because of its hyperbole and hysteria, which in turn facilitated the massive expansion of the Eid al-Fitr celebration in September 2013. This rose from twenty-five to thirty-five in the previous year to around five hundred, of whom two hundred were Indonesians, Filipinas and Filipinos, and a handful of Thai and Vietnamese. All of these participants believed that celebrating Eid al-Fitr would benefit migrants as a whole, so long as a consciousness of solidarity was consolidated. TIWA and Lennon Wong, solely representing the Taiwan Confederation of Trade Unions, played major roles in organising the three hundred or so Taiwanese supporters of the September 2013 celebrations.

The protestors occupied the cordoned-off region of the Station's lobby and defied the food ban. IPIT led the chant: 'Give the space back to the people, give freedom back to migrant workers.'[50] If there were any migrants involved in the Railway Station protests who had

---

48 Loa 2012a, 3.

49 Loa 2012b, 3.

50 Quoted in Shan 2013, 3.

once presumed that Indonesians were docile, then these people now questioned and rejected such a perspective.

Ultimately, the bureaucracy surrendered to the Indonesians' persistent demands, leading to massive, consecutive expansions in Eid al-Fitr attendance at the Station. On 19 July 2015, between 10,000 and 20,000 migrants amassed at Taipei Main Railway Station to share the Indonesians' triumphs in the battle to construct their own political-cultural space for Eid al-Fitr, a twenty-to-forty-fold increase over the five hundred or so who had participated in September 2013.[51]

Such forms of inter-ethnic unity have been impressive. But overall, Taiwan's transnationals have shown little interest in forming their own labour unions because they see little benefit in unionisation without a six-day week.[52] The exceptional case is the fishers.

Stratagems of Resistance: The Fishers

As stated earlier, men from Indonesian villages represented around three-quarters of the 10,146 documented migrant fishers in Taiwan during the first month of 2016. Data for so-called runaway migrant fishers in Taiwan are elusive, but some fragments of evidence, again anecdotal, suggest that deep sea trawling is an industry in which undocumented migrants may well exceed those whose papers are legitimate. The highest proportion – perhaps even the vast majority – of the undocumented migrant fishers, however, are of a nationality which is not even party to Taiwan's guest worker programme: Mainland Chinese.

Working conditions in deep sea trawling are arguably the worst in Taiwan's occupational sector. The Reverend Bruno Ciceri, representing the Vatican's Apostleship of the Sea and formerly based in Taiwan, has described Taiwan's trawlers as 'floating coffins'.[53] The Reverend Ranulfo Salise, who manages the Stella Maris Seafarers' Center in Kaohsiung, claims that most of the fishers at the Shelter have provided 'narratives of physical beating, verbal abuse, [of being] forcefully

---

51 Shan 2015, 3.

52 O'Neill, telephone interview, 15 December 2014.

53 Ciceri 2001.

fed with expired noodles, of unpaid and unaccounted salary for 6–7 months, [of] back-breaking work.'[54]

Conditions at sea have at moments reached emotional and political flashpoints. This may explain the disappearance of two Taiwanese men on the vessel *Te Hung Hsing No. 368*, in French Polynesian waters in late July 2013, after eight months of almost continuous stretches at sea. Their disappearance coincided with arguments between the Taiwanese and Indonesians about 'work assignments'.[55] The case reveals some disturbing elements, namely the ferocity of racist anger against the Indonesian crew, demonstrated by Taiwanese citizens when the vessel docked at Yilan Harbor, the protracted imprisonment of the Indonesians awaiting trial for murder, and the immediate presumptions of guilt by the Coast Guard, prosecutors and mass media. The police ultimately concluded that the murder allegations lacked any substance and in December 2013 they instead indicted eight Indonesians for manslaughter.

Javanese and other migrant fishers also experience conflicts with undocumented fishers from Mainland China. They have complained about aggressive harrying by the Mainland Chinese in Kaohsiung, conduct encouraged and joined in by Taiwanese crews. In spite of political tensions across the Taiwan Strait, the ethnic and linguistic ties between Taiwanese and Mainland Chinese crews have legitimated practices of bullying Indonesian fishers.[56] The latter are quite familiar with racist stigmatisation from other guest workers. Filipinos, for instance, have been known to accuse them of docility, in ways somewhat analogous to the labels applied by Filipinas to caregivers. Culpability, however, cannot be confined to the Filipinos. As Mark Erdmann has noted, several Asian nationalities in deep sea trawling have long been prepared to dismiss Indonesians as 'too poor and ignorant' to be effectual fishers and seafarers.[57]

---

54 Salise, letter to the author, 17 December 2014.

55 'Eight Indonesian Fishermen Indicted for Manslaughter'. *Taipei Times*, 27 December 2013, 3.

56 Salise, letter to the author, 17 December 2014.

57 Erdmann 2000.

Prior to mid-2013, transnationals and their supporters spent years demanding legislative reforms enabling the extension of labour unionism to Taiwan's migrant workforce. On 25 May of that year, the first – and hitherto the only – migrant union was established, courtesy of the eighteen months of struggle by eighty-nine Filipino fishers in Yilan County in the northeast of Taiwan. The Filipino fishers named it the Yilan County Fishermen's Union.[58] The union has expanded since then, as illustrated by the 4.5-fold increase in membership in December 2014, compared with that of the inaugural meeting. Notwithstanding this impressive gain, only one quarter are active in the union.

Inter-ethnic unity has always been one of the fisher union's prominent goals. The union, however, has not up to now succeeded in this endeavour. In the main, the relatively minor involvement of Javanese fishers can be attributed to fear of repatriation, which broker firms are adept at whipping up. The hostility of the brokers to a rally of more than one hundred Javanese fishers against placement fees in 2011, only days after the formation of the union, revealed how merciless the former can be: in response, Taiwan's brokers arranged for the firing and early repatriation of ten fishers.

Despite this setback, there seems little reason to suppose that the Javanese cannot feasibly achieve effective unionisation, forging robust political links with other migrant nationalities. Some optimistic Filipinos in the Yilan union feel that it is only a matter of time before this is achieved.

Conclusion

Taiwan's labour market is intensely racialised, as illustrated by persistent rigidity in the types of occupations in which documented and undocumented migrants work. The state will not authorise migrants to break out of these jobs. Javanese migrants are the most ghettoised migrants on the island as well as the most exploited. Indonesian caregivers, who constitute the bulk of migrant women unable to access the benefits of minimum wage increases, are the first to attest to the injustices of legislative regulation. Offensive prejudicial labels, signifying

---

58 Lin 2013.

so-called intellectual inferiority, are inflicted upon Javanese migrants, which have the effect of reinforcing their economic subordination, not only in the outlook of the Taiwanese but also in the mindset of other migrant nationalities, especially those from the Philippines.

Although relations between Indonesians and those from the Philippines have been laced occasionally with tension and hostility, it is also true that the two groups have achieved remarkable solidarity. Caregivers and domestics have demonstrated the ability to protest in support of one another, with Filipinas defending the right of caregivers to take comfort and pleasure in the festivities of Eid al-Fitr and with caregivers joining rallies devoted to overturning state initiatives which might lead to the victimisation of Filipinas and Filipinos alike. Inter-ethnic solidarity in the struggle for unionism is also of great importance. Unlike the caregivers and domestics, the fishers have formed their own union, although it is clearly evident that up to the present time Indonesians have been considerably less active in it. Several structural factors have conspired to weaken Indonesian involvement, particularly the threats and fears imposed by broker firms.

Migrants of all nationalities and occupations need to unite *en masse* in order to overcome or at least reduce the fear of deportation, experienced particularly by transnationals on their first visas. A plethora of NGOs in Taiwan, together with some union activists, have long provided support against the brokers, whom they despise almost as much as do the guest workers themselves. The introduction of direct hiring arrangements, which are needless to say long overdue, will become an important element in this struggle for migrant rights for wage justice, fair conditions and union rights.

References

Bales, K. 2007. *Ending Slavery: How We Free Today's Slaves*. Berkeley: University of California Press.

Chang, R. 2007. 'Taiwan's Coast Guard Intervenes in Conflict at Sea', *Taipei Times*, 14 March: 2.

Chen, H-Y. 2013. 'Placemaking in between Urban Redevelopment: "Little Indonesia" in Taipei'. In *Transcultural Cities: Border-crossing and Place-making*, ed. J. Hou, 274–284. New York: Routledge.

Cheng, S.-J. A. 2006. *Serving the Household and the Nation: Filipina Domestics and the Politics of Identity in Taiwan.* Oxford: Lexington Books.

Ciceri, B. 2001. 'Fisherman: The Forgotten Seamen', *People on the Move: Pontifical Council for the Pastoral Care of Migrants and Itinerant People* 85, April. [www.vatican.va/roman_curia//pontifical_councils/migrants/pom2001_85_87/rc_pc_migrants_pom85_ciceri.htm]

Coplan, D. 2006. '"I've Worked Longer than I've Lived": Lesotho Migrants' Songs as Maps of Experience', *Journal of Ethnic and Migration Studies,* 32(2): 223–241.

Du Yu 2013. 'Violence Puts Spotlight on Fishing', *Taipei Times,* 8 August: 8.

Erdmann, M. V. 2000. 'Leave Indonesia's Fisheries to Indonesians', *Inside Indonesia.* 6 (July–September). [www.insideindonesia.org/leave-indonesias-fisheries-to-indonesians-3]

Huang, S. 2010. 'Foreign Workers Rally for Religions', *Taipei Times,* 17 May: 2.

—— 2011. 'Filipinos Rally against Retaliation', *Taipei Times,* 7 March: 3.

International Organization for Migration 2010. *International Migration and Migrant Workers' Remittances in Indonesia.* Makati City: International Organization for Migration.

Kennedy, J. 2012. 'Female Indonesian Domestic Workers in Taiwan'. M.A. thesis, Taipei Medical University.

Killias, O. 2010. '"Illegal" Migration as Resistance: Legality, Morality, and Coercion in Domestic Worker Migration to Malaysia', *Asian Journal of Social Science* 38: 897–914.

Lai, M.-Y. 2010a. 'Dancing to Different Tunes: Performance and Activism among Migrant Domestic Workers in Taiwan', *Women's Studies International Forum* 33: 501–511.

—— 2010b. 'The Sexy Maid in Indonesian Migrant Workers' Activist Theatre: Subalternality, Performance and Witnessing', *Performing Ethos,* 1(1): 21–34.

Lan, P.-C. 2006. *Global Cinderellas: Migrant Domestics and Newly Rich Employers in Taiwan.* Durham: Duke University Press.

Lin, I.-F. 2013. 'Fishermen Organize First Migrant Workers' Union in Taiwan', *Global Voices,* July. [globalvoicesonline.org/2013/07/06/fishermen-organize-first-migrant-workers-union-in-taiwan/]

Loa I.-S. 2008. 'Indonesians Celebrate Eid-al-Fitr at Da-an Park', *Taipei Times,* 6 October: 2.

—— 2012a. 'Group Slams Racist Rail Station', *Taipei Times,* 13 September: 3.

—— 2012b. 'Workers Protest Station Measure', *Taipei Times,* 17 September: 3.

Lovebrand, A. 2004. 'Positioning the Product: Indonesian Migrant Women Workers in Taiwan', *Journal of Contemporary Asia* 34(3): 336–48.

Ministry of Labor 2017a. 'Table 1-1: Major Labor and Economic Indicators', [statdb.mol.gov.tw/html/mon/c1010.htm]

—— 2017b. 'Table 12-4: Foreign Workers in Productive Industries and Social Welfare by Industry and Nationality, End of June 2017', [statdb.mol.gov.tw/html/mon/c12040.htm]

—— 2017c. 'Table 12-6: Foreign Workers in Productive Industries and Social Welfare by Nationality and Sex, End of June 2017', [statdb.mol.gov.tw/html/mon/c12060.htm.]

—— 2017d. 'Table 12-7: Missing Persons in Productive Industries and Social Welfare by Nationality and Sex, End of June 2017', [statdb.mol.gov.tw/html/mon/c12070.htm].

Pressman, S. 2007. 'The Decline of the Middle Class: An International Perspective', *Journal of Economic Issues* 41(1): 181–200.

Shan, S. 2013. 'Protesters Say Station Ban Targets Overseas Workers', *Taipei Times*, 16 September: 3.

—— 2015. 'Ramadan Feast Celebrated in Taipei Railway Station', *Taipei Times*, 20 July: 3.

Tierney, R. 2007. 'The Guest Labor System in Taiwan: Labor Market Considerations, Wage Injustices and the Politics of Foreign Labor Brokerage', *Critical Asian Studies* 39(2): 229–254.

—— 2008. 'Inter-Ethnic and Labour-Community Coalitions in Class Struggle in Taiwan since the Advent of Temporary Immigration', *Journal of Organizational Change Management* 21 (4): 482–496.

—— 2011. 'The Class Context of Temporary Immigration, Civic Nationalism and Racism in Taiwan', *Journal of Contemporary Asia* 41(2): 289–314.

CHAPTER 7

From Java to Saudi Arabia and Dubai

Precarious Itineraries of Indonesian Domestic Workers

Rachel Silvey

Women from West Java have left their origin communities in rapidly growing numbers in recent decades to work in Saudi Arabia, the United Arab Emirates (UAE),[1] as well as other countries of the Gulf Cooperation Council (GCC) and East Asia. As their numbers have grown, so too has a dominant narrative about the dangers that they may face while abroad. Specifically, NGOs and the popular media have highlighted the horrific stories of human rights abuses suffered by migrant domestic workers. As Aihwa Ong puts it, 'The underpaid, starved, and battered foreign maid . . . has become the image of the new inhumanity in the Asian metropolis.'[2] This image has been especially pronounced in the literature on migrant workers in the GCC countries, including Saudi Arabia[3] and the UAE.[4] Studies of domestic labour in the GCC find that legal protections for migrant workers are particularly weak in the region, and acknowledge that this institutional setting opens the door to widespread and extreme abuse of migrant domestic workers.[5]

---

1 The UAE was established in 1971. The country is a federation of seven emirates: Abu Dhabi (which serves as the capital), Ajman, Dubai, Fujairah, Ras al-Khaimah, Sharjah and Umm al-Quwain.

2 Ong 2006, 195.

3 Human Rights Watch 2007.

4 Human Rights Watch 2007 and 2014, 624–625.

5 Fernandez and De Regt 2014.

My research with Rhacel Parreñas has analysed the legal production of indentured servitude, its persistent precarity, and its
texture among migrants in everyday life in Dubai.[6] In this chapter,
I build on Parreñas's attention to the legal frameworks that enable
indentured servitude, to ask what political work is accomplished by
the circulation of abuse narratives in the lives of migrant women.[7]
How does migrant women's awareness of abuse affect the ways they
perceive and manage their labour market precarity, the conditions of
their work, their poverty, and their transnational lives? In addressing these questions, I illustrate some of the texture of everyday life
among migrant domestic workers, and contribute to explaining why
so many Indonesian women continue to migrate abroad, despite
their awareness of the risks entailed by their journeys. The analysis
stands in contrast to arguments put forward by Andrew Gardner,
whose research on Bangladeshi migrant construction workers
in Bahrain argues that workers continue to enlist themselves in
overseas work because they lack knowledge about the dangers and
abuses of working abroad.[8] On the contrary, among Indonesian migrants the information about abuses is widely known, but growing
numbers of people nonetheless continue to want to try their luck in
the transnational labour market in the GCC.

How do migrant workers make sense of the spectacle of the
domestic worker as a subject of gendered transnational exploitation
and violence? I argue in this chapter that most migrants see similar
risks at home to those they are told exist overseas. The main difference between staying home and going abroad in their view is the
possibility of earning more income abroad than ever will be possible
at home. Many are pushed by persistent poverty and unemployment
at home to seek the slim chance of a better income abroad. In addition, many seek to leave the tedium of their rural lives in order to
see something – anything – other than what they know. For most
overseas migrants from West Java to the Gulf, 'home' is associated
with experiences of poverty and boredom. The majority of women

---

6   Parreñas and Silvey 2015, 2016a, 2016b.

7   Parreñas 2017.

8   Gardner 2012.

I interviewed had little desire to return to Indonesia, at least not in the short-term future. Those who could find a way to migrate felt compelled – socially and materially – to do so, and most viewed Java as a place remaindered for those 'left behind'.

This chapter explores brief portions of the journeys of two women who migrated from West Java, one to Saudi Arabia, and one to Saudi Arabia then Dubai, both as domestic workers. I begin by tracing the migrants' memories of two sites (a training camp in Jakarta and an informal 'runaway house' in Dubai), excerpts that shed light on the ways they narrated their journeys. In particular, I explore the co-ethnic social networks shaping their migration itineraries and experiences. In addition, I examine migrants' signifiers of religious propriety – headscarves, modest dress and bodily comportment – as respondents mobilised them in everyday mobility practices in the spaces of the city. I follow the migrants' memories with some reflections on the implications of these migration histories for understanding the production of the gendered transnational labour market linking Indonesia with the GCC.

The Unhappy Marriage of Feminism and West Javanese Women's Migration

When migration scholars first turned serious attention to women's migration and the gender politics of global mobility, liberal, second-wave feminism drove the theoretical agenda. The primary concerns of this feminist migration research were gender inequalities in labour markets, gendered household divisions of productive and reproductive labour and the differential implications of these for women's and men's migration. In international migration studies, women of colour feminists provided particularly crucial insights into the intersections of gender with race, nation, class and ethnicity, enabling scholars of transnational migration to understand the international division of social reproduction[9] as organised around intersecting global inequalities. In part because it appears that inequalities based on racialised and gendered differences travel so persistently across national borders, feminists have expressed some

---

9 Parreñas 2001.

ambivalence about what transnational migration can offer to women.[10] Indeed, for migrant domestic workers, transnational travel often entails greater socio-spatial entrapment – and disempowerment – than staying at home might entail. However, their spatial entrapment does not operate neatly in the same way everywhere, nor is 'home' itself necessarily a site of relative safety or power for migrant women.

The spatial logics of liberal feminist theory are insufficient for the task of understanding the subjects and spaces of transnational migration.[11] The liberatory subject of feminist genealogy, upon entering the transnational spaces demands fresh approaches to power, approaches that transect state-centred notions of empowerment and rights.[12] Indeed, for the Indonesian–GCC circuits of female domestic workers, transnational feminist frameworks are complicated further because of the central, overt and complex role that religion plays in these sending and receiving contexts.

Although the specific role of religion is beyond the scope of discussion here, Caroline Nagel's more general call to expand explicitly spatial analyses of gender issues in relation to religious communities and practices is relevant to understanding Indonesian migrants in the GCC.[13] Indeed, Nagel's call is particularly relevant to understanding how Indonesian migrant women, the majority of whom are Muslim, view spaces of jurisdiction as interpolated by gendered and religious moral discourses. Their itineraries are shaped by, among other forces, the deepening development and pluralisation of the transnational pan-Islamic *umma* (community); the effects of the

---

10 Pratt and Yeoh 2003.

11 The limitations of liberal feminist migration research are not characteristic of Mark Johnson's (2015a, 2015b) important research, which has developed empirically grounded and theoretically sophisticated insights into the specific gendered complexities of migrant workers' subjectivities through his focus on migrants from the Philippines in Saudi Arabia. In particular, he examines pastoral power as a form of care that tends to be carried out by male migrants, the affective dimensions of migrant infrastructure, and the ways that surveillance practices intersect this gendered migration culture.

12 Brown 2010.

13 Nagel 2001.

expanded use of information and communication technologies; the religious and secular tensions at the heart of how and where human rights are defined and for whom;[14] and the poor fit of Western feminist notions of the liberal subject with the modes of agency and practice associated with religious piety movements.[15]

In Indonesia, Islam is invoked in many cases in explicit support of human rights and women's rights. Robert Hefner has termed Indonesia's religiously inflected democratisation movement 'civil Islam', a phrase he coins in order to disrupt conflations of Islam with oppressive authoritarianism.[16] Research that disarticulates religion from states (or at least tries to understand this disarticulation as complex) has a special role in public debates since the beginning of the U.S.-led 'war on terror' in 2001, when neo-Orientalist views of Islam as congruent with 'the oppression of women' were deployed as justification for military invasion and occupation in Afghanistan and Iraq, and as Islamophobic detentions and sentiments rose in the United States and Europe.[17]

In contrast to the ideology of the 'war on terror', Muslim women activists in Indonesia are deploying Islam as they participate publicly in re-envisioning the Indonesian nation[18] and the nation-state's responsibilities to transnational workers.[19] In October 2013, in response to a widespread public outcry about the abuses of migrants abroad, the Indonesian government placed a moratorium on sending domestic workers to the UAE, and in recent years to other GCC countries as well. The ban is meant to stay in place until Memoranda of Understanding (MOU) can be developed between Indonesia and the various receiving countries to better protect the rights of overseas workers. As of February 2016, newly registered domestic workers continue to be banned from migrating to work in the Gulf. Despite the ban, in practice, migrants have continued to seek work in the

---

14 Asad 2000.

15 Mahmood 2005.

16 Hefner 2000.

17 Rana 2011.

18 Rinaldo 2008, 1782.

19 Silvey 2012.

UAE in large numbers, travelling primarily on tourist visas, over-staying these visas, and then finding work as undocumented labour-ers. In this context (and also prior to it), the Indonesian embassy in the UAE receives approximately one hundred 'runaway housemaids' seeking repatriation each month, while in Saudi Arabia between 400 and 600 women per month seek some form of support from the embassy. These numbers are high relative to the overall numbers of Indonesians estimated to work in the region.[20] My interviews with these 'runaways' in Dubai confirm the findings of other scholars that turning to the embassy is often the least desirable option in their assessment, one they accept only when they feel that all other avenues for staying on in Dubai have been exhausted.[21] But most of the women staying at the embassy would prefer not to be repatriated if other options were available to them; they are there for shelter, food and escape from intolerable workloads and employers. Indeed, as I discuss further below, most do not desire to return to Indonesia, much less to their 'home' communities. As Johan Lindquist has argued, returning to one's village without earnings from abroad is a source of shame in the cultural logic of migration in Indonesia, and the shame of failure, in conjunction with the material pressure of labour market precarity, compels people to migrate repeatedly or to refuse to return to their origin communities.[22]

Between Abuse and Sociality: Training and Travelling Together

The numbers of Indonesians involved in the transnational labour market have grown rapidly in recent decades, with Saudi Arabia receiving the largest numbers of registered migrants and the UAE growing into an increasingly popular destination. Saudi Arabia ranks first (1,428,000 between 2006 and 2012) and the UAE ranks the fifth

---

20 Estimates vary widely, but Tirtosudarmo (as cited in Bachtiar 2012) esti-mates that between two and four times as many Indonesians may be living abroad as the oft-cited estimate of 6.5 to 9 million registered workers over-seas. For the UAE, popular media list approximately 65,000 Indonesian 'housemaids' (Ruiz 2012), and approximately 1,260,000 in the GCC.

21 Killias 2014, Mahdavi 2011.

22 Lindquist 2013.

(220,000 between 2006 and 2012) in the list of countries receiving the most migrant workers from Indonesia,[23] while Malaysia, Taiwan and Singapore also rank in the top-five destinations. The distinct majority of these migrants in all of these countries are women employed as domestic workers.

Like the Philippines, the Indonesian government is interested in sending nationals abroad in order to earn much-needed foreign exchange, and it has developed programmes to recruit and train women in particular to fill the demand for paid domestic labour in East Asia and the GCC. While receiving states welcome the entry of low-cost temporary labour, they refuse to extend citizenship or labour protections to the incoming workers. Many migrants thus face a range of problems, including: 'exclusion from coverage of labour and social legislation, the absence of grievance mechanisms, and/or coverage under restrictive and discriminatory policies and law [... as well as extremely high rates of ...] abuse, violence and exploitation.'[24] The issues of overwork, underpayment of wages and sexual violence are particularly acute among migrant domestic workers, and the plight of women who work as domestics has captured the attention of international human rights advocates[25], interstate organisations (United Nations Development Fund for Women known as UNIFEM, International Labor Organisation), and national and local NGOs.[26]

In November, 2014 an advocate from an NGO, the Centre for Indonesian Migrant Women, introduced me to Sirani[27] in her rural home community in Sukabumi, West Java, Indonesia. Sirani had recently returned home to Sukabumi from a job as a domestic worker in Saudi Arabia, where she had cut short her two-year contract to escape the intolerable violence to which she had been subjected by her employer. The introduction was uncomfortable, at least from my perspective, because while Sirani sat quietly in front of us, the NGO advocate introduced her to me with these words:

---

23 www.bnp2tki.go.id/read/9081/Penempatan-Per-Tahun-Per-Negara-2006-2012.html, accessed 25 February 2015.

24 Alcid 2004, 169.

25 Human Rights Watch 2004, 2007.

26 Piper 2004.

27 All names are pseudonyms in order to protect the anonymity of respondents.

Take her picture! Tell *her* story back to your friends in America!
She is a casualty of the Indonesian government's overseas migration programme. Look! She worked as a maid in Saudi until she
was abused so badly by her boss that she ran away. Just finally
climbed out of a window of the house and ran away! She is lucky
to be alive. Her boss tortured her, held a hot iron to her face, and
burned her so badly she is *blind* in one eye and can't hear any
more in her left ear. And our government does not even care!
Tell *that* to people when you get home.

Sirani maintained her silence, and her face remained expres-
sionless, as the introduction wound down. A few moments after we
began talking, her husband joined us and held her hand. She had
been seriously disfigured and disabled by the severity of the burns.
It appeared to me from her demeanour that she was accustomed to
having her injuries openly discussed in her presence. It also seemed
that she, her husband and the NGO activist shared an interest in
communicating with me about the violence that had been done to
her: Sirani by sitting stoically and embodying the crime, her husband
shaking his head in equal parts sympathy and disbelief and the NGO
representative providing the narrative.

After we had been together for several more days, Sirani began
to tell me her own version of events. Religion was central to Sirani's
desire to work in Saudi Arabia rather than in other possible destinations, such as Singapore or Hong Kong. As she put it, 'It's the Holy
Land, and I'm a Muslim. So of course my whole life I have dreamed
of making the *hajj* [pilgrimage]. To be able to work in Saudi would
mean I would be near Mecca, and my boss and neighbours would
also be practising Muslims.' In addition, in her description of each
stop along her migration journey, Sirani invoked religion as important to her social map and her sense of belonging. She was shocked
by the way she had been treated by her Saudi employer, and indeed
especially stunned that her wounds had been inflicted by a fellow
Muslim. Her understanding was informed by her faith: 'Islam does
not allow any human being to abuse another person the way my boss
did me. What she did to me was sinful no matter where it happens.'
Whereas the NGO advocate had sidestepped religion, emphasising
instead the role of the government in failing to protect Sirani from
violence, Sirani underscored religion as both what had motivated

her to choose to migrate to Saudi and what had informed her sense of the injustice and violence to which she had been subjected.

In Sirani's community in Sukabumi she and almost all of her neighbours were practising Muslims. When I visited her a second time in 2009, a large new mosque was under construction there with funds from a Saudi investor, and a newly constructed *pesantren* (Islamic boarding school) was set to open for over one hundred middle-school students in the new school year. Sukabumi has a long history of ties with Saudi Arabia, based primarily on the outmigration of religious leaders and scholars who undertook advanced religious education there.[28] It is only since the 1980s, however, that large numbers of villagers, predominantly women (approximately 75 per cent) as well as some men, have circulated between Sukabumi and the GCC as labour migrants. By 2005, overseas migrants' remittances had grown into the largest source of revenue for the community, and each year more local people enlisted to take their chances abroad.

In 2002, a neighbour of Sirani's who worked informally as a recruitment agent for a labour contractor in Jakarta, approached her with the possibility of overseas employment. She remembered the conversation, held in the front room of her family's home, as a very brief exchange: 'He told me there was a job opening in Jeddah. I was so excited. I didn't ask many questions. It was my lifelong dream to visit the Holy Land, and I just said, "Yes! How much will it cost me to go?"' Sirani's view of Saudi as a particularly desirable destination because of its sacred status is one that is widely shared among Muslims in Indonesia, who make up the distinct majority of the world's fourth most populous nation.

The Indonesian Islamic revival over the past several decades has involved a proliferation of types and spaces of Islamic practice, and multiple relationships to the concept of the *umma*[29] as well as strengthening transnational networks based on increasing Indonesian-Saudi migration and communication flows.[30] In Sukabumi, migrants' notions of gendered rights and aspirations vis-à-vis their labour are intertwined with their religious subjectivities and communities.

---

28 Mandal 2002.

29 Hefner 2000.

30 IAIN n.d.

As I have described in some of my previous work, religion plays an important role among recruitment agents in the marketing of particular destinations, including especially Saudi Arabia, to potential migrants[31], and the notion of sharing a religion with one's employer is a major selling point. As Sirani explained:

> My mother and father and my husband agreed that it was good for me to go [to Saudi] because the Saudis practise the same religion as we do. Everyone in Sukabumi is very devout (*beragama kuat*), so everyone wants to make the pilgrimage. For people like us, sorry, people who don't have much [in the way of capital or assets], the only way to make the hajj is to work as a migrant labourer.

One month after agreeing to sign a two-year contract, Sirani packed her bag and piled into her neighbour's van accompanied by her family members for the trip to the training camp in Jakarta. The training camps are managed by labour recruitment companies and loosely regulated by the Indonesian government.[32] Prior to departure for their stints abroad, migrants are required to undergo courses that introduce them to some basic vocabulary and phrases in the language of their destination country, and to learn the skills necessary for their future jobs. The training periods last between two weeks and several months, and NGOs for the most part view the training camps as sites where migrants face inhumane treatment. Indeed, the trainings themselves are geared towards indoctrinating workers into servile subject positions. In addition, migrant rights advocates have reported cases of forced labour, physical abuse and confinement of migrants in the training camps.

In one report by Human Rights Watch, an interview with a migrant who had worked in Malaysia documented her pre-departure ordeal:

> The agent came to my house and promised me a job in a house in Malaysia (. . .) He promised to send me to Malaysia in one month, but [kept me locked in] the labour recruiter's office for six months (. . .) I think one or two hundred people were there. The gate was locked. I wanted to go back home. There were two

---

31 Silvey 2005.

32 Lindquist 2010.

or four guards, they carried big sticks. They would just yell. They would sexually harass the women.[33]

Some migrants I have interviewed have reported hearing about similar abuses in the pre-departure trainings camps. However, many migrants also recollected relatively positive experiences during their time in the training centres. Sirani was escorted to the gate of the training camp by her agent, who introduced her to the guard, who escorted her into the dormitory, filled with bunkbeds, where approximately 200 other women were staying during the pre-departure training period. She remembers seeing the dormitory in the training facility this way:

It was just like home. So many friends. Lots of talking and laughing. Totally boisterous. Our sleeping spots were small and we had to scoot over to make room for each other, but we liked it. Almost all of us were Sundanese [the predominant ethno-linguistic group in West Java], so we made friends quickly.

RS: What was the place itself like?

Sirani: It was just normal. Just a place to sleep and learn about our jobs. There were a few big rooms beside the one where we slept, two classrooms with chalkboards for the teachers, and one kitchen with some rice cookers, dishes and sinks, a room for praying, things like that. . .

RS: Did you stay in the facility for the full two months, or did you sometimes take walks outside?

Sirani: Oh, we just stayed. All of us were new to Jakarta, and we weren't brave enough to go out.

RS: Even though you were there for two months?

Sirani: . . .We were learning how to use washing machines, vacuum cleaners, how to speak [minimal] Arabic. It was a really lively (*ramai*) place, and we were in a lively group (*beramai-ramai*).

RS: Really?

Sirani: Yes. Why [do you ask]?

---

33 Interview with Fatma Haryono, age thirty, returned domestic worker, Lombok, Indonesia, 24 January 2004 (Human Rights Watch 2004, 21).

RS: Well, I've just read that the training camps are very crowded and dirty, and that the trainers can be quite strict.

Sirani: Well, maybe I was lucky because my teachers were nice [laughs again.] Oh, it was tight! But most of us were pretty compatible with each another. We just adapted and moved over for each other. Sundanese people are good at that [laughs again].

RS: Good at tolerating each other in close quarters?

Sirani: That's not tolerating. We were *enjoying* being together!

This interview stood out in part because it challenged some common assumptions about what makes the training centres problematic spaces.[34] I had persisted in questioning Sirani about whether the training camp had provided her with enough personal space, whether she had been forbidden to leave the camp, and whether the training period had been difficult. In contrast to my concerns, she painted a picture of the camp as a positive space of social contact. Sirani, and many migrants I have interviewed, placed great value on the time spent with fellow Indonesians, noting that as long as they are not alone, they can cope with other difficult aspects of their journey. The social life of the group of fellow migrants remained important to Sirani when she travelled to the airport and boarded the airplane:

I had never been to an airport before, so I was lucky to be with my friends. We travelled as a group. We were all wearing our company's [uniform] shirts, so we wouldn't get left behind by our agent (. . .) Our agent showed us where to wait and which papers we needed for each line. He held all our visas and tickets for us. We were mostly quiet then, just looking around (. . .) I was thinking about whether my boss in Saudi would be a nice person, and I was a little afraid to get on the airplane. It was my first time flying.

RS: Were other people afraid too?

Sirani: Actually, I think we were all feeling the same way. Some of my friends began praying (. . .) I was just grateful to God that

---

34 The camps remain deeply problematic, often abusive, spaces for migrants, as Rudnyckyj (2004) has shown, as NGOs have detailed (Human Rights Watch 2007, 2014) and as Silvey (2004) has underscored in previous work.

we were all together (*bersyukur bersama-sama*). When we got on the plane, we were just totally silent almost the whole way – because I think we were scared of separating [from one another once arriving at our destination]. We filled up almost the whole plane with just us all.

The sociality of the training camps and the travelling was what made them tolerable, or even, as Sirani insisted about the camp, enjoyable. For scholars of gender and transnational migration, attention to sociality implies a shift in register away from liberal questions of resistance and empowerment and towards more complex conceptions of desire, power and possibility. In part because scholars, advocates and journalists have repeatedly found the Indonesian-GCC labour market to be rife with human rights abuses, and because there is widespread information circulating about the extent of the abuses, it is important to ask what drives so many Indonesians to continue to see the place relatively favourably and pursue work there, and what sorts of hidden transcripts about migrants' motivations and coping practices might exist. These less-frequently-told narratives capture something of value to migrants in a context where their possibilities are extremely limited. As the following section discusses, some clues to possible futures may be decipherable in the spaces migrants choose and create as sites of escape.

Runaway Spaces: Finding Sociality in the Margins

After almost six months of abuse by her employer in Saudi Arabia, Sirani decided that she had little choice but to run away. She climbed out of the window in the middle of the night and began walking in the direction of the highway overpass in the centre of town:

> My friends back home had told me about the overpass before I had left. They said that sometimes you could find other Indonesians sitting there under it –people who had run away from their jobs. They told me if I was ever in a bad situation that I should either go to the Embassy or go to the overpass. I couldn't find the Embassy, so I looked for the overpass. I had passed it a few times when my boss had taken me with her to the mall, and luckily it wasn't too far from the house. When I got there (. . .) I heard people speaking Indonesian (. . .).

RS: Did you see anyone you knew ?

Sirani: No (. . .) nobody I had ever met before (. . .) But I was standing there alone for just a short time and people just (. . .) started asking me if I was alone and why I was alone *(sendirian)*?

RS: And then . . .?

Sirani: I just started talking and talking, and they gave me some water. There were so many people there. We just sat down and started telling each other so many things. One woman told me she knew someone who was from my village and said she would help me find her. It was (. . .) really (. . .) lively.

RS: Lively?

Sirani: Yes (. . .) like that *(begitu)*. Because we were all so relieved to be able to talk to each other. The whole time I had been working before I ran away, I didn't have anyone to talk to in Indonesian. My 'madame' [employer] had been really sharp-tongued *(cerewet)*. Then under the overpass everyone had run-away *(semuanya kaburan)* (. . .) and we were just talking non-stop about everything to each other. Everyone was venting *(curhat [mengeluarkan isi hati])*.

Sirani's memories of finding people with whom she could speak Indonesian, and later also Sundanese, were part of her survival story. The social contact with people from her own community provided relief that coincided with the escape from the abuse of her employer, but mattered, in her telling, because it was a relief from the social, linguistic, physical and emotional isolation she had endured in her employer's home.

Sundanese migrants in Dubai also emphasised the importance of social contact with co-ethnics.[35] Ibu Soraya had worked abroad

---

35 In 2013 and 2014 I conducted collaborative qualitative fieldwork with Rhacel Parreñas on Indonesian and Filipina migrant domestic workers in Dubai and Singapore. The project compares the meanings of 'servitude' for domestic workers from the Philippines with those from Indonesia. I have focused my own research for the last fifteen years on the themes of gender and migration as they play out in West Java in particular. My longest term and most extensive research is based in Sukabumi, where growing numbers of women in particular have migrated abroad in recent

for twelve years without ever returning to Indonesia. She was, she estimated, 'about forty years old', and she had left one son, now an adult, back in Sukabumi when he was six years old. Her son's father had passed away when her son was a toddler, and in order to earn an income to cover her son's and her own basic needs, she sought work abroad. Her first contract was for a two-year period in Saudi Arabia. She, like Sirani, explained her willingness to leave Java for Saudi Arabia in particular as underpinned by a belief that Saudi Arabia's religiosity would mean she would be protected by people who shared her faith. Unlike Sirani, however, Soraya was under no illusion that the faith of her employer would translate into being treated well on the job. As she put it, 'Oh, I'd heard so many stories, seen so many people come back in bad shape, I knew I wouldn't necessarily be safe, but I still wanted to go to the holy land.'

Soraya's employer in Saudi Arabia turned out to be a decent employer in her view ('*Alhamduhlillah, baik*'), and she completed her two-year contract with some modest savings. Rather than returning to Java at the end of the contract, she asked her contact at the labour recruitment agency if he could find her another position in a country other than Saudi Arabia. She did not want to return to Sukabumi nor did she want to stay in Saudi Arabia. Her agent informed her that she could pay him – it was not clear how much – to obtain a tourist visa for her to enter Dubai. There, she might be able to find work on her own, but he could not find her a placement nor would he be responsible for her.

According to Soraya, she was glad to pay the agent to arrange the tourist visa, and she felt confident that she would be able to find work once she arrived. She knew that in Dubai, unlike in Saudi Arabia, she could move around the city without a *muhrim* (male relative,

---

decades. Our research team carried out collaborative interviews with community leaders, family members, labour recruiters and neighbours of migrants, as well as return migrants (from Saudi Arabia, Jordan, the UAE, Singapore and Hong Kong), aspiring migrants and people who claim not to wish to migrate abroad. I base this chapter on material and observations from my previous research in Sukabumi, and draw also on ten weeks of ethnographic work carried out with women migrants from Sukabumi who live and work in Dubai.

required as chaperone for women in Saudi Arabia). So, she paid the agent some of her savings, and prepared for her journey. Her agent introduced her to an acquaintance who promised to rent her a room once she arrived in Dubai. Once she arrived, she settled in quickly and developed a reputation as a hard-working, honest, selfless and morally upstanding house-cleaner. She wore her headscarf and modest clothing every day, and presented herself – deliberately, she told me – as a pious person by holding her body tightly, hands clasped, head down. She lived in her rented room and cleaned several houses per day for non-Emirati foreigners ('I said no locals [that is Emiratis] and no Saudis', she explained with reference to the nationalities for whom she refused to work) on a live-out basis at a lower cost than would be charged for a full-time live-in domestic. She met other Indonesian people at the public events held by the Indonesian embassy, and at the Indonesian restaurants and specialty shops.

For ten years, she remained undocumented, having overstayed her thirty-day tourist visa at the end of the first month after having arrived. Through her networks, she met many former domestics who had run away from their employers in the UAE for various reasons, and who did not want to be repatriated. She began to serve as a sort of anchor for a large network of runaway migrant domestic workers, particularly those from West Java, in part because she had saved enough money to offer loans to women in dire financial straits. Her leadership role in the runaway community also appeared to be enhanced by her reputation as trustworthy and devout. People knew about Soraya. She received calls every day during our Dubai research from women who wanted to run away or who had already run away and were desperate to find a place to sleep. They were also desperate for wage earning work, which Soraya could also arrange for them. Prospective employers called Soraya every day as well, asking her if she had any new recruits. Indeed, she had a list of cell phone contacts that included over one hundred employers and more than 500 Indonesian women who had been in Dubai looking for work at one time or another over the last decade.

Soraya's social network included a Dubai Police officer from Yemen and a rental car business operator from India, both of whom helped her to find jobs and safe places to stay for the women she called her *anak buah* (fictive children). She was able to rent rooms in villas to stay temporarily with the women in her charge, sometimes twelve at a time. It was in these rooms where the runaway Sundanese women recreated a sense of 'home'. They cooked Sundanese food, ate together, chatted in their mother tongue, and watched DVDs of Sundanese music and dance (*jaipongan*) and soap operas. Their lack of legal work visas and their 'illegal' renting of rooms meant that they lived a highly insecure everyday existence. They had to move to a new house every few weeks to avoid raids by the police. So, they kept their bags packed, ready to flee and relocate at a moment's notice. Soraya managed these relocations with information and support provided by her Yemeni friend in the police force, who would warn her prior to planned raids.

For Soraya and her *anak buah*, given the extreme structural constraints under which they operated, living on the run was preferable to going home to Java. They worked part-time cleaning houses or giving massages, or sometimes both. Soraya claimed not to allow any of her *anak buah* to participate in sex work or to have boyfriends because she wanted to keep her reputation 'clean'. Most of the women in her charge eventually earned enough money to send some back to family members. They could not have earned these incomes at home in Java. In response to questions about whether they wished to return, they commonly said that there was 'nothing' (*nga ada apa-apa*) to which to return. They preferred the quest for new experiences in Dubai to their memories of 'being bored in the house' in Java. For them, departing from Java was driven by a desire to escape what they knew, and staying away – even with extremely insecure status – was preferable to repatriation. A widely shared sentiment was that once one 'made enough money', estimated to take 'about five more years', one might consider returning to Java, but there was little speculation about what sort of livelihood they would have upon return. Life on the run in the company of fellow Sundanese women was more than tolerable; it was better than being 'back home'.[36]

Concluding Thoughts

A transnational lens contributes to understanding the contemporary local and national dynamics of immigration regulation, gendered

---

36 See Lindquist 2013.

subject formations and religiously inflected politics. This is a critical point in time for research and teaching about these issues, as religious difference, gender politics and immigration futures are at the forefront of both controversial government agendas and public debate. The Indonesian-Saudi and -Dubai cases provide an example through which to examine some assumptions and misconceptions at the centre of these debates. In addition to focusing on the ways that migrant domestic workers highlight the importance to them of social contact, this chapter has attempted to inquire more generally into the implications of their narratives for theorising gendered spatial regulation, empowerment and migration. The interstitial spaces claimed by transnational migrant women workers represent both the extremely limited space of manoevre available to them as workers multiply marginalised in the global economy, as well as spaces of contact in which they can help each other cope, connect, and sometimes – as long as they are together – possibly even have fun.

Gendered space is produced through webs of social relations that themselves take shape at multiple scales ranging from the local to the global.[37] All bodies participate on highly unequal terms in the production of socio-spatial belonging and exclusion, such that for a body to travel through a space is for it to be a part in the making of group boundaries and power relations.[38] The social meanings of gendered space are contingent not only on specific histories and geographies of difference that attach to bodies (as inscribed by race, ethnicity, class, gender, sexuality, nation, religion et cetera) but also importantly on the ways in which these embodied distinctions take on different valences in the specific lived places and moments that migrants inhabit and travel through. Juxtaposing the spatial imaginaries that circulate in human rights literature with some migrants' memories of their everyday lived spaces permits discussion of the interstices in the margins of state efforts to control migrant spatialities. In addition, it directs attention towards the ways that micro-spaces of social contact matter in migrants' own cartographies of survival, refuge and coping in a transnational space characterised predominantly by gendered exploitation and violence.

---

37 Massey 1993.

38 Cresswell 1996.

References

Alcid, M. L. 2004. 'The Multilevel Approach to Promoting Asian Migrant Workers' Rights: The MFA Experience'. *International Migration* 42(5): 169–176.

Asad, T. 2000. 'What Do Human Rights Do? An Anthropological Enquiry'. *Theory & Event* 4(4): 5–25.

Bachtiar, P. P. 2012. 'Chaotic Statistics of Indonesian Migrant Workers'. *The Jakarta Post*, 26 January. [www.thejakartapost.com/news/2012/01/26/chaotic-statistics-indonesian-migrant-workers.html].

Brown, W. 2010. *Walled States, Waning Sovereignty*. New York: Zone Books.

Cresswell, T. 1996. *In Place/Out of Place: Geography, Ideology, Transgression*. Minneapolis: University of Minnesota Press.

Fernandez, B. and M. de Regt 2014. 'Chapter 1: Making a Home in the World: Migrant Domestic Workers in the Middle East'. In *Migrant Domestic Workers in the Middle East: The Home and the World*, ed. B. Fernandez, M. de Regt, and G. Currie, 1–26. New York: Palgrave Macmillan.

Gardner, A. 2012. 'Why Do They Keep Coming? Labor Migrants in the Gulf States'. In *Migrant Labor in the Persian Gulf*, ed. M. Kamrava and Z. Babar, 41–58. London: C. Hurst and Co.

Hefner, R. 2000. *Civil Islam: Muslims and Democratization in Indonesia*. Princeton: Princeton University Press.

Human Rights Watch 2004. 'Bad Dreams: Exploitation and Abuse of Migrant Workers in Saudi Arabia'. [hrw.org/reports/2004/saudi0704/index.htm]

—— 2007. 'Swept Under the Rug: Abuses against Domestic Workers around the World'. [hrw.org/reports/2006/wrd0706/]

—— 2014. 'United Arab Emirates: Trapped, Exploited, Abused Migrant Domestic Workers Get Scant Protection'. [www.hrw.org/news/2014/10/22/united-arab-emirates-trapped-exploited-abused]

Johnson, M. 2015a. 'Gendering Pastoral Power: Masculinity, Affective Labour and Competitive Bonds of Solidarity among Filipino Migrant Men in Saudi Arabia'. *Gender, Place and Culture A Journal of Feminist Geography* 24(6): 823–833.

—— 2015b. 'Surveillance, Pastoral Power and Embodied Infrastructures of Care among Migrant Filipinos in the Kingdom of Saudi Arabia'. *Surveillance & Society* 13(2): 250–264.

Killias, O. 2014. 'Intimate Encounters: The Ambiguities of Belonging in the Transnational Migration of Indonesian Domestic Workers to Malaysia'. *Citizenship Studies* 18(8): 885–899.

Lindquist, J. 2010. 'Labour Recruitment, Circuits of Capital and Gendered Mobility: Reconceptualizing the Indonesian Migration Industry'. *Pacific Affairs* 83(1): 115–132.

Lindquist, J. 2013. 'Rescue, Return, in Place: Deportees, "Victims", and the Regulation of Indonesian Migration'. In *Return: Nationalizing Transnational Mobility in Asia*, ed. B. Xiang, B. S. A. Yeoh, M. Toyota, 122–140. Durham: Duke University Press.

Mahdavi, P. 2011. *Gridlock: Labor, Migration, and Human Trafficking in Dubai*. Stanford: Stanford University Press.

Mandal, S. K. 2002. 'Forging a Modern Arab Identity in Java in the Early Twentieth Century'. In *Transcending Borders: Arabs, Politics, Trade and Islam in Southeast Asia*, ed. H. de Jonge and N. J. G. Kaptein, 163–184. Leiden: KITLV Press.

Massey, D. 1993. 'Power-Geometry and a Progressive Sense of Place'. *Mapping the Future: Local Culture, Global Change*, ed. J. Bird, B. Curtis, T. Putnam, L. Tickner, 59–69. London: Routledge.

Nagel, C. 2001. 'Contemporary Scholarship and the Demystification – and Re-Mystification – of "Muslim Women"'. *Arab World Geographer* 4(1): 63–72.

Ong, A. (2006). *Neoliberalism as Exception: Mutations in Citizenship and Sovereignty*. Durham: Duke University Press.

Parreñas, R. S. 2001. *Servants of Globalization: Women, Migration and Domestic Work*. Stanford: Stanford University Press.

—— 2017. 'The Indenture of Migrant Domestic Workers'. *Women's Studies Quarterly* 45(1–2): 113–127.

Parreñas, R. and R. Silvey 2015. 'Not One of the Family: The Tight Spaces of Migrant Domestic Workers'. *Harvard Design Magazine*, 'Family Planning No. 41, F/W 2015 (5 pages).

—— 2016a. 'Domestic Workers Refusing Neo-slavery in the UAE'. *Contexts* 15(3): 36–41.

—— 2016b. 'The Indentured Mobility of Migrant Domestic Workers: The Case of Dubai'. In P. Kotiswaran (ed.), *Revisiting the Law and Governance of Trafficking: Forced Labor and Modern Slavery*, 503–523. Cambridge: Cambridge University Press.

Piper, N. 2004. 'Gender and Migration Policies in Southeast and East Asia: Legal Protection and Sociocultural Empowerment of Unskilled Migrant Women'. *Singapore Journal of Tropical Geography* 25(2): 216–231.

Pratt, G. and B. S. A. Yeoh 2003. 'Transnational (Counter) Topographies'. *Gender, Place and Culture* 10: 159–166.

Rana, J. 2011. *Terrifying Muslims: Race and Labor in the South Asian Diaspora*. Durham: Duke University Press.

Rinaldo, R. 2008. 'Envisioning the Nation: Women Activists, Religion and the Public Sphere in Indonesia'. *Social Forces* 86: 1781–1804.

Rudnyckyj, D. 2004. 'Technologies of Servitude: Governmentality and Indonesian Transnational Labor Migration'. *Anthropological Quarterly* 77(3): 407–434.

Ruiz, R. 2012. 'Indonesian Envoy Wants Fewer Maids Sent to UAE'. *The National, UAE*, 30 May. [www.thenational.ae/news/uae-news/indonesian-envoy-wants-fewer-maids-sent-to-uae].

Silvey, R. 2004. 'Transnational Domestication: State Power and Indonesian Migrant Women in Saudi Arabia'. *Political Geography* 23(3): 245–264.

—— 2005. 'Transnational Islam: Indonesian Migrant Domestic Workers in Saudi Arabia'. In *Geographies of Muslim Women: Gender, Religion, and Space*, ed. G. Falah and C. Nagel, 127–246. New York: Guilford Press.

—— 2012. 'Gender, Difference and Contestation: Economic Geography through the Lens of Transnational Migration'. In *The Wiley-Blackwell Companion to Economic Geography*, ed. T. Barnes, J. Peck, and E. Sheppard, 420–430. Malden: Wiley-Blackwell.

CHAPTER 8

East Javanese Housemaids in Saudi Arabia, 1990s–2010s

Transnational Labour Migration, Survival, Social Networks and Identity

NURCHAYATI

Introduction

The village of Pranggang lies in the sub-district of Plosoklaten, which belongs to the district of Kediri in East Java. Pranggang is nine kilometres to the south of Pare, the district's capital town, and twenty-four kilometres to the east of the city of Kediri. A network of roads, large and small, connects the village to East Java's major towns and cities. To the east of Pranggang stands Mount Kelud, a volcano whose eruptions give fertility to the soil of the surrounding plains. Endowed with about ten natural springs, and made up of six hamlets, Pranggang occupies an area of seven square kilometres. Its population of 8,768 is mostly Muslim by religion and Javanese by ethnicity.[1] Most of its inhabitants are junior high school graduates by education and farmers or service sector workers by occupation.[2]

Migration is one of the key factors that have shaped Pranggang's history. The village was established in the 1890s during the Dutch colonial era, when Javanese migrants from Central Java cleared the forest in the western slopes of Mount Kelud to build houses and rice fields for their families. Later in the post-colonial era, from the early 1980s onwards, with Pranggang having become densely populated, the desire for a village-centric good life – one that depends on the ownership of a home and a plot of farmland – has driven quite a few of its poor, unskilled and undereducated women to engage in

---

1   BPS Kabupaten Kediri 2017, 19.

2   BPS Kabupaten Kediri 2015, 21–22.

transnational labour migration.[3] These women have gone to work as domestic helpers in Malaysia, Singapore, Hong Kong, Taiwan, South Korea and Saudi Arabia.[4]

This chapter examines how, in pursuing their goals, those Javanese women of Pranggang who worked in Saudi Arabia managed to survive physically and mentally, as well as to preserve and/or refashion their sense of ethnic identity.[5] It is argued that these women toiled abroad to become what they saw as better versions of themselves, that is, to become better *Javanese* women. It was their hope that they would return to their communities of origin as Javanese women who could enjoy more wealth, command greater respect, exercise more influence and lead a more meaningful life. But how did they go about accomplishing this mission? How did they tackle the physical, mental, social and cultural challenges that they faced as migrant workers? What sorts of connections to the homeland did they try to maintain abroad? How did they attempt to form networks of Javanese migrant workers in the diaspora? And in what ways did these strategies that they used as well as the cultural encounter that they experienced in Saudi Arabia affect their sense of identity as Javanese? These are the questions that this chapter seeks to examine by employing the experiences of several Javanese women (three as primary informants) from Kediri who worked as domestic workers in Saudi Arabia.

This contribution is based on the fieldwork that I carried out in the village of Pranggang, Kediri, East Java in November–December 2009, February–March 2011 and December 2013–September 2014.[6]

---

3 For example, village records show that 30 Pranggang women did so in 2006, 13 in 2007, 12 in 2009 and 18 in 2011. Since only a small portion of migrant workers from Pranggang follow the legal procedure when they go for work overseas, these numbers do not give a precise reflection of reality.

4 Nurchayati 2017, 38–43, 121–123. To place these Pranggang women's migration experiences in the wider context of government policy, national economy and Indonesia's performance in labour export, see *Tempo* 1983, Fardah 2012, Johan 2012, Sugiyarto and Pernia 2012, Suhariyanto, Sugiyarto and Avenzora 2012, Azwar 2014, Palmer 2014, 56–70, Bank Indonesia 2015a, 2015b, 2017 and BNP2TKI 2007, 2008, 2017.

5 This chapter is partly based on Nurchayati 2010 and 2011.

6 Kediri is one of the major domestic-worker-exporting districts in East Java.

My key informants were Sarinah, Lestari and Ratih, all of whom had a primary school education, were married Muslim Javanese housewives and (at the time) made a living as farmers.[7] A 56-year-old mother of two children, Sarinah had been to Saudi Arabia twice. In her first stint (1990–1993), she served as a domestic worker in the household of a retired officer in Riyadh, who had a wife and eight children. During her second sojourn, she worked in the village of Taif from 1997 to 1999, this time as a domestic worker for a young couple with three children. Lestari, a 51-year-old mother of two children, had also worked twice in Saudi Arabia. Her first period of employment (1993–1996) was as a domestic worker for a bookseller's family in Dhahran. Her employers had eight children and she was the only domestic worker they hired. After spending a year back home, she returned to work in Saudi Arabia again. In this second stint (1997–2000), Lestari served as a domestic worker in Riyadh for a retired gardener and his wife. Ratih, aged 41, was married to a bricklayer, with whom she had two children. She had spent the years 2005–2007 in Saudi Arabia, serving as a domestic worker for an expatriate Syrian couple who worked as physicians in Abha. She babysat their children and took care of the house but was not required to cook.

This study draws on biographical and ethnographic data to examine how my informants' lives have interacted with their changing society. I conducted in-depth, structured interviews in Javanese with my informants to reconstruct their life stories, relying on their memories, which were selective, incomplete and sometimes inaccurate. The reader is thus best advised to read the following accounts of Javanese housemaids' experiences in Saudi Arabia critically, that is, as a mixture of what actually happened and what the informants felt to have happened. In order to assemble an ethnographic picture of the village, I interviewed more than seventy locals, including, among others, the key informants, their husbands and relatives, other return migrant workers, the village chief and his assistants, and other villagers. Besides observing sites of collective activities (the market, village office, water reservoirs, rice fields, food stalls, mosques, orchards and house yards), I took part in prayers,

---

7   I use pseudonyms to protect the privacy of my informants.

campaigns for the district head elections, palavers at local food stalls and informal gatherings.

Working Conditions in Saudi Arabia

During the reign of King Faisal (1964–1975), the Saudi government began a programme of economic modernisation. One of the obstacles it faced was a shortage of manpower. To solve this problem, the government offered competitive wages to attract foreign workers, whom the country needed to run development projects.[8] Saudi Arabia soon experienced an influx of migrant workers, who constituted over 50 per cent of its workforce in the early 1970s.[9] The number of foreign workers grew from 4.5 million in 1995 to 5.6 million in 2008.[10] This trend led some in the government and citizenry to perceive migrants as a threat to the Saudi way of life.[11] Since the mid-1980s, the government has been trying to address the demographic imbalance by Saudising the country's manpower.[12]

This programme of economic modernisation has resulted in the rise of a middle class whose members hire domestic workers for prestige and convenience.[13] About 80 per cent of Saudi households nowadays rely on migrant workers to deal with household chores.[14] This is common practice even where households do not need the extra help. Rukmini, an ex-migrant domestic worker in her fifties was aware of the Saudi practice of using domestic workers as a status symbol:

> My employers in Medina were a teacher and his wife, a homemaker and mother of two. Less well-off than their neighbours, they lived in a small rented house, where the amount of chores was too negligible to justify hiring a domestic worker. To make the most of the wages they paid me, they made me do laundry work for their relatives.

8   Shaw and Long 1982, 42.
9   Bowen 2008, 119.
10 Ramady 2005, 356, North and Tripp 2009, 81.
11 Kapiszewski 2006, 4–11.
12 Feiler 1987, 308, Zuhur 2011, 72.
13 Oishi 2005, 47, Gulati 2006, 56.
14 O'Kane 2009, 3.

The Saudi government also pursues a restrictive immigration policy.[15] Offering no tourist visa, it allows only five categories of foreigners to visit the country: entrepreneurs, workers and their dependents, Muslim pilgrims, diplomats and the citizens of Gulf Cooperation Council (GCC) countries.[16] To limit foreigners' mobility, the government enforces housing segregation between citizens and non-nationals, prefers non Arab aliens and supports short term work contracts and the *kafala* system.[17] Under the *kafala* system, all foreigners need a Saudi sponsor to get an entry or exit visa approval when entering or leaving the country. Upon entering Saudi Arabia, they must submit their passport to their Saudi sponsors, who in turn provide them with an *iqama* or temporary residence permit.[18] Their passport is returned when the employment contract expires and they must leave the country.[19] In compliance with the *kafala* system, Sarinah, too, had to submit her passport to her employer, who also acted as her sponsor:[20] 'During my stay in the country, my employers kept my passport and I could only have its copy.'

The *kafala* system creates unequal labour relations. Sarinah's employer could terminate the contract at any time, forcing her to leave the country immediately without paying some of her wages. This sponsorship system turns migrant domestic workers into 'illegal' aliens the moment their employers end their contracts or when they run away from their abusive employers.

Foreign domestic workers usually enter into a renewable two-year contract that requires them to undergo a three-month probation period. This is a time of uncertainty and increased vulnerability because they must work for free and under their employers' constant and close scrutiny. If a migrant domestic worker passes the probation period, she will receive wages for nine instead of twelve months in

---

15 Scully 2010, 826–827, O'Kane 2009, 1.

16 Rayburn and Bush 1997, 31, North and Tripp 2009, 113.

17 Beaugrand 2010, 4.

18 Rayburn and Bush 1997, 31–35.

19 O'Kane 2009, 2.

20 In most cases involving foreign domestic workers, their employers act as their sponsors.

their first year.[21] Employers have high expectations of their domestic workers because besides being charged expensive recruiting fees by employment agencies, they must also pay for the workers' visas and work and residence permits.[22] If an employer finds his new worker's performance unsatisfactory, he can send her back to the recruiting agency and demand a replacement. This system enables rogue recruiters to make more money by urging workers to flee their employer's house a few days just after their trial period ends. In this case, the employers remain responsible for covering the recruitment cost. The rogue agents then send the domestic workers to work for other employers whom they charge with recruitment fees.[23] On the other hand, rogue employers can abuse the system by transferring a domestic worker around among themselves before the probation period ends, thereby forcing her to work for free for multiple employers.

Migrant domestic workers find no protection in Saudi laws. They are, in fact, excluded from the Labour Law of 1969 and the Royal Decree No. M/51 of 27 September 2005.[24] If their employers mistreat them, it is difficult for them to get legal aid. Law enforcers do not handle cases of severe physical abuse of women domestic workers unless the international media and human rights activists mobilise pressure campaigns. For instance, the employers who tortured the Indonesian domestic worker Keni binti Carda in September 2008 were not brought to trial until the case received considerable international attention.[25]

The Probation Period and the Challenges of Adjustment

The probation period exposed the Javanese female informants of this study to the challenges of cultural adjustment that working overseas entailed. The challenges appeared in such areas as language,

21 According to a report by the London School of Economics Middle East Centre (2014, 5), the *kafala* policy first appeared in Saudi Arabia's Residency Law of 1950.
22 Varia 2008, 29, Saudi Arabia Ministry of Labor 2006, 4.
23 Bradley 2005, 129.
24 Scully 2010, 827, Sherry 2004, 27.
25 Human Rights Watch 2010, 13.

dress codes and working conditions. This trial period, which was the initial episode in the interpersonal and cross-cultural encounter between the Javanese domestic workers and their Saudi employers, often exposed the former to moments of discomfort, confusion, shock and stress. The Javanese housemaids must learn the basics of their employers' culture. The sudden 'transplantation' from their small village world to an overseas metropolis such as Riyadh and Jeddah came to them as quite a shock.

One of the triggers of the 'culture shock' that the informants suffered during their probation period was the foreign language. Consisting of numerous regional dialects and having an intricate grammar, Arabic is a difficult language to learn.[26] Sarinah, Lestari and Ratih reported to me that the two-week language course they took during their pre-departure training in Indonesia left much to be desired. The teachers in Jakarta taught them standard Arabic but their Saudi employers spoke colloquial Arabic. Thus, for the first six months of their encounter, the first-time Javanese migrant workers and their Saudi employers found each other mutually unintelligible. The employers, for their part, felt angry and cheated, having spent much money hiring a domestic worker who – unable to understand and perform even the simplest of all orders – seemed beyond training and good for nothing. Some employers reacted to their frustration by abusing their Javanese housemaid verbally or physically, or by sacking her. Lost in a linguistic limbo, their job security hanging by a thread, as first-time domestic workers the informants kept their cool, politely grinning and bearing the angry words their frustrated madams hurled at them every so often. Through the day-to-day interaction with their employers and their children, the Javanese housemaids picked up the colloquial Arabic. It was by employing this grin-and-bear strategy that Sarinah, Lestari and Ratih survived their probation period on their first stint. 'Though at the time I [Ratih] didn't understand Arabic, the tone of their speech left little doubt that they're grumbling about me. I noticed that in her grumblings my madam said certain words over and over again. I committed these words in memory. It was a few months before I discovered that

---

26 North and Tripp 2009, 192–195.

they were terms of abuse. Once the madam's kids got close to me, they revealed to me the meaning of all those words.'

By the time they started their second stints in Saudi Arabia, the informants had learned their lessons so well that they now had at their disposal the social knowledge they could draw upon to bolster their bargaining positions vis-à-vis their employers. When Sarinah returned to the country in 1997, for example, she was no longer the greenhorn she had been in 1990. She deliberately misled her employers to believe that she knew no Arabic so they would lower their guard and unwittingly reveal the otherwise hidden attitudes they had towards her. The knowledge of these attitudes helped Sarinah design and deploy various ways to 'tame' her employers.

> Not knowing that I spoke Arabic, she made fun of me and spat out insults at me, calling me filthy names, comparing me to animals. I tried not to take it to heart, though, because I was away from home, from my family and relatives and I had nowhere else to go. So I tried to make it feel like I was home and did whatever my madam told me to do. Her nasty words offended me, to be sure, but since I was still in my probation period, I knew better than to quarrel with her. Had I done so, she would've sent me home immediately. So I remained silent, keeping cool until my probation period was over and I was in a position to talk back to her.

The second cultural challenge was the dress code. The Saudi custom prescribes that men and women wear their traditional clothing when they go outdoors: the *gutrah* and the white *thobe* are for men while the *abaya* and the veil are for women. When they reach puberty, girls must conceal their face in the presence of men who are not members of their immediate family. All migrant domestic workers are required to comply with the Saudi dress code.

Sarinah, Ratih and Lestari found the Islamic dress codes in Saudi Arabia uncomfortable and impractical. While the sort of Islam they embraced as Javanese women in Kediri did not require them to cover their head and face, in Saudi Arabia women had to don the *burqa* – which covered the whole body save the hands and eyes – in the presence of males who were not their immediate relatives, at home and in public. The cumbersome burqa made it difficult for the domestic workers to perform their chores. In their own home in Java they would have worn a short-sleeved duster dress and have needed neither headscarf nor face-cover. In a Saudi household they could remove their headscarf only when all members of their employers' family were out. Seeing it as part of her job requirements, Lestari complied stoically with the dress codes. 'It was for survival's sake', she explained. By contrast, for safety reasons Sarinah could not do what Lestari did:

> In compliance with [the local interpretation of] Islamic dress code, my madam was adamant that I wear the burqa at all times, especially when we went outside the house. The problem was, the face-cover blocked my eyes and blurred my vision. [...] On [one] occasion the burqa I wore made me so clumsy that I fell down the stairway along with the baby I was carrying in my arms. Thank God, neither of us sustained any serious injury. But this accident led my madam to change her mind and let me stop wearing the burqa.

As it turned out, my informants regarded themselves as Javanese Muslim women and not as Saudi ones. In general, they felt more comfortable with the Javanese interpretation of the proper dress style for Muslim women. Later, after they had passed the probation period, they would take off their burqa for a time if and when the opportunity to do so came their way.

Saudi food customs also posed a cultural problem for Sarinah, Lestari, and Ratih, as well as all my other informants. Coming from rural East Java, they were accustomed to three meals a day (breakfast at eight, lunch at twelve, and dinner at seven), each consisting typically of steamed rice served with soup, greens, and a piece of bean curd, *tempeh*, salted fish, chicken, or meat. The eating habits in Saudi Arabia differed from those in Indonesia: people breakfasted at ten in the morning, lunched at four in the afternoon, and dined at ten in the evening. As Javanese women, Sarinah, Lestari and Ratih found most dishes in Saudi cuisine unpalatable. It was hard for them to eat mashed spinach, raw vegetables, or rice cooked in sweetened milk. Sarinah tried to live on fruit alone, which did not work, for such a diet rendered her too weak to work. She soon abandoned the method. Finally, like Lestari, she taught her body to adapt to Saudi cuisine. To survive the probation period both of them adopted a functional approach to eating whereby they had meals not for pleasure but for the mere calories they needed to perform their daily tasks. Compared to them, Ratih was luckier in that her employers provided her with enough foodstuffs such as rice and instant noodles that she could use to prepare her own meals. She seldom cooked for her madam, boss, and their children, for they relied mostly on take-away food for their daily sustenance.[27]

Like other female migrant workers in Saudi Arabia, Javanese housemaids, too, had to suffer from severe constraints on their mobility. Ratih reported that her boss and madam never let her go outdoors. 'Whenever they went out', she said, 'they would shut me in the house.' She added that her friend, a woman from Gringging, received even worse treatment from her employers. Once she was done with her chores, they would lock her up in her bedroom, furnished with a TV and a bathroom.

The isolation of women domestic workers exposes them to higher risk of abuse, exploitation and sexual harassment, and makes it harder for them to seek help from the police and other authorities.[28] Some Indonesian women domestic workers in Saudi Arabia sustained serious injuries and died on the run from the abusive employers who confined them.[29] Most of the 4,550 Indonesian migrant workers deported from Saudi Arabia between 19 September and 24 October 2011 were women domestic workers running away from their employers, who had subjected them to non-payment of wages, physical abuse or sexual harassment.[30]

---

27 Another of my informants, Laras (aged forty-one), told me that after they had survived the probation period, Javanese women migrant workers would be able, once in a while, to reestablish their cultural bonds with their motherland through Javanese and/or Indonesian cuisine and conviviality by attending the parties or Islamic feasts organised by the local network of Indonesian migrants where people served the Javanese and/or Indonesian dishes and desserts they loved, such as goat *satay* and *bakso* (noodle-and-meat-ball soup) (Laras personal communication 8 April 2014).

28 Varia 2010, 10.

29 Sherry 2004, 67–68.

30 *Metro TV News*. 'Konjen RI Jedah Pulangkan 4.550 TKI Bermasalah' 25 October 2011, www.metrotvnews.com/read/news/2011/10/25/69393/Konjen-RI-Jedah-Pulangkan-4.550-TKI-Bermasalah (accessed 25 November, 2011).

In other cases, women were required to work outside the home, despite the fact that their contracts stipulated that their duties would be confined to domestic work. As Ratih remembered, despite the stipulation in their contracts that as domestic workers they were to serve in a domestic setting, some wound up toiling in the sun as shepherds or farm hands, or serving their employers as shop-assistants at local bazaars.

> There was this friend of mine from Banyuwangi who left for Saudi Arabia shortly after she got married. She wound up working there as a shepherd. By the time she finished her contract and returned to Indonesia, prolonged exposure to the sun had tanned her skin to a dark brown. In this respect, Saudi Arabia is not unique, though, for my neighbour Nina, who worked in Hong Kong, also ended up becoming a kind of a field labourer.

That some Javanese women migrant workers hated getting a suntan is culturally understandable because the prevailing Javanese idea of feminine beauty included possessing, among other bodily features, fair skin colour.[31] During the pre-departure training, the recruiting agents had advised the migrants to refuse work if the actual working conditions overseas differed from those specified in their contracts. Yet despite serious discrepancies between contract and reality, the informants decided to comply with their employers' wishes. 'It would have been foolish to have done otherwise', Ratih explained to me. 'We had made a lot of sacrifices just to arrive there. So we had better stay, keep the job and make the best of a bad situation.'

Sarinah and Ratih recalled that their employers viewed their relations with them in such a way that to hire a domestic worker meant to 'buy' her as a human being.[32] Once, while angry, Ratih's madam complained that after spending much money to 'purchase' her, she still had to pay her regular wages. The madam considered it

---

31 Prasetyaningsih 2007, 63–157.

32 Since slavery was not abolished in Saudi Arabia until 1962 (Zuhur 2011, 52), it 'has existed within the lifetime of many present-day Saudis', with the result that 'a semblance of the slave-owner mentality sometimes lingers on' among them (North and Tripp 2009, 79). Owing to the recent legacy of slavery, too, the Saudi labour system 'smacked of indentured servitude' (O'Kane 2009, 2).

fair that migrant domestic workers should work for free during their probation period even though their contracts did not require them to do so. Under the contract, the employer could use the probation period to appraise the worker's personality and job qualifications. One of the ways the madam assessed her domestic worker's character was by testing her honesty. The madam would put a bit of money or jewellery in spots where the worker would stumble upon it easily. Sarinah recalled one of the tests she underwent: 'I was tidying up the clothes in one of those closets when I found a bundle of money. I picked it up and delivered it immediately to Madam. Had I not done so, I would've flunked the character test.' On the whole, the informants experienced the probation period as a time of fear and hope. Lestari, for one, remembered being haunted by the constant fear that her madam might ship her back to Indonesia.

Life and Work Abroad: Survival, Networking and Identity

The post-probationary phase in the stints of the Javanese women migrant workers in Saudi Arabia partly differed from and partly replicated the probationary one. On the one hand, after surviving the tryout, they now enjoyed greater job security: the threat of sudden dismissal no longer haunted them. On the other hand, in both the probation period and the rest of their stint in the country, Sarinah's, Lestari's and Ratih's everyday life revolved around roughly the same themes: handling the encounter of two cultures as both challenge and opportunity; joining and contributing to the Javanese and/or Indonesian communities-in-diaspora; and struggling for control over time, space and labour. Two new issues, however, did not appear until the probation period concluded. These were the sexual dimensions of overseas domestic labour and money management.

Three months' immersion in a Saudi household was too short for the informants to develop proficiency in Arabic. Their command of the language did not go beyond a few words and simple phrases. Consequently, their interaction with their employer was so full of misunderstanding that they failed to perform their daily chores competently. Sarinah could not suppress her laughter as she recalled how so much was lost in mistranslation between her and her employers:

Man, was I stupid or what? I had spent three months [there] but understood nothing. Every time my employers issued an instruction, I did not know exactly what to do. I made so many mistakes my madam decided to teach me some instructions in Arabic. But for quite some time even this didn't work. I kept on misunderstanding her [. . .]. At first the madam laughed at the funny mistakes I made. After some time, though, she broke down and cried – perhaps out of frustration at my slow progress. There were times when I doubted whether I had what it took to keep the job. I then decided that I should stop and think it out before responding to any of my madam's orders. This was how things were until the sixth month.

In response to the failure of verbal communication, there were times when Sarinah's employers resorted to body language. Sometimes this strategy worked; sometimes it caused complications:

I was always cautious, preparing for the worst. One day my boss followed me around with some clothes in his hand. I had no idea what's on his mind but I was afraid he's going to do me harm. I took a knife from the kitchen drawer for self-defence and ran away. But he kept following me, waiving his hand at me. I ran around inside, trying to avoid the man. Finally, he realised that a terrible misunderstanding was going on between us, whereupon he made a few gestures to indicate that all he wanted was for me to wash his clothes. I was like, 'God, was I stupid!' The moment I understood what's going on, I was very embarrassed.

It took these Javanese women nine to twelve months to become competent speakers of Arabic. They soon realised they could use their newly acquired language skill as a weapon to protect themselves from physical abuse by their employers. They could do this by demonstrating to their employer in Arabic their understanding of the terms of their contract. For instance, when their madams were going to lay a hand on them, Sarinah and Ratih responded by challenging them to send them home to Indonesia. Speaking in Arabic, they showed their madams that they understood an article in their contract which said that by physically abusing her domestic worker, the employer rendered the contract void. By doing so, she would at her own expense have to send the worker home and pay her wages for her work until the termination of contract plus three months' salary. It would be difficult for employers to find a new domestic worker as reliable as the one they had to send home.

The cultural encounter between these Javanese women migrant workers and their Saudi employers was not a one-way-street. Over time, some of the madams and bosses developed a taste for certain Javanese dishes that their maids cooked but that they initially disliked. As Laras told me on 8 February 2014,

> At first, whenever I prepared *sambal trasi* [chili sauce with shrimp paste] for myself, my madam would complain, 'What on earth is this? It smells like shit! You're making the kitchen smell like a filthy bathroom!' She then told me to spray all the rooms in her home with a deodoriser. After some time, though, she developed a fondness for Javanese food, such as fried chicken with rice and *sambal trasi*. Every Ramadan, she would ask me to cook this dish for her. Somewhat shamefaced, she also got hooked to *iwak pindang* [boiled-salted fish].

Months of immersion in the local culture did not lead the Javanese women of this study to adopt the kind of Islam practised by their Saudi employers. Some of my informants continued to practise their syncretic variant of Islam during their stint in Saudi Arabia. For example, when she worked in several stints in Saudi Arabia in the 1990s, Widati, now aged fifty, brought with her some of the same prayer books that she and her neighbours used in their regular prayer-group meetings in Pranggang, her village of origin. One of these prayer books contained the *Salawat Nariyah*, 'a prayer of intercession' about how 'God blessed the Prophet Muhammad' and cleared troubles from his way.[33] One day, upon seeing Widati reciting the book in her free time, her madam remarked that it was a heretical act, adding that Muslims must 'look to the Koran alone for guidance'. Speaking in a polite tone, Widati replied, 'It's all right, Madam; I just love this [prayer].' Since the days prior to her stints in Saudi Arabia, Widati has kept this practice up; it is part of who she is as a Javanese Muslim woman.

Besides facing the challenges of adjusting to an alien culture, some Javanese women migrant workers were also exposed to the real

---

33 Woodward and Rohmaniyah 2014, 161.

danger of being physically abused by their employers. As Ratih once explained to me, 'Some Saudi employers were physically abusive. If we were afraid of them, they would often lay a hand on us. But if we resisted them, they would think twice.' It should be pointed out that it was not only the madams and the bosses who maltreated their maids. Sometimes, Sarinah recalled, it was the employers' children who committed the physical abuse.

Sometimes conflict erupted between Indonesian migrant domestic workers and their employers. The common triggers of domestic worker-employer conflict included the madam's jealousy of the worker, unsatisfactory service, quarrels over childcare, complaints from the employer's children about the worker, sexual harassment of the worker by her boss, and linguistic misunderstandings. Depending on the causes, the temperament of the people involved, and their methods of handling it, the conflict could either end quickly or last long. In some cases, minor mistakes on the part of the domestic worker caused her to receive severe corporal punishment from the employer. For example, Keni binti Carda – an Indonesian domestic worker working in Saudi Arabia – was badly abused and mutilated by her madam who was disappointed with her performance.[34]

Some Saudi madams do not like seeing their domestic workers idle.[35] No sooner does a domestic worker finish with her chore than her madam finds her another task to keep her busy. Some tasks are ridiculous and unnecessary. For example, some madams make their domestic workers wash the walls several times a week or dust the furniture and wash the carpet every day. A work regime like this pushes the workers beyond their endurance. After a few months,

---

34 *Suara Merdeka*, TKI Disiksa Majikan, Sekujur Tubuh Disetrika' 1 April 2009. www.suaramerdeka.com?beta1/index.php?fuseaction=news.detaiNews& id_news=20555, (accessed 13 July 2009); Joewono 2011.

35 Although in the 20th century gender-based segregation required that middle- and upper-class Saudi women stay mostly at home, it was a mark of status for them *not* to do domestic chores. Whereas before the abolition of slavery in 1962, they depended on slaves for domestic labour and as a status symbol, in the post-abolition era they relied on foreign domestic workers (Al-Khateeb 1998, 182). In this context, a domestic worker who was 'idle' might look, in the eye of her madam, as if she were misappropriating the latter's status symbol.

some become so bored and exhausted they quit their job or run off. Others decide to stay and keep the job while devising some tricks to cope with the terrible workload. For example, Sarinah regulated her work pace in such a way that she could take a rest secretly:

> My first madam hated seeing me idle even for a minute. She wanted to see me busy all the time. To deal with this, I used a trick: Once I was done with my major chores, I kept carrying around this piece of cloth, which I used from time to time to wipe every stupid thing I could lay my hands on. The point was to look busy all the time. Whenever I could, I would politely refuse my madam's invitation to go with her to parks or malls. As soon as she and the kids were out, I took a nap. I would wake up the moment I heard them coming home. I would pretend as if I had been busy doing the house chores all along.

In general, domestic workers commonly work from fifteen to twenty hours a day in Saudi Arabia.[36] An Indonesian migrant worker named Siti, for example, told the daily *Jakarta Post*: '[My madam] did not allow me to rest more than two hours. She also overload[ed] me with tasks.'[37] One of the reasons was that the Saudis enjoyed holding family gatherings, which started at 10:00 P.M. and ended at 2:00 A.M. Friends and kinfolk came to visit, bringing their own domestic workers with them to help those of the host and hostess to organise the event. It was a physically exhausting event for the workers as they had to cook many dishes to accommodate the guests. As a result, they rarely had enough sleep during their stints in Saudi Arabia. As Lestari once put it, 'After hours I felt like a flat tyre.' In 2009, the Shura Council attempted to pass a law on domestic workers' working hours but this attempt failed because the proposed law was deemed inimical to 'the needs and traditions of Saudi families.'[38]

Family gatherings, which the Javanese housemaids found exhausting to help organise, also brought benefits, as they provided them with the chance for networking with their compatriots. On such

---

36 Zuhur 2011,162.

37 *Jakarta Post*, 'Journey of 2,349 Migrant Workers on the Labobar Ends'. 5 May 2011, www.thejakartapost.com/news/2011/05/05/journey-2349-migrant-workers-labobar-ends.html

38 Varia 2010, 15.

occasions, they would meet with one another and share information, ideas, knowledge and experiences of recreational and strategic importance. Such opportunities were precious because Saudi employers forbade their domestic workers to socialise.

Besides their employer's family gatherings, my informants could also meet their Javanese colleagues at shopping centres and amusement parks. Their Saudi employers visited such places from time to time with their children. Usually, while the madams and bosses were busy shopping, they told the workers to look after the children. While doing their job on such an occasion, the workers could meet and talk with other workers. They took care not to make this communication too conspicuous lest their employers intervene and dismiss it. Some madams and bosses were less strict and let their domestic workers get together with their colleagues provided that they did not neglect the children. On the social networks that she and her co-workers established in Saudi Arabia, Ria, a former migrant worker now in her early forties who had once run away from her employer and worked illegally in Jeddah in the early 1990s, said, 'Even though we lived in different districts, we formed chains of friends and got together once in a while.'

The importance of these 'windows of opportunity' for Javanese women migrant workers to build social networks cannot be underestimated. Javanese housemaids used such networks to get in touch with more experienced colleagues who could teach them some of the effective methods for enhancing their bargaining position vis-à-vis difficult employers, as well as some useful tips on how to better adjust to the Saudi society. Also, in times of trouble, members of these ethnic communities in diaspora could provide these Javanese housemaids with the support that they needed if they ever had to run away and, therefore, become 'illegal'. The kinds of support given included helping them escape from what they considered as exploitative and/or abusive employers; giving them a place to hide especially during their first three months as runaway migrant workers; and finding them a new, undocumented job. In addition, diasporic networks provided some of the cultural artefacts that Javanese women migrant workers needed for the preservation of their ethnic and national senses of identity.

The theme of sexuality also figured in informants' narratives about their experiences living and working in Saudi Arabia. Their overseas

225

employment revolved around, but cannot be reduced to, the economic encounter between the migrant domestic worker and the host
employer in which labour was exchanged for cash, and either party
did what he or she could to maximise his or her results. Intended
or unintended, consensual or coerced, the intrusion of sexuality
into the encounter could render it more complicated. For example,
Indonesian-Saudi cultural differences concerning non-verbal behaviour sometimes lead to sexuality-related misunderstandings that
make domestic worker-employer relations difficult. It is common in
Indonesia to see women and men smile and nod to each other to express respect and politeness. In the Saudi context, however, smiling
and nodding between opposite sexes can be interpreted as gestural
expressions of sexual interest. In this regard, a manual for expatriates living and working in Saudi Arabia notes, 'Women should not
be overly friendly to Arab men in public. It may be misinterpreted as
a "come on".'[39] It also warns the reader that 'Looking directly at men
and smiling can be misconstrued. Should you receive any unwanted
advances, make some *immediate verbal reaction*. Simply ignoring an
advance is considered tantamount to approval.'[40]

A handbook for Indonesian migrant workers in Saudi Arabia
provides tips on how a good domestic worker should behave towards
her boss, lowering her gaze in his presence. Under no circumstances
should she steal a glance at him or nod and smile to him because to
make any of these gestures is to act in a seductive manner, to present
oneself as a loose woman[41] and to risk inviting sexual advances
from men. Some Indonesian migrant workers, however, do not
understand this gestural code or, if they do, they simply forget to
translate their message (deference) from the Indonesian to the Arab
code. In some cases, this lack of understanding and this failure of
translation expose domestic workers to sexual harassment by their
male employers.

Cultural misunderstandings are not the only factors contributing
to the sexual harassment of Indonesian domestic workers by their

39 Rayburn and Bush 1997, 27.

40 Rayburn and Bush 1997, 97.

41 Saad 2005, 29–30.

Saudi employers. There are some who treat their domestic workers as sexual objects. As Rukmini recalled, one day she was home alone with nobody else but her boss. The man opened his robe and displayed his genitals to her.

When Indonesian migrant domestic workers had the chance to gather together, one of the things they did was learn from each other the tips and tricks for protecting themselves from sexual harassment. As Sarinah explained to me, one of these tactics was for the domestic worker never to say or do things that could be misconstrued as signs of sexual availability. Another tactic was for her to mount a physical counter-attack against a stubborn sexual harasser. When the son of her employers sought to harass her, Sarinah hit him with a broomstick and threatened that she would report the incident to his mother. Some fellow domestic workers armed themselves with a basin of water that they would throw at their boss and his son if they tried to molest her. Ratih recalled how this tactic often worked. The botched attempt at sexual harassment would leave its traces in the house, such as spots on the floor drenched with water. Seeing this, the madam would ask the domestic worker what had happened and the domestic worker would tell her the story, protesting her innocence. In some cases, this led to the development of mutual trust between the domestic worker and the madam. The third tactic was for the domestic worker to stay as far away physically as possible from all the adult male members of the family she served. If any of these asked her for a sexual favour, she would turn down the request firmly and assertively. Lestari did this when one of her employers' relatives asked her for a kiss on the cheek.[42]

In a few cases, it was the migrant domestic workers who were guilty of sexual harassment or, at least, sexual provocation. Some domestic workers took a sexual interest in their bosses and made

---

42 In some cases, assertiveness could even protect 'illegal' women migrants from sexual abuses. For example, Ria responded with a firm refusal when her boss demanded her to provide him with sexual services. Aware of her 'illegal' status, he threatened to turn her over to the authorities. She silenced him by pointing out that the authorities would find him guilty of a more serious offence: employing an illegal worker.

advances towards them,[43] which made their madams so bitterly jealous they subjected the domestic workers to various forms of physical abuse. Representatives of Indonesian recruiting agencies based in Saudi Arabia have received reports from some male employers who complained that their domestic workers had seduced them and their sons.[44]

Some of the stories the informants told me suggest that some sexual encounters between domestic workers and their male employers were consensual. Women migrant workers are sexual beings with sexual needs. Some focus on their work and delay the gratification of these needs until their stint is over and they reunite with their husbands; a few others seize the opportunity for sexual enjoyment that presents itself overseas. For the latter, such recreation may alleviate the dehumanizing effects of having to work overtime and stay at home almost every day. The domestic worker-male employer sexual liaison can be doubly rewarding for the domestic worker if she receives money from her boss in exchange for the sexual favours she does for and with him. This means extra money, a generous addition to her official wages, a supplement she can negotiate with her boss so as to make these favours a regular activity. Sarinah reasoned that some migrant domestic workers performed sexual services for their employers as 'a side job': 'We can count how much money we earn by working in Saudi Arabia. I have worked in Saudi twice, you see, but this is all I have. I tried to save as much money as I could. My family led a simple life, surviving on a frugal diet. If a maid earned that much money, it was really unusual. She might have done a "side job" in addition to working as a housemaid.'

Occasionally, the altercations between return migrant domestic workers in their home village were shot through with allegations that their interlocutors earned extra income in Saudi Arabia by providing sexual services. For example, one morning, sitting on the bamboo bench in the porch of his home, my research assistant Pandu witnessed a quarrel between two former migrant domestic workers in which they launched a vituperative attack on each other.

---

43 Kula and Alsagoff 1991.

44 Tobing et al. 1990, 95–96.

One party of this quarrel shouted to the other, 'Cut out that holier-than-thou attitude, will you? When we were there [in Saudi Arabia], you and I were *lonté* [whores].'

All the aforementioned tactics that the Javanese women of this study employed to stay alive, develop diasporic networks and maintain their ethnic roots and identities in Saudi Arabia were part of the larger struggle that had motivated them to work overseas in the first place: their search for a better future for their families. They learned from others that overseas work could ameliorate the standards of life of people like them. Whether or not they could make their dream come true depended not only on their physical, mental and cultural survival overseas and on the actual income they generated by working there, but also on the prudence and acumen with which they managed this income.

The informants negotiated with their employers for what they considered as the better ways of administering their wages. Sarinah, for example, would rather receive her paycheque once every few months. Once she indicated to her employers that she wished now to receive her wages, the latter would escort her to the bank where she could not only cash her cheque, but also send the money to her husband in Indonesia. Sarinah's colleagues managed their incomes differently, preferring to receive their wages monthly. Lestari, for one, knew that some fellow Indonesian domestic workers had trouble having their wages paid, especially if their employers faced financial difficulties. She also had heard stories of unfinished money business between Indonesian domestic workers and their employers even after the contract had expired and the domestic workers had returned home. In such cases, even though they were about to depart for Indonesia, the migrants had not received their full wages. Lestari was determined that this kind of trouble should not happen to her. She decided that the sooner she received her wages, the better she could manage her hard-earned income on her own. Experience had taught her that the employer could just renege on certain items in his or her contract with the worker. Her own employers, for example, failed to take her to Mecca to perform the *hajj* at the end of her contract just because one of them fell ill. (There is a clause in the labour contract that requires an employer to help the Muslim employee to perform the hajj.) Now she was worried that they would betray her trust again if she entrusted them with keeping her wages for her.

There seems to have been a cultural price that my informants had to pay for their survival abroad and economic success at home. It is doubtful that these Javanese women emerged completely unchanged from the transnational labour migration that they had carried out. In some cases at least, sojourns in Saudi Arabia seem to have brought about certain changes (real and potential) in the ways in which my key informants thought about themselves and their society. Aside from changing their living standards and social status, the transnational labour migration that some Javanese women of Pranggang carried out broadened their life's horizon, improved their bargaining position vis-à-vis their husbands and increased their control over family resources. Working and living for a while in Saudi Arabia opened these women's eyes to at least one different form of gender relations. This exposure allowed them to see in a comparative perspective the wife-husband relations in their own households. As a result, these began to appear relative and open to some changes. In this regard, Sarinah had an interesting recollection to share:

> Once married, Saudi women stay home, eating and sleeping; there was no need for them to work. Married women in Indonesia are different; they face tons of problems, having to make sacrifices so their households survive. As if that was not enough, they have to put up with their husband's nasty words. But the law [shari'ah] is the same here in Indonesia as it is in Saudi Arabia: it says that husbands must not neglect their wives; that men must never make life hard for women. Indonesian husbands are the most laid-back in the world. To make ends meet, Indonesian women are willing to help their husbands make a living.

However, as Sarinah, Lestari and Ratih soon realised, the downside to Saudi gender relations was that the wives did not enjoy freedom of movement in the public sphere. They had to spend the bulk of their daily life indoors, as they were forbidden to travel outdoors without their husband or a *mahram* to escort them.[45] In contrast, though Indonesian women fared worse financially, they fared better

---

45 A *mahram* is a male relative whom a woman is forbidden to marry.

in terms of freedom of movement; they were free to move around in their village, free to visit their neighbours almost any time during the day.

As several studies have discovered, one of the consequences of working overseas is that it can change women migrant workers' bargaining positions vis-à-vis their husbands, parents and siblings.[46] This finding is confirmed by Lestari's experience. Owing to the large sum of money she made abroad, her contribution to her family's income far exceeded that of her husband. As a result, she began to have a greater say in the decision-making processes in her own nuclear family and in the extended family. For example, she told her husband to till their own land and raise cattle rather than work for other people.

Dress styles are another area where we can look for signs of change and continuity in connection with transnational labour migration. Very few Javanese Muslim women in Pranggang followed as strict a dress code as their Saudi counterparts did. My informants admitted that they did not like the Saudi dress style. It did not fit in with what they considered as Indonesian culture. Having considered the pros and cons, my informants made up their mind that it was better to be Javanese women than to be Saudi women.

Some Javanese women migrant workers in Pranggang have succeeded in becoming what they felt to be better versions of themselves, that is, they have changed their lives for the better. In their own eyes and in those of their neighbours, they have emerged as successful, respectable, middle-class women. And this is an accomplishment. As an illustration of what such Javanese women look like, consider the case of Asri (aged 42), who has spent a total of eighteen years working mostly in Saudi Arabia. Her home in the village of Pranggang is a modest-looking brick house, whose living room (where guests are received) showcases a cluster of objects that Asri has brought home with her from her stints in Saudi Arabia. These imported artefacts, meant to win and express prestige, included tablecloth, carpet, a ceramic flower vase, wallpaper, a tapestry showing the Prophet's Mosque, Arabic calligraphy and (under the coffee table) a stack of the Arabic edition of the women's magazine *Marie Claire* (which

---

46 Williams and Widodo 2009, 136–137, Gambulrd 2000, 192.

Asri cannot read). And, if this is one of your first visits, Asri will offer you cold Coca Cola (served in a crystal glass) and some Javanese snacks. Well-dressed, wearing gold jewellery around her neck, in her ears and on her fingers, she will conduct a light and pleasant conversation with you, in which she may refer to her experience as a migrant worker in the Middle East. Perhaps she will mention that during Eid al-Fitr (the festival of the breaking of the Ramadan fast) in the village she serves her guests with pizzas, which she prepares in her kitchen using ingredients, utensils and appliances that she bought while in Saudi Arabia. She will say that she feels good if her home is clean and orderly.

Conclusion

In pursuit of wealth, respect, influence and meaning, it was not enough for Javanese women migrant workers from Pranggang to survive physically and mentally in Saudi Arabia. It was necessary too that while overseas they join and help build networks of Javanese migrants in diaspora, as well as preserve their ethnic and national sense of identity, although the *kafala* system quite severely restricted their geographical mobility. The Javanese women of this study employed several strategies to attain physical and mental survival while working in Saudi Arabia. In resisting the oppressive and exploitative acts that their employers committed against them, they used their employers' language (Arabic) against them. These women protected themselves by talking back to them in Arabic, engaging in counter-intimidation and negotiating for better labour relations and a better method of salary payment. In addition, they resisted their more powerful employers by engaging in dissimulation. For instance, they pretended they did not yet understand Arabic. This enabled them to eavesdrop on their employers' conversation to discover their real thoughts, feelings and attitudes, which in the future they could use against them. Moreover, they wielded other 'weapons of the weak', such as faking constant diligence in the presence of their employers; pretending to prefer work at home to travel outdoors with employers so they could take a nap while the latter were out; and protecting themselves from sexual harassment by consistent avoidance and assertive refusal.

In order to participate in and help establish Javanese and Indonesian communities in diaspora, they made use of two 'windows of opportunity': they secretly engaged in networking activities and the exchange of strategic information with fellow Indonesian domestic workers at malls and amusement parks (while their employers were busy shopping or having fun), as well as in the kitchens of their employers (while the latter held their family gatherings). In addition, to maintain their connections with their home village and motherland and preserve their cultural sense of identity, these Javanese women continued, while in Saudi Arabia, to practise certain elements of their Javanese culture. Not only did they cook and enjoy Javanese food in the home of their employer; they also attended the parties or Islamic feasts (e.g., Eid al-Fitr and Eid al-Adha or Sacrifice Feast) that the local network of Indonesian migrants held in which they could savour Javanese and/or Indonesian cuisine and conviviality. But of course they could not live on food and beverages alone. Thus, in such gatherings they also consumed Indonesian popular culture and conducted conversation in Javanese. To the consternation of their Saudi madams, these women continued to practise the 'traditionalist' variety of Islam which was predominant in their home village.

Finally, the transnational labour migration these women undertook not only provided them with the opportunity to see their home village community from a distance and from different angles but also exposed them to an encounter between their own Javanese culture and that of the host Saudi community. This kind of experience has compelled them to not only preserve but also (to some degree) transform their way of life and social relationships. Some accomplished upward social mobility and joined the middle class of their village, in the process adopting certain elements of the middle-class lifestyles that they had observed among their Saudi employers. Some also managed to strengthen their bargaining position vis-à-vis their husband in family decision-making. On the other hand, to remain themselves, most of them stayed committed to the version of Islam prevalent in their village and continued to speak the local version of proper Javanese (rather than show off their Arabic).

To conclude, this chapter contends that these Javanese women from Pranggang, Kediri, undertook transnational labour migration to generate the wealth and prestige which they needed to become better *Javanese* women. It was their hope that they would return to their home village as Javanese women who could enjoy more wealth, command greater respect, exercise more influence and live a more meaningful life.

References

Al-Khateeb, S. A. H. 1998. 'Women, Family and the Discovery of Oil in Saudi Arabia'. *Marriage and Family Review* 27(1/2): 167–189.

Azwar, H. A. 2014. 'Remitansi TKI berdampak perkuat ekonomi daerah'. *InfoPublik*, 8 July. [infopublik.org/read/83388/remitansi-tki-berdampak-perkuat-ekonomi-daerah.html]

Bank Indonesia 2015a. *Statistik Ekonomi Keuangan Indonesia = Indonesian Financial Statistics* 17 (12).

—— 2015b. *Laporan Perekonomian Indonesia*. Jakarta: Bank Indonesia.

Bank Indonesia 2017. 'Indonesian Financial Statistics – June 21, 2017'. [www.bi.go.id/en/statistik/seki/bulanan/Pages/SEKI-June-2017.aspx]

Beaugrand, C. 2010. 'Nationality & Migrations Control in the Gulf Countries'. *Hyperarticles en ligne: Science de l'homme et de la société*, 27 August. [halshs.archives-ouvertes.fr/docs/00/51/19/53/PDF/Nationality-migration_cbb.pdf]

BNP2TKI 2007. *Peraturan Kepala Badan Nasional Penempatan dan Perlindungan Tenaga Kerja Indonesia No. Per-45/KA/XII/2007 tentang Tatacara Pelaksanaan Pembekalan Akhir Pemberangkatan*. Jakarta: BNP2TKI.

—— 2008. 'TKI Sektor Unggulan Ketiga'. 22 October. [bnp2tki.go.id/content/view/584/231/]

—— 2017. 'Data Penenpatan dan Perlindungan Tenaga Kerja Indonesia Tahun 2016'. 14 August. [www.bpn2tki.go.id/uploads/data/data 08-02-2017 111324 Data-P2TKI tahun 2016.pdf]

Bowen, W. H. 2008. *The History of Saudi Arabia*. Westport: Greenwood Press.

BPS Kabupaten Kediri 2015. *Kecamatan Plosoklaten dalam Angka 2015 = Plosoklaten District in Figures 2015*. Kediri: BPS Kabupaten Kediri.

—— 2017. *Kecamatan Plosoklaten dalam Angka 2017 = Plosoklaten Subdistrict in Figures 2017*. Kediri: BPS Kabupaten Kediri.

Bradley, J. R. 2005. *Saudi Arabia Exposed: Inside a Kingdom in Crisis*. New York: Palgrave.

Cribb, R. and A. Kahin 2004. *Historical Dictionary of Indonesia*. 2nd ed. Lanham: Scarecrow Press.

Fardah 2012. 'Remittances from Migrants Soften Global Economic Crisis Blow'. *Antara News*, 9 August. [www.antaranews.com/en/news/83864/remittances-from-migrants-soften-global-economic-crisis-blow]

Feiler, G. 1987. 'Arab Labor Mobility in the Middle East in a Period of Economic Recession, 1982–87'. In *Middle East Contemporary Survey*, vol. 11, ed. I. Rabinovich and H. Shaked, 298–317. Boulder: Westview Press.

Gamburd, M. R. 2000. *Kitchen Spoon's Handle: Transnationalism and Sri Lanka's Migrant Housemaids*. Ithaca: Cornell University Press.

Gulati, L. 2006. 'Asian Women Workers in International Labour Migration: An Overview'. In *Migrant Women and Work*, ed. A. Agrawal, 46–72. New Delhi: Sage.

Human Rights Watch 2010. *Rights on the Line: Human Rights Watch Work on Abuses against Migrants in 2010*. New York: Human Rights Watch.

Joewono, B. N. 2011. 'Sariam dipukul, disetrika, hingga cacat'. 21 January. [regional.kompas.com/read/2011/01/21/21213713/Sariam.Dipukul..Disetrika..hingga.Cacat]

Jordan, M. 2012. 'Migrants' Cash Keeps Flowing Home'. *The Wall Street Journal*, 23 September. [online.wsj.com/news/articles/SB10000872396390443995604578004280591669350]

Kapiszewski, A. 2006. 'Arab versus Asian Migrant Workers in the GCC Countries'. Paper presented at the United Nations expert group meeting on international migration and development in the Arab region, 15–17 May, Beirut, Lebanon.

Kula, R. and H. Alsagoff, eds 1991. *Behind Closed Doors: Maids in Singapore*. Singapore: Knightsbridge Communications.

London School of Economics Middle East Center 2014. *Addressing the Demographic Imbalance in the GCC States: Implications for Labor Markets, Migration, and National Identity*. London: LSE Middle East Center. [www.lse.ac.uk/middleEastCentre/publications/other/DemographicImbalanceinGCC.pdf]

North, P. and H. Tripp 2009. *Culture Shock! Saudi Arabia: A Survival Guide to Customs and Etiquette*. 3rd ed. Tarrytown: Marshall Cavendish.

Nurchayati 2010. 'Foreign Exchange Heroes or Family Builders? The Life Histories of Three Indonesian Women Migrant Workers'. MA thesis, Ohio University, Athens, USA.

—— 2011. 'Bringing Agency Back In: Indonesian Migrant Workers in Saudi Arabia'. *Asian and Pacific Migration Journal* 20(3/4): 479–502.

—— 2017. 'Sociocultural Change and the Life Cycle: A Study of Javanese Village Women's Decisions on Transnational Labour Migration and Their Impact'. PhD dissertation, The University of Sydney.

Oishi, N. 2005. *Women in Motion: Globalization, State Policies, and Labor Migration in Asia*. Stanford: Stanford University Press.

O'Kane, M. 2009. *Saudi Arabia Labor Law Outline*. Riyadh: The Law Firm of Salah al-Hejailan.

Palmer, W. 2014. 'Discretion and the Building of Institutions: A Critical Examination of the Administration of Indonesia's Overseas Labour Migration Programme'. PhD dissertation, The University of Sydney.

Prasetyaningsih, L. A. S. 2007. 'The Maze of Gaze: The Color of Beauty in Transnational Indonesia'. PhD dissertation, University of Maryland, College Park, USA.

Ramady, M. A. 2005. *The Saudi Arabian Economy*. New York: Springer.

Rayburn, R. and K. Bush 1997. *Living and Working in Saudi Arabia: How to Prepare for a Successful Short or Long Term Stay*. Oxford: How-To Books.

Robinson, K. 2009. *Gender, Islam, and Democracy in Indonesia*. London: Routledge.

Rubiyanto 2011. *Profil desa tahun 2011 desa Pranggang kecamatan Plosoklaten*. Kediri: Pemerintah Kabupaten Kediri.

Saad, H. M. 2005. *Panduan buruh migran (Tenaga Kerja Indonesia/TKI) di Arab Saudi*. Jakarta: Komnas HAM.

Saudi Arabia Ministry of Labor 2006. *Guidebook for Expatriates Recruited for Work in the Kingdom of Saudi Arabia*. Riyadh: Kingdom of Saudi Arabia Ministry of Labor.

Scully, K. 2010. 'Blocking Exit, Stopping Voice: How Exclusion From Labor Law Protection Puts Domestic Workers at Risk in Saudi Arabia and Around the World'. *Columbia Human Rights Law Review* 41(3): 825–882.

Shaw, J. A. and D. E. Long 1982. *Saudi Arabian Modernization: The Impact of Change on Stability*. Washington, DC: Center for Strategic and International Studies, Georgetown University.

Sherry, V. N. 2004. *Bad Dreams: Exploitation and Abuse of Migrant Workers in Saudi Arabia*. New York: Human Rights Watch.

Sugiyarto, G. and E. Pernia 2012. 'Effects of Global Crisis on Remittance and Poverty in Asia'. In *Global Crisis, Remittances, and Poverty in Asia*, ed. Asian Development Bank, 5–30. Mandaluyong City: Asian Development Bank.

Suhariyanto, Kecuk, G. Sugiyarto, and A. Avenzora 2012. 'Indonesia'. In *Global Crisis, Remittances, and Poverty in Asia*, ed. Asian Development Bank, 64–77. Mandaluyong City: Asian Development Bank.

Tagaroa, R. and E. Sofia 1998. *Buruh migran Indonesia mencari keadilan*. Bekasi: Solidaritas Perempuan, Lembaga Advokasi Buruh Migran Indonesia.

Tempo 1983. 'Mengais Devisa dari Arab'. 28 May.

Tobing, M. et al. 1990. *Perjalanan nasib TKI-TKW: Antara rantai kemiskinan dan nasib perempuan*, ed. Y. P. Utomo. Jakarta: Gramedia.

Varia, N. 2008. *As If I'm Not Human: Abuses against Asian Domestic Workers in Saudi Arabia*. New York: Human Rights Watch.

—— 2010. *Slow Reform Protection of Migrant Domestic Workers in Asia and the Middle East*. New York: Human Rights Watch.

Williams, C. P. and A. Widodo 2009. 'Circulation, Encounters, and Transformation: Indonesian Female Migrants'. *Asian and Pacific Migration Journal* 18(1): 123–142.

Woodward, M. and I. Rohmaniyah 2014. 'The Tawdry Tale of "Syech" Puji Luftiana: Child Marriage and Polygamy on the Boundary of the Pesantren World'. In *Gender and Power in Indonesian Islam: Leaders, Feminists, Sufis and Pesantren Selves*, ed. B. J. Smith and M. Woodward, 157–175. New York: Routledge.

Zuhur, S. 2011. *Saudi Arabia*. Santa Barbara: ABC-CLIO.

CHAPTER 9

Javanese in Suriname

Between Multi-ethnicity and Nationalism

Peter Meel

In a 2017 television speech celebrating Eid al-Fitr the Surinamese minister of Home Affairs Mike Noersalim characterised Ramadan as a training period inducing Muslims to perform virtuous actions, demonstrate affectionate and caring behaviour, and purge the human spirit. He confirmed that the joyful termination of the fasting month was unmistakably a Muslim event, but elucidated that spiritual upliftment and values such as justice and solidarity transcended the circles of those who adhered to Islam: they linked up to the needs and ideals of the entire Surinamese community.

According to this official it was of crucial importance to acknowledge that tolerance towards different cultures and creeds was embedded in the Surinamese constitution and duly respected by successive Surinamese governments. However, he wished to add that complying with these stipulations was only meaningful when Surinamese took into account that full integration of all ethnic and religious groups was required to become a powerful people. Nation building called upon the readiness of all citizens to cooperate and put individual and collective assets at the service of the developing nation-state.[1]

In his speech minister Noersalim – of mixed Hindustani-Javanese descent and a dedicated Christian – demonstrated an inclination to harmonise multi-ethnic views on society with nationalist principles pertaining to the role of the state.[2] As a matter of fact, his stand

---

1 www.starnieuws.com/index.php/welcome/index/nieuwsitem/42054 (accessed 3 August 2017).

2 Both supporters of multi-ethnicity and nationalism acknowledge the connection between the Surinamese plural society and the Surinamese

displayed the outcome of the protracted integration process of the Javanese in Suriname that allowed them to firmly position themselves in the political arena of their country of settlement. From the inception of parliamentary democracy in Suriname in the late 1940s they have established political parties and have been a vital link in the power-sharing system. In this respect Surinamese Javanese occupy a unique position within the Javanese/Indonesian diaspora.[3]

A high degree of fragmentation as exemplified by partisan goals and ideas and a corresponding large number of political organisations have determined Suriname's governance landscape.[4] Persistent

---

nation-state and the need to make ethnic identities and the national identity compatible. However, advocates of multi-ethnicity prefer to emphasise existing (ethnic) diversity and the respectful prolonging of cultural heterogeneity, whereas proponents of nationalism like to depict the nation as a supraethnic or nonethnic community, stressing the (legal) equality of all citizens (Eriksen 2002, 115–120).

3   The most recent demographic data on Suriname were collected in 2012 by the census office of the Algemeen Bureau voor de Statistiek in Suriname. Distribution of ethnic groups: Hindustani 148,443 (27.4%), Maroons 117,567 (21.7%), Creoles 84,933 (15.7%), Javanese 73,975 (13.7%), mixed 72,340 (13.4%), other 40,985 (7.6%). Distribution of religions over the Surinamese population: Christian (48.4%), Hindu (22.3%), Muslim (13.9%), other/none (12.3%). www.statistics-suriname.org/index.php/statistieken/ downloads/category/30-censusstatistieken-2012 (accessed 3 August 2017).

4   In the 2015 general elections no fewer than twenty-two political parties engaged in a battle for fifty-one parliamentary seats. The majority of these parties had strategically allied with other parties forming combinations that were expected to have better prospects to gain power. Single political parties mainly appealed to a particular segment of the populace, be it an ethnic group, a social class or a mixture of both. As part of a combination they generally delivered a multiethnic or a nationalist message. The main combinations were V7 and the Alternatieve Combinatie (Alternative Combination). V7 consisted of six parties as the Kerukunan Tulodo Prenatan Inggil (Party for National Unity and Solidarity of the Highest Level, KTPI), discontented with its positions on the candidate lists, abandoned ship before the elections. V7's key players were the Vooruitstrevende Hervormings Partij (Progressive Reform Party, VHP), the Nationale Partij Suriname (National Surinamese Party, NPS) and Pertjajah Luhur (Full of Confidence). The Alternatieve Combinatie was composed of three parties and included the KTPI and the Partij voor Democratie en Ontwikkeling

cleavages are commonly attributed to the prevailing ethnic and religious pluralism and socio-economic inequalities in the former Dutch colony. Apart from Javanese particularly Creoles (descendants of former enslaved Africans), Hindustani (descendants of former indentured labourers from India) and Chinese (partly descendants of former indentured labourers, but increasingly 'new migrants' from China) have left their mark on Surinamese society. From the late 20th century Maroons (descendants of former enslaved Africans who escaped the plantations to establish communities of their own in the Surinamese interior) have progressively extended their presence and influence nationwide. Ethno-political entrepreneurs of different backgrounds have gained access to the legislative and executive powers to safeguard the interests of their support base and productively cope with a weak administrative infrastructure. Up to the present political parties have held a preponderate position in the Surinamese polity as promoters of factional interests, distributors of spoils and vehicles of emancipation.[5]

In this chapter I will track the development of the Javanese population group in Suriname, examining their political parties, the acts and convictions of their leaders, and the interests they have defended. More importantly, I will assess the role of Javanese politicians in the integration process of their group and their efforts to relate to the aspirations of their followers and of Surinamese society at large. Identifying points of friction, fracture and change, major attention will be paid to the gradual shift from ethnically inspired ways to play politics to more nationalist orientations. In this respect notions and considerations of Surinamese born after the country obtained sovereignty in 1975 have been of decisive importance. I will centre on the accomplishments of four political leaders: Iding and Willy Soemita (KTPI), Salikin Hardjo (Pergerakan Bangsa Indonesia Suriname, Union of Indonesians in Suriname, PBIS) and Paul Somohardjo (Pertjajah Luhur). Put on a pedestal by their supporters

---

(Party for Democracy and Development, PDO). The Nationale Democratische Partij (National Democratic Party, NDP) was the foremost single party.

5   See Dew 1978, 1994 for Suriname's political system and political culture. On ethno-political entrepreneurs, see Brubaker 2002, 166.

and more than willing to tolerate these expressions of reverence and admiration, they have shaped the image of Javanese politics and the vicissitudes of their ethnic group in the past seventy years.

Early Forms of Organisation

Initially successive groups of Javanese workers who arrived in Suriname under the indentured labour system considered their stay in the host society a temporary one. In Java recruiters of the Dutch colonial regime and private agencies had persuaded them to abandon their burdensome existence and grasp the opportunity to build a better future in an overseas location, which they shrewdly promoted as the proverbial land of milk and honey. Although Javanese male and female young adults left for different (often personal) reasons, escaping economic hardship, debts and social exclusion were among the chief motives triggering them to try their luck in a new environment.

From 1890 onwards, Javanese workers focused on fulfilling the five-year contract on the plantations where they had been assigned to. In Suriname's coastal area they had to perform arduous manual labour, cope with poor living conditions and endure the strict control exercised by the plantation regime and the colonial government. Following the expiration of their contract indentured labourers could sign a new contract and extend their stay in Suriname on the same basis, accept a plot of land and resort to subsistence farming, or return to Java and attempt to reintegrate in their native communities. Despite the harsh and humiliating treatment they had encountered, more than 75 per cent of the Javanese indentured labourers who had arrived in Suriname between 1890 and 1930 decided to prolong their stay in the colony.[6]

There are a number of reasons to explain their decision to stay in Suriname. First of all, the workers weighed the pros and cons of a continued residence in the colony. On the negative side there were their low social status, the disrespect shown by residents belonging

---

6 Following the indentured labour period free labourers from Java entered Suriname in the 1930s. In the period 1890–1939 a total number of 32,962 Javanese labourers migrated to Suriname (Hoefte 1998, 44–55, 61–62).

to other ethnic groups and their isolation in the rural areas. But
at the same time Suriname could provide something Java was
definitely short of: the possibility to obtain land and pursue a life as
a small farmer. This proved to be a major incentive. Furthermore,
the workers increasingly found out that returning to Java for many
of them most likely would be a mixed blessing. Culturally and
spiritually they would experience a sense of homecoming, but re-
entering the networks and institutions considered crucial in Javanese
village life would be difficult. Moreover, the colonial government
in the Netherlands East Indies was not able to offer returnees jobs,
housing and social services because of overpopulation. In the
1930s, the reluctance of the Dutch authorities in Suriname to pay
a free return passage to Java and their policy to transform Javanese
indentured labourers into reliable colonists helped to convince
many Javanese that permanent settlement in Suriname would be a
viable option.

Given that the majority of Javanese workers were poorly educated and had to focus on sheer survival, the establishment of
new institutions among members of this group developed slowly.
Opportunities for political representation were lacking – except for
the colonial elite – and the local authorities anxiously kept tabs on
immigrant initiatives to ensure that they did not challenge the status
quo. Nevertheless, on the plantations workers managed to establish
associations in an attempt to ameliorate their living conditions. The
issues they addressed included wage questions, maltreatment by
plantation overseers and expenses related to birth, illness or death.
Equally important were organisations controlling the observance
of rules and obligations linked to Islam.[7] Mostly these were confined to practical matters such as the provision of Quran learning
classes and the building of mosques. In the 1930s, the residence of

---

7   Well-known associations were Tjintoko Muljo (Elevated in Calamity),
    established in 1918 on the Mariënburg plantation and mainly involved in
    solving social and labour issues, and the Perkumpulan Islam Indonesia
    (Indonesian Islamic Association, PII), founded in 1932 by (among others)
    Salikin Hardjo and initiator of the building of the first mosque in Paramaribo
    for reformist Javanese Muslims (Hoefte 1998, 180–183; Breunissen 2001,
    15–17, 155).

Javanese Muslims in the Caribbean caused internal debate about the correct way to worship. Ultimately these disputes culminated in a split between traditionalists worshipping as in Java with their heads facing West and reformists worshipping with their heads directed towards Mecca, thus East.[8]

Notwithstanding the absence of grassroots political organisations Javanese workers demonstrated a keen interest in political affairs. First they supported progressive socio-political programmes. When the left-wing activist Anton de Kom – of Surinamese origin, but residing in the Netherlands – visited his country of birth in 1933 he was received with much enthusiasm. Working-class Creoles, Hindustani and Javanese believed that De Kom would bring an end to their misery, which had been severely aggravated by the global economic crisis. Despite his black complexion and Creole roots many Javanese identified De Kom with the mythical Ratu Adil, a righteous prince, who was believed to have come from Java to terminate their exile by awarding them a free return passage to their home country. Javanese hopes, however, proved illusory. The arrest and expulsion of De Kom by the local authorities thwarted his anti-colonial and anti-imperialist agenda.[9]

Further proof of Javanese political concern in Suriname was the engagement Javanese displayed with the nationalist struggle of their compatriots in Indonesia. They particularly followed the activities of the Partai Nasional Indonesia (PNI) led by Sukarno. Like-minded sailors stopping by in Paramaribo clandestinely distributed Javanese and Malay periodicals among Javanese and provided information on the Indonesian independence movement. Irregular exchanges of letters and occasional visits of go-betweens strengthened ties between progressive forces in both countries. In Suriname sympathy for *Indonesia Merdeka* (Free Indonesia) was most visibly expressed by pictures of Sukarno decorating the walls of Javanese homes.[10]

---

8 This controversy has ceased to arouse heated debate, but is still a feature of Javanese religious life (Hoefte 2015).

9 De Kom recorded his experiences in his acclaimed *Wij slaven van Suriname* (We slaves of Suriname) (1934). See Woortman & Boots 2009, 99–135.

10 Meel 2015, 233–236.

The Emergence of Javanese Political Parties

World War II marked the end of migration from Indonesia to Suriname and the beginning of Javanese emancipation in their host country. During the war years Suriname experienced developments towards urbanisation, economic differentiation and administrative reform. Prime movers behind this turn of events were the U.S. military presence in Suriname (to protect the country and its resources from attacks by Nazi Germany and Vichy-French Guiana), the booming bauxite industry (bauxite providing basic material for the production of U.S. military aircraft) and the promise of political autonomy announced by the Dutch government (under pressure from the U.S. and U.K. administrations). For the Surinamese population these changes opened up avenues for social mobility and a better standard of living.

Attempting to climb the social ladder, many Javanese left their rural districts and moved to the capital of Paramaribo and to the small bauxite mining town of Moengo.[11] These internal migration movements lifted them out of their isolated and ethnically homogeneous agrarian communities and situated them in multi-ethnic and more vibrant urban settings. Accompanied by their family members, Javanese now lived in the proximity of Creoles, Hindustani and (numerically smaller groups of) Chinese. They no longer were exclusively employed as subsistence farmers, but also held jobs in the bauxite industry, the army and retail trade. Javanese vendors and *warung* (food stand) keepers became a common phenomenon in the Paramaribo streetscape. Other Javanese found employment as drivers, gardeners, garbage collectors or domestic servants.[12]

The political restructuring of the Caribbean parts of the Dutch colonial empire took twelve years to accomplish.[13] In 1954, Suriname and

---

11 On Moengo, with special reference to the then occupational and social hierarchies and the segregated residential patterns, see Hoefte 2014, 113–132.

12 Van Wengen 1972, 107–165. From the 1970s Javanese started to run small restaurants. These further popularised Javanese dishes among all ethnic groups, stimulated inter-ethnic contact and fostered Javanese integration (Patmo-Mingoen 1990, 62).

13 The Dutch government wished to settle her dispute with Jakarta over Indonesian independence first. The decolonisation of the Caribbean

the Netherlands Antilles became autonomous parts of the Kingdom of the Netherlands and thus responsible for their own domestic affairs. Earlier, in 1948, universal suffrage had ended eighty years of elite rule; free parliamentary elections were organised for the first time in 1949.[14] These made way for the first local government based on a fair consultation of the adult population and responsible to a parliament executing rights considered fundamental in a liberal democracy.

In anticipation of the 1949 elections, leaders of the main population groups started to establish political parties. Previously ad hoc political associations had organised the election of representatives of the highest strata of Surinamese society. The introduction of parliamentary democracy, however, required the building of political institutions to serve the needs of their supporters on a more permanent basis and to fully engage in state affairs. Considering the successive arrival of the different population groups and the divide and rule strategies they had been subject to for a long time, it is not surprising that the new political parties were founded on the basis of ethnicity and religion. The main parties were the Nationale Partij Suriname (National Surinamese Party, NPS), a mainly Creole Protestant party, the Progressieve Surinaamse Volkspartij (Progressive Surinamese People's Party, PSV) a Creole Roman Catholic party, and the Verenigde Hindostaanse Partij (United Hindustani Party, VHP), a party bringing together Hindus and Muslims of Indian descent.[15]

The Kaum Tani Persatuan Indonesia (Indonesian Peasants' Party, KTPI) completed the category of major parties.[16] The KTPI, established in 1948 and in all respects directed at the hearts and minds of Surinamese Javanese, was known for the powerful leadership of

---

parts of the Kingdom of the Netherlands did not gain momentum until the early 1950s.

14 Prior to 1948 only 2 per cent of the Surinamese population had voting rights, as this right was restricted to citizens who paid a certain amount of tax and had reached a minimum level of secondary education.

15 The VHP changed its name twice and from 1973 became known as the Vooruitstrevende Hervormings Partij (Progressive Reform Party). On the emerging political landscape of the late 1940s, see Mitrasing 1959.

16 In 1987, the KTPI renamed itself Kerukunan Tulodo Prenatan Inggil (Party for National Unity and Solidarity of the Highest Level).

Iding Soemita. In 1925, at the age of seventeen, Soemita had moved to Suriname as an indentured labourer. In the early years of its existence the KTPI dealt with fierce competition from the Pergerakan Bangsa Indonesia Suriname (Union of Indonesians in Suriname, PBIS) founded in 1947. Salikin Hardjo, chairman of the PBIS, in 1920 at the age of nine had set foot in Suriname in the company of his parents, who had been recruited as indentured labourers. Differences in social background, leadership style and political programme between Soemita and Hardjo provoked disagreement and hostility within the Surinamese Javanese community.

Soemita – who was born in West Java and raised in a Sundanese village community – worked as a male nurse in the hospital of the Mariënburg sugar plantation in the Commewijne district.[17] Although functionally illiterate his social and organisational skills gave him a good reputation and allowed him to build up a substantial network particularly after the establishment of the Persatuan Indonesia, forerunner of the KTPI, in 1946. The Persatuan Indonesia presented itself as the main vehicle for Javanese ex-indentured labourers who had lost the formal right to a free return to Java, but who expected financial support from the colonial government to get back to their native soil. They considered this a proper compensation for the poverty and despair they had experienced. After all, these conditions were in sharp contrast to the prospects presented by recruiters in Java. The organisation also stood up for those who were still waiting for the authorities to keep their promise of a free return passage to Java. World War II had made it impossible to fulfil this commitment, but after transportation and communication lines had been restored, former indentured labourers insisted that the colonial regime should charter a ship that would take them back to what they perceived as their homeland.

The Persatuan Indonesia actively responded to the repatriation urge many Javanese felt. Experiencing neglect and exclusion, lacking formal training and still occupying the lower ranks of society, members of the Javanese community proved to be susceptible to the idea of return and eagerly adopted the *Moelih nDjowo* (back to Java)

---

17 Soemita's childhood and adolescence are obscured by mystery, see Meel 2015, 223–225, 229–230.

ideology that Iding Soemita offered them. The captivating image of their island was further enhanced by Sukarno's proclamation of independence on 17 August 1945 and the subsequent decolonisation wars their countrymen were fighting against the Dutch. Not only did these provoke a strong engagement with the fate of their overseas kinsmen, the Indonesia merdeka ideal also held out the promise of a new beginning which particularly appealed to those on the verge of (re)migration.

In 1948, the Persatuan Indonesia was transformed into the KTPI. This political party aimed to champion the interests of the 'common' Javanese. It vowed to uphold and protect traditional Javanese culture (mixing Islam with ideas and rituals derived from Hinduism, Buddhism and animism), concentrate on the back-to-Java policy, vigorously promote the introduction of full universal suffrage in Suriname and critically scrutinise the Dutch rulers there. In order to make up for the lack of intellect within the party organisation Iding Soemita joined forces with Mohamed Ashruf Karamat Ali, a lawyer of a prominent Hindustani family who acted as his main adviser. This close cooperation with a non-Javanese met with ambivalence within the Javanese community. Besides, groups of co-ethnics rejected Soemita's authoritarian leadership style, the militant behaviour he allowed party members to display towards exponents of rival parties, his inability to comprehensively attend to state affairs and his murky business operations, which had induced the colonial administration to monitor his actions. His supporters, however, admired Soemita's simple lifestyle, his knowledge of Javanese culture and his command of high Javanese[18], his rhetorical gifts and charisma, and his cunningness and sense of humour.[19]

---

18 Among Surinamese Javanese three types of Javanese were spoken: low, middle and high, corresponding with informal, formal and highly formal language. Javanese political, cultural and religious leaders usually used the latter, also called *krâmâ* or *krâmâ inggil*. Most Javanese spoke low Javanese (or *ngoko*) and (increasingly) Sranantongo (the Surinamese vernacular) and (Surinamese) Dutch. See Vruggink 2001, xvii, xxix–xxxiii; Gooswit 1994, 174–176.

19 On Soemita's Javaneseness, see Meel 2015, 230–233.

Soemita's main political opponent Salikin Hardjo – born in East Java, but also a resident of Central and West Java for some time – was raised in a relatively well-to-do family. His father – who was fluent in reading and writing Javanese – earned a living as a mechanic, a watchmaker, a goldsmith and a contractor successively. Although of Javanese descent Hardjo was familiar with Sundanese customs and traditions and had maintained cordial relations with members of this very small group in Suriname. In Moengo, where his father worked on a five-year contract as a mechanic in the bauxite industry, Hardjo went to primary school. In Paramaribo he attended secondary school which at that time made him one of the best educated Javanese in Suriname. At the age of twenty-one he started working in a printing office and between 1932 and 1935 he contributed articles to a newspaper in which (using a pseudonym) he called attention to the difficult living conditions of the Javanese on the Surinamese plantations. In 1936 Hardjo accepted a position as public relations officer at the ministry of Public Health. He travelled the country explaining contagious diseases and their prevention. Meanwhile he remained involved in activities that aimed to promote the well-being and emancipation of his fellow Javanese.[20]

The PBIS, like the KTPI, directed its activities towards the entire Javanese community, but its operations were hampered by its elitist image. This was a result of the level of education of its leadership and some of the opinions the political party favoured. The PBIS supported a gradual extension of the suffrage, not universal suffrage, on account of the illiteracy of large sections of the Surinamese population. In their opinion the Javanese in particular would be the object of manipulation and deceit once they were allowed to vote. Another feature of the PBIS programme was the ambition to fulfil a mediator's role between their supporters and the colonial authorities. This stand made the PBIS prone to the accusation that they were collaborating with a regime that was responsible for the prolonged suffering of the Javanese. Furthermore, the PBIS not only welcomed adherents of traditional Javanese culture, but also orthodox Muslims and Christians. This made the party less appealing in the eyes of

---

20 Breunissen 2001, 1–13. Hardjo's newspaper articles are collected and commented upon in Breunissen 2001, 19–24, 141–162.

most Javanese. The PBIS's downplaying of the idea of returning to Java, however, constituted the main difference with the KTPI. The PBIS called on their followers to build a future in Suriname and encouraged them to get an education, save money, abstain from gambling and expensive festivities such as the *tayub* (a dance party) and start profitable businesses. However, stressing private initiative, capital accumulation and the importance of making a difference caused unease among many Javanese. They considered these recommendations at odds with their collective work ethic beliefs, more specifically with the principles of *rukun* (harmony and unity) and *gotong royong* (mutual collaboration and aid).[21]

In the 1949 elections the KTPI easily beat the PBIS, leaving the latter without a single seat in parliament. The vehement campaigning against the PBIS, the assurance that Javanese cultural traditions would be safeguarded and the undisputed leadership of Iding Soemita were the basis of the KTPI's victory. According to PBIS officials the Javanese had voted with their hearts, not their minds. They had been spellbound by the idea of (re)settlement in Java and were insufficiently aware that their extensive daydreaming would detract from their chances to become respectable citizens of Suriname. The controversy between the KTPI and the PBIS continued to split the Javanese community and ultimately produced a remarkable outcome. In the face of the KTPI's supremacy it was Salikin Hardjo, together with over one thousand PBIS sympathisers, who left Suriname and in 1954 established the village of Tongar in Western Sumatra. The Indonesian authorities had declined them permission to (re)migrate to Java due to persistent problems of overpopulation on the island.[22]

Conversely the KTPI, convinced that return to Java was not a valid option any more and conscious of the challenges Suriname autonomy had in store for them, now started to give priority to the improvement

---

21 Breunissen 2001, 34–55.

22 On the establishment and development of the village of Tongar, see Breunissen 2001, 56–139, 184–211. Salikin Hardjo's decision marked the last mass migration movement of Surinamese Javanese back to Indonesia. See also personal recollections by return migrants, including Hardjo's daughter, in Djasmadi, Hoefte and Mingoen 2010.

of the living conditions of the Javanese in Suriname.[23] Between 1949 and 1967 the KTPI under Iding Soemita would be represented in parliament, boosting the political power and the socio-economic progress of the Javanese population group. The distribution of land, welfare facilities and educational provisions were the party's primary goals. However, in the course of the 1960s Javanese youngsters increasingly questioned Soemita's political performance. They emphasised the need for the modernisation of the party leadership, denounced – what they termed – Soemita's self-serving clientelistic strategies, and pressed him to speed up the integration of Javanese into Surinamese society. In both the 1967 and the 1969 elections the KTPI failed to win any seats and was no longer represented in parliament. Instead their parliamentary seats were held by the Sarekat Rakyat Indonesia (Union of Indonesians, SRI) consisting of Soemita critics, former members of the PBIS, and Javanese who earlier had found refuge with non-Javanese political parties. These electoral defeats demonstrated the waning authority of Iding Soemita and paved the way for a change of the guard within the KTPI.[24]

Independence and the Consolidation of Javanese Political Parties

In the 1970s a new generation of Javanese politicians embodied by Willy Soemita and Salam Paul Somohardjo entered the political arena. Willy Soemita had been politically trained by his father and had succeeded him as chairman of the KTPI in 1972. Paul Somohardjo

---

23 From the moment the Dutch handed over sovereignty to Indonesia on 27 December 1949, Iding Soemita encouraged Surinamese Javanese to adopt Indonesian citizenship. Most Javanese followed his advice, which meant that they lost their voting rights. Both the Surinamese and the Dutch governments considered the presence in Suriname of a large group of inhabitants holding foreigner status and lacking political rights as unjust and undesirable, the more so since Javanese mass repatriation to Indonesia seemed increasingly illusory. To remedy this situation, parliaments in Suriname and the Netherlands created provisions allowing Surinamese Javanese to opt for Dutch citizenship easily and free of charge. The great majority of Surinamese Javanese made use of this opportunity (Mitrasing 1959, 214, 247–248).

24 Meel 2011, 101–102.

left the (Javanese presidium of the) NPS to found his own political parties: the Pendawa Lima (1977) and Pertjajah Luhur (1998).[25] Since the 1970s both men have competed for the political leadership of the Surinamese Javanese, using various tactics, championing different issues and displaying distinctive leadership styles.

Like their predecessors, Willy Soemita and Paul Somohardjo thoughtfully honoured values pre-eminent in traditional Javanese culture. These included respectful dealings with the macrocosmic principles of life and presupposed the dependency of the Javanese on a *bapak* (father figure), who derived his leadership from divine powers and could offer them wisdom, guidance and protection. The two politicians also tapped into the need of their co-ethnics to adhere to the moral codes and mutual support offered by their community, and correspondingly rejected anti-social and disrespectful behavior.[26] Moreover, Soemita and Somohardjo confirmed and reinforced the reliance of Javanese on their Muslim identity. Javanese visibly expressed this part of their worldview through building mosques and providing religious services, running Islam-based associations and celebrating the Eid al-Fitr (the feast at the end of Ramadan, in Suriname often called Bodo) and Eid al-Adha (the Feast of Sacrifice) festivals.[27] They also exhibited aspects of their

---

25 Presidia were ethnic based administrative sections of the NPS and primarily meant to represent non-Creole voters.

26 Anderson 2006; Mulder 1978.

27 Among Surinamese Javanese the main Muslim associations are the Stichting Islamitische Gemeenten in Suriname (Foundation of Islamic Congregations in Suriname, SIS) and the Federatie Islamitische Gemeenten in Suriname (Federation of Islamic Congregations in Suriname, FIGS). Despite their differences of opinion on the prayer direction towards Mecca and on the need to adhere to Islamic orthodoxy, both organisations offer religious education in the *serambi*, the roofed porch attached to the front or side of the mosques that are connected to their associations. In these classrooms the emphasis is on learning Arabic and Quran recitations under the supervision of a *guru* (also named *ustadz* or *sheikh*). In addition to these Islamia schools SIS runs four primary schools (one in Paramaribo, the others in the districts of Commewijne, Para and Marowijne) providing a regular Surinamese curriculum, but teaching the basics of Islam during the one hour per week scheduled for religious education (Interview with S.

Muslim identity during the commemoration of Javanese Arrival Day (9 August).[28]

Apart from sustaining sociocultural and religious traditions that bolstered group cohesion, both Soemita and Somohardjo more emphatically contextualised their authority. They added a firmer drive towards emancipation and integration to their repertoire, acknowledging the challenges of Surinamese society and grasping opportunities to collectively move forward. In this respect they linked up to the Western lifestyles Javanese youngsters were increasingly exposed to and to the more national outlook they were acquiring while receiving secondary and tertiary education in Paramaribo. The strategy of the KTPI and the Pendawa Lima was targeted at endorsing Javanese religious and socio-cultural traditions and securing the Javanese an equal position in the evolving Surinamese nation-state.[29]

Willy Soemita, nicknamed Willy the Silent, exemplifies that rare category of politicians who were pushed to take up the leadership of a political party against their will.[30] Having had no formal position within the KTPI and not craving any political career, he was nevertheless expected to replace his father after he had retired.[31] Soemita, who had been working as a rather nondescript

---

Soeropawiro, head of the department of Religious Affairs of the ministry of Home Affairs, Paramaribo, 30 June 2016). The interrelationship between Muslim associations and Javanese political organisations is examined in Derveld 1982, 127–144.

28 Javanese culture does not feature prominently in Suriname's national identity and public space. Javanese Arrival Day is not a public holiday. The most important Javanese monuments are located outside the centre of Paramaribo – at Sana Budaya – and at Mariënburg, in the Commewijne district. Mariënburg hosts a large figurative statue honoring the first 94 Javanese indentured labourers who entered Suriname in 1890. On 9 August during the Day of the Wong Jawa (organised by Pertjajah Luhur) people meet here. See also Gowricharn 2015b.

29 Continuities and changes in Javanese music, dance, dress, language, literature, art and cuisine are discussed in Meel 2011.

30 Originally this nickname is connected to William of Orange (1533–1584), founding father of the Dutch Republic and a diplomat and strategist who knew when to keep his mouth shut.

31 According to Soemita's version of the story, see Brave 2012.

civil servant under his father's tutelage, introduced an open-door policy, attempting to persuade talented young Javanese to (re)join the KTPI and work towards modernisation. In 1973, the KTPI won two seats in the parliamentary elections and managed to obtain two ministerial posts in the new NPS-led government. Soemita himself became minister of Agriculture, Animal Husbandry and Fisheries, a position that allowed him to effectively supervise the distribution of jobs, grants, permits and land among the KTPI rank and file.[32]

On 15 February 1974, the Prime Minister and NPS chairman Henck Arron announced that Suriname would become independent the next year. This message provoked serious friction between Creole and Hindustani politicians, the former dominating the government, the latter – headed by VHP-leader Jagernath Lachmon – constituting the parliamentary opposition. The Hindustani – demographically and economically the dominant population group in Suriname – denounced independence, fearing Creole hegemony if the Dutch were to cut political ties with their country. Significant portions of then third ethnic population group, the Javanese, shared this point of view. While Soemita supported independence, behind the scenes his father was making a strong case for the continuation of the Dutch presence in Suriname in order to secure ethnic peace. Iding Soemita admired Paul Somohardjo, who had launched a forceful crusade against independence, left the NPS to join the opposition and fervently pushed for the emigration of Javanese to the Netherlands. In Somohardjo's opinion the metropole was obliged to offer his people a safe haven, protecting them from selfish politicians who were driven by a sheer lust for power. Despite the many protests against independence, the Arron administration kept the course it had set and with the support of The Hague Suriname became independent on 25 November 1975. Among the over 50,000 Surinamese who had taken refuge in the Netherlands in the preceding two years, Hindustani and Javanese were overrepresented. As for the latter group, their outmigration laid the foundation for a distinct Surinamese Javanese

---

32 At that time the Surinamese parliament consisted of thirty-nine representatives.

Netherlandish community, maintaining strong connections with Suriname.[33]

Early in 1977, Soemita had to step down as minister following an impeachment process.[34] He was incarcerated on charges of extortion. After the 1977 parliamentary elections the KTPI, having won three seats, was awarded two ministerial posts and a deputy minister position in the second Arron administration. In Soemita's absence the KTPI continued to be a coalition partner, but after his release from prison its chairman pledged support to the opposition and quit the government. A KTPI split-off under the name Partij Perbangunan Rakjat Surinam (Progressive Party of the Construction of Suriname, PPRS), however, allowed the government to retain its parliamentary majority. Nevertheless, animosities continued to fuel political relations and the Arron administration failed to offer the population substantial economic development and improved social services. One month before the 1980 elections – which were expected to become a confrontation between an Arron-led combination including the PPRS and a Lachmon-headed alliance including the KTPI and Somohardjo's Pendawa Lima (see below) – a group of sixteen non-commissioned officers under the command of Desi Bouterse staged a *coup d'état* and took over power.[35]

In contrast to Willy Soemita, Paul Somohardjo was a self-made man who had started his political career in the 1960s in the NPS. As leader of the Javanese presidium of this party he built a reputation as a flamboyant politician who in 1973 was elected to the Surinamese parliament. Somohardjo was known for his organisational skills and entrepreneurial operations, which focused on Miss Jawa contests, Pasar Malam (night markets) and fairs, recreation and education facilities for youngsters, and social activities like lotteries and cook-outs for seniors. Due to disagreement over the party's drive towards independence Somohardjo broke with the NPS and in 1977

33 Meel 2014, 125–128 and chapters IV and V. For data on Surinamese emigrants to the Netherlands between 1960 and 1985 see Oostindie 1988, 63. In the mid-1970s the Surinamese population totaled 380,000.

34 His father, while being a member of parliament, in 1956 had been sentenced to prison on charges of swindle in a rice deal. Dew 1978, 113, 115.

35 Meel 2014, 260–267, 331–332, 367–372.

established the Pendawa Lima. The name of the party referred to the five Pandawa brothers, key characters of the Mahabharata, the famous epic popular among Hindustani and Javanese.[36] In its founding year the Pendawa Lima, having incorporated the SRI, obtained three seats in parliament, but Somohardjo had teamed up with the VHP and much to his dismay was forced to side with the opposition. Somohardjo was clearly determined to shake off the stigmas of 'backwardness' and 'docility' that had impeded the Javanese in Suriname for decades. Instead, he wished to use the ongoing integration of his group to lay claim to a fair share of the political cake and be accepted as an equal competitor for high state positions. Whereas Soemita took a cautious stance and quietly and imperturbably worked towards his goals, Somohardjo demonstrated self-confidence and boldness by pushing himself forward to call attention to the Javanese cause.[37]

The military regime led by Desi Bouterse between 1980 and 1987 abolished parliamentary democracy, introduced new administrative bodies controlled by the National Army and prosecuted 'old school' politicians suspected of corruption. A military court sentenced Soemita to prison on the same charges of extortion that he had already been legally punished for in 1977–1978. He was badly treated during his detention. Meanwhile Somohardjo engaged in an attempted overthrow of the Bouterse regime in 1982. The operation failed and Somohardjo was subjected to severe torture while being interned.[38] He managed to escape the country and stayed in exile in the Netherlands between 1982 and 1993. Here he conducted business operations, joined the resistance movement

---

36 This reference was interpreted as a deliberate attempt by Somohardjo to connect both to his supporters and to proponents of the VHP. Interestingly, Sukarno was associated with two of the Pendawa brothers, namely Bima, the mythic warrior famous for his bravery, stubborn will and single-mindedness, and Arjun, the semi-divine lover possessing the qualities of extreme refinement and charm. See Willner 1984, 65–72. A Somohardjo-Bima connection might consciously or unconsciously have been in the mind of Pendawa Lima supporters.

37 Competition between Javanese political parties in the 1970s and the influence of kinship, patronage, culture and religion are examined in Derveld 1982 and Suparlan 1995.

38 Dew 1994, 75–77.

against Bouterse and explored collaboration opportunities with the controversial Raymond Westerling.[39]

Since the mid-1980s Soemita, together with Arron and Lachmon, had participated in negotiations with Bouterse about a return to democratic rule. These high-level discussions produced a new constitution and new parliamentary elections in 1987. The latter were won by the Front voor Democratie en Ontwikkeling (Front for Democracy and Development), a combination consisting of the NPS, VHP and KTPI. In the new government Soemita became minister of Social Affairs and Public Housing, and in this capacity contributed to the ending of the war in the interior, which devastated Suriname between 1986 and 1992.[40] Soemita retained his position as minister of Social Affairs and Public Housing in the second Front government, but in 1996 the KTPI unexpectedly withdrew from the Front combination and joined the Bouterse-led Nationale Democratische Partij (NDP). The Front leadership deemed this an act of betrayal. Soemita's constituency also had difficulties understanding this move. It allowed the KTPI to remain in power and to cater to its followers, but how could cooperation with the NDP be reconciled with Soemita's humiliation by the military in the early 1980s? Ever since the demise of the unstable NDP administration in 2000 the

---

39 Dutch military officer Raymond Westerling (1919–1987) fought in the Indonesian war of independence (1945–1949) and was accused of ordering his troops to disproportionally resort to brutal force and summary executions, particularly in South Sulawesi. Westerling always denied allegations of war crimes and was never prosecuted, but in the 1980s still enjoyed a questionable reputation. Moreover, it is hard to find logic in Surinamese Javanese wishing to cooperate with a reputed executioner of Javanese, albeit in a different time period and under dissimilar circumstances. Interview author with former Surinamese ambassador to Indonesia S. Rasam, Paramaribo, 3 November 2011.

40 The war in the interior – mainly occurring in East Suriname – was fought between Bouterse's National Army and the Jungle Commando of Ronnie Brunswijk, a former bodyguard of Bouterse. The conflict took many lives, uprooted people, disrupted socio-cultural structures, ruined infrastructure, aborted development projects and enhanced the intertwining of legal and illegal networks of administration and business. See Hoogbergen and Kruijt 2005.

simmering grudge against the KTPI leadership within sections of the Javanese community has intensified, causing the proportional decline in support for the party.[41]

After his return to Suriname legal obstacles prevented Somohardjo from running for parliament in 1996. Two years later, grave dissension over the control of the Pendawa Lima caused Somohardjo to establish a new political party, the Pertjajah Luhur. Being part of the Front combination between 2000 and 2010 Pertjajah Luhur participated in two government coalitions in which the party held three ministerial positions. Somohardjo correctly considered himself the political leader of the Surinamese Javanese, blending political and entrepreneurial initiatives and demonstrating a distinct feel for public relations.[42] However, his erratic political behaviour and sometimes ambiguous transactions met with scepticism in the media, although rumours of shady business operations never resulted in any legal proceedings. Somohardjo's involvement in some eye-catching incidents unmistakably damaged his reputation. His harassment of a Miss Jawa contestant in 2003 – leading to a two-month suspended sentence – forced him to resign as minister of Social Affairs and Public Housing. Video recordings of Speaker Somohardjo beating up a member of the opposition during a meeting of the National Assembly in 2007 went global.[43]

On the one hand Somohardjo identified himself as a true Surinamese politician. 'The man with the red jacket,'[44] as he was routinely

---

41 Sedney 2010, 231–250.

42 In this period Somohardjo started to spread a story about his suspended animation as a baby and his awaking shortly before his burial. Apparently he wished to present this as testimony of a predestined leadership and a reference to the divine source of his power. See www.youtube.com/watch?v=vu4oAlihTCo (accessed 5 May 2015).

43 See www.youtube.com/watch?v=F90iT8sakF8 (accessed 5 May 2015). This seemed to echo a much talked about incident in which Somohardjo fought a political opponent on Dutch public television in 1984, see www.youtube.com/watch?v=L94yCS8VooY (accessed 5 May 2015).

44 The colour is part of the red/white Pertjajah Luhur flag, mirroring the Indonesian flag. The party leadership considered red symbolic with courage and white synonymous with (ethnic) peace. According to Pertjajah Luhur

labelled by journalists, chairing what he himself termed 'the party that never sleeps', pointed out that he was not only advocating the interests of people who phenotypically looked like him. Copying a 1960s and early 1970s NPS strategy he introduced presidia in the Pertjajah Luhur and offered representatives of non-Javanese groups (particularly people of Surinamese Chinese and Indigenous origin) positions within the party organisation. Speaking (Surinamese) Dutch, (low) Surinamese Javanese, but usually the country's lingua franca Sranantongo, he liked to reach out and engage himself with society at large. Streetwise, boyish and energetic, he acknowledged the need to take into account national developments and the advancement of all Surinamese.

On the other hand Somohardjo attempted to boost relations with both the Surinamese Javanese in the Netherlands and the Javanese of Indonesia. This commitment distinguished the Pertjajah Luhur from the KTPI. Ever since the dissolution of the back-to-Java movement in the early 1950s, the Indonesian diplomatic mission in Paramaribo has been crucial in keeping Suriname and Indonesia in touch. However, in the 21st century initiatives to prolong and deepen these connections have increasingly shifted to the governments of both countries. Following up on their policy and reaping the fruits of the ICT revolution and the improved and cheaper means of transportation, Somohardjo has particularly invested in solidifying the cultural and religious bonds between the Javanese in Indonesia, Suriname and the Netherlands.[45]

Jakarta and Paramaribo also aim to benefit more substantially from human resources abroad to obtain economic advantages and buttress regional prestige. As part of their respective Indonesian

---

opponents Somohardjo's other nickname, *tjekre tjekre* – after the well-known dice game – indicated his inclination for political gambling.

45 The Surinamese embassy in Jakarta became operational in 2002. Three years later the Sultan of Yogyakarta (Protector of Javanese culture) and Somohardjo visited each other in Commewijne and Yogyakarta and established ties of friendship between the two locations. In the slipstream of these meetings cultural exchanges between Indonesia and Suriname intensified. In this context Soewarto Moestadja – anthropologist, politician and minister on behalf of the KTPI, Pertjajah Luhur and the NDP respectively – presented himself as a cultural broker as well.

and Surinamese diaspora policies Jakarta focuses on Surinamese Javanese in Suriname and Paramaribo on Surinamese Javanese in the Netherlands. Apart from exploring opportunities to collaborate, representatives of both Surinamese Javanese communities have proposed changes to immigration legislation – including arrangements such as dual nationality and dual citizenship. Although generally the status of overseas members of the Indonesian and Surinamese 'families' has taken a turn for the better – accusations of disloyalty and betrayal are voiced less frequently when references are made to those who live outside the homeland territory, except for politicians who wish to arouse nationalist sentiments – and some legal provisions have been introduced to encourage 'family-oriented' mobility, in both countries a diaspora policy embedded in an elaborate and long-term development policy is still lacking.[46] Depending on their place of settlement and degree of integration, Surinamese Javanese mainly identify with Suriname and the Netherlands, with Indonesia providing additional homeland features, largely of a symbolic nature.[47]

In 2010, having reached an agreement with a number of rival Javanese parties (among them the Pendawa Lima) about a merger with the Pertjajah Luhur and having stabilised the party's position following parliamentary elections, Somohardjo expressed his sup-

---

46 A Surinamese delegation attended the first and second Indonesian Diaspora Congress (2012 and 2013), but was absent during the third and fourth (2015 and 2017). A Surinamese branch of the Indonesian Diaspora Network – which came into being in 2012 – is still non-existent. In the Netherlands this branch is involved in nine fields of interest including health care, migrant workers, and youth and education. See www.idn-nl.com/ (accessed 26 October 2015). Interview by author with former Surinamese ambassador to Indonesia Angelique Alihusain-del Castilho, Leiden, 25 May 2013 and complementary e-mail correspondence 14 October 2015. Currently Jakarta and Paramaribo allow members of their diasporas to stay for an extended period of time in their countries without requiring them to apply for a visa or a residence permit (Reeve 2014; Gowricharn 2015a).

47 Meel 2011, 108–117 and 2017. In the mid-1990s, with the support of the KTPI, the Surinamese government attempted to establish stronger economic ties with Indonesia. Later Somohardjo personally tried to promote trade relations between the two countries, without any significant results so far.

port for the NDP to form a new government.⁴⁸ For many pundits this confirmed that Somohardjo's selection of coalition partners ultimately depended on their ability to guarantee him a position in the power centre.⁴⁹ The Pertjajah Luhur joined the NDP-led government, but in 2014 President Bouterse accused Somohardjo of blackmail and forced Pertjajah Luhur to leave the coalition. Somohardjo denied that he had claimed more favours, permits and positions than Bouterse argued he was entitled to. He revengefully turned his back on the NDP and reunited with the Front. Under the name V7 this combination, however, lost the 2015 elections. The Pertjajah Luhur won five seats, but it was immediately confronted with two of their elected representatives who challenged Somohardjo's authority, established a separate parliamentary group and backed the second Bouterse administration. In this government the current minister of Home Affairs Mike Noersalim is their political ally. The failure of the KTPI and two Javanese splinter parties to gain seats showed that an important part of the Javanese electorate had put their trust in the NDP, which had won a landslide victory securing Bouterse's re-election as president.⁵⁰

---

48 Pertjajah Luhur participated in the elections under the name Volksalliantie (People's Alliance)/Pertjajah Luhur. Apart from Pertjajah Luhur this combination consisted of four (tiny) political partners. Following the elections the Volksalliantie quickly disintegrated as a consequence of Pertjajah Luhur's monopolisation of the negotiations with the NDP and its exclusive claim to the available ministerial positions.

49 Many people were taken aback by Somohardjo's move since he was known to be a long-time critic and fierce opponent of Bouterse. The year before as Speaker he had deprived Bouterse of his mandate as member of parliament (Sedney 2010, 257–265). Somohardjo's decision in 2010 to cooperate with Bouterse resembled Soemita's 1996 initiative to cross the floor.

50 The Javanese splinter parties were the Nieuwe Stijl KTPI (New Style KTPI, NSK), presided by Oesman Wangsabesari, a KTPI split-off that had joined forces with the NDP, and the Partij voor Democratie en Ontwikkeling (Party for Democracy and Development, PDO), led by Waldi Nain – a former Pendawa Lima dignitary – and affiliated with the Alternatieve Combinatie. Pertjajah Luhur won 7 per cent of the votes (13 per cent in 2010). Judging from the size of the Javanese group (totaling 13.7% of the Surinamese population) this indicated that besides votes for Pertjajah Luhur, the KTPI, the NSK and the PDO a considerable number of Javanese

For the Javanese population group the disappearance of the KTPI and the Soemita dynasty from the political stage demonstrated the bankruptcy of old-school ethnic politics. The party leadership was considered to have outlived itself and to have lost touch with contemporary developments. The rather poor election results of Pertjajah Luhur indicated that many Javanese had become tired of the daredevilish and often unpredictable manoeuvring of Paul Somohardjo, despite the more modern and inclusive image of his party. Javanese support for the (Javanese candidates of the) NDP can be explained as evidence of their full integration into Surinamese society. Yet, their backing of Bouterse also displayed a desire to play safe. They cast their votes for a political leader who was expected to remain in power and who most likely would tend to their needs once he was in the driver's seat again.

Both the KTPI under the evasive and aloof Willy Soemita and Pertjajah Luhur under the outspoken and forceful Paul Somohardjo have continued to apply rent-seeking traditions awarding jobs, goods and benefits to their political supporters. Taking the socio-economic background of the Javanese as their point of departure, and connecting to the worlds that Javanese are materially and spiritually familiar with, they preferred to control the ministry of Agriculture, Animal Husbandry and Fisheries and the ministry of Social Affairs (and Public Housing) to remove barriers, distribute favours and allow Javanese to climb the social ladder.[51]

---

had cast their votes for the NDP. Source: dagbladdewest.com/2015/07/08/ondermaatse-verkiezingsresultaten-v7-partners-nps-en-pl/ (accessed 9 July 2015).

51 Other departments KPTI and Pertjajah Luhur ministers regularly were in charge of included Home Affairs, Trade and Industry, Environmental Planning, Land and Forestry, and Education (Sedney 2010). As far as education and employment are concerned in the past decades Javanese to large extent have caught up with Creoles and Hindustani. Currently Javanese are well represented in all types of secondary and tertiary education. Agriculture and mining as 'traditional' Javanese employment niches have vanished. Javanese perform a wide variety of jobs in sectors such as agriculture, industry, construction, transport, trade, education and (particularly) government. See census data 2012 unstats.un.org/unsd/

The performance of Javanese ministers varied highly in terms of effectiveness, transparency and accountability. Allegations of mismanagement, favouritism and corruption have haunted many of them, frequently as a consequence of the operations and directives of their political superiors. In the long run, however, it cannot be denied that government participation by both the KTPI and Pertjajah Luhur has contributed to the well-being and integration of the Javanese group. The current presence of Javanese in all social classes and occupational groups as well as their residential differentiation, notably in Paramaribo, is an apparent manifestation of this. Yet, this progress seems to be primarily the fruit of education and private initiative, paths of advancement already championed by the PBIS in the late 1940s and early 1950s.[52]

Level of education together with age and place of residence have become important factors determining the stand Javanese take towards 'their' political leaders. Generally they perceive the ebbs and flows of the Surinamese political theatre as a fact of life and a source of both support and concern. Knowing the rules of the game and being aware of the intertwining of socio-cultural and political networks, many Javanese feel attracted to politicians who are well versed in the way of life they consider emblematic for their ethnic group. In most cases their socio-economic position does not permit them to escape political leaders who to a large extent control the distribution of resources over their constituents.

Senior Javanese, particularly those with a modest educational background and living outside the capital, display great respect for the leadership qualities of their bapak. They tend to endorse their operations, follow in their footsteps and turn a blind eye to acts of misconduct committed by them. Younger and better educated Javanese, primarily those who reside in Paramaribo, question these in-group solidarity reflexes, have more confidence in their individual judgement and do not shy away from criticising leaders who underperform. They feel free to support likeminded politicians,

demographic/sources/census/wphc/Suriname/SUR-Census2012-vol2.pdf (accessed 8 September 2017).

52 Hoefte 2014, 172–181 and www.statistics-suriname.org/index.php/statistieken/downloads/category/30-censusstatistieken-2012 (accessed 3 August 2017).

irrespective of the ethnic group they belong to. If they vote for Javanese candidates this does not necessarily imply that these have to represent a Javanese political party. However, experience has shown that their room for manoeuvre is limited. Demonstrating independent conduct is contingent on a political system and a political culture based on the maintenance and cultivation of dependency relations.

Concluding Remarks

At present fragmentation is still a feature of Javanese politics, as it is of Surinamese politics in general. Caught between multi-ethnicity and nationalism Javanese political leaders and their supporters perform a balancing act. They demonstrate an unwavering focus on Javanese culture and turn to forms of identity politics and corresponding ideas of belonging to a Javanese diaspora. Simultaneously, they aspire to the full inclusion of the Javanese in Surinamese society and subscribe to the view that in a globalised world a small country can only achieve progress by applying concerted action as a unified nation. The resulting in-between position does not so much produce anxiety or discomfort among Javanese, but rather leads to patient and astute pragmatism. Javanese adhering to Pertjajah Luhur and the NDP – currently their political homes – increasingly resort to multi-ethnicity *and* nationalism, taking into account the persistence of long-standing traditions, but at the same time attempting to come to terms with present-day realities.

Although ethnicity as the principal characteristic of a political party and the alpha and omega of their operations is in retreat, it is still a powerful yet subtly deployed instrument to mobilise people. Multi-ethnic and nationalist parties deal strategically with ethnicity to ensure that all population groups can come on board and that the widest possible support base can be obtained.[53] Apart from organisational power and ideology this requires engaging leadership. The success of a political party invariably depends on the

---

53 This electoral strategy provoked many Javanese and Hindustani politicians to term the NDP a pseudo-nationalist party, which unjustly equated 'Surinamese' and 'Creole' while disqualifying non-Creoles as quasi-Surinamese.

performance of its chair. Salikin Hardjo, Iding and Willy Soemita, and Salam Paul Somohardjo have dominated Javanese politics in the past seventy years and have had a decisive share in the successful emancipation and integration of their population group into Surinamese society. Particularly following independence, Soemita junior and Somohardjo have presented themselves as Javanese *and* Surinamese, working both for and beyond their ethnic group.[54] The principle of gotong royong prevailed, but was extrapolated to non-Javanese groups in order to transcend ethnic boundaries and forge a sense of extended community.[55] In light of the overwhelming NDP victory in 2015 it remains to be seen if the waning power of ethnically rooted parties will persist and if nationalism in Surinamese politics will finally supersede multi-ethnicity.

References

Anderson, B. 2006. 'The Idea of Power in Javanese Culture'. In *Language and Power: Exploring Political Cultures in Indonesia*, ed. B. Anderson, 17–77. Jakarta: Equinox. [Orig. 1972.]

Brave, I. 2012. 'Willy Soemita'. *Parbode* 6(71): 22–26.

Breunissen, K. 2001. *Ik heb Suriname altijd liefgehad: Het leven van de Javaan Salikin Hardjo*. Leiden: KITLV Uitgeverij.

Brubaker, R. 2002. 'Ethnicity without Groups'. *Archives Européennes de Sociologie* 43(2): 163–189.

Derveld, F. E. R. 1982. *Politieke mobilisatie en integratie van de Javanen in Suriname: Tamanredjo en de Surinaamse nationale politiek*. Groningen: Bouma's Boekhandel.

---

54 This does not imply that stereotyping ('Javanese politicians do not pass the test when it comes to reliability, credibility and integrity') has vanished altogether. *Parbode*, Suriname's sole critical opinion magazine, shortly before the 2015 elections assessed the performance of members of the legislature, awarding none of the parliamentarians of Javanese descent a single star, out of a maximum of five stars. Ranking: 23 members gained no star, 15 members 1 star, 7 members 2 stars, 5 members 3 stars and 1 member 4 stars (Redactie *Parbode* 2015). After the elections the magazine tendentiously (and erroneously) argued that more than other ethnic groups the Javanese had suffered from political dissension (Snijders 2015).

55 Pertjajah Luhur 2010; 2015.

Dew, E. M. 1978. *The Difficult Flowering of Surinam. Ethnicity and Politics in a Plural Society*. The Hague: Martinus Nijhoff.

—— 1994. *The Trouble in Suriname, 1975–1993*. Westport: Praeger.

Djasmadi, L., R. Hoefte and H. Mingoen (eds), 2010. *Migratie en cultureel erfgoed: Verhalen van Javanen in Suriname, Indonesië en Nederland*. Leiden: KITLV Uitgeverij.

Eriksen, T. H. 2002. *Ethnicity and Nationalism: Anthropological Perspectives*. 2nd ed. London: Pluto Press.

Gooswit, S. M. 1994. 'Veranderde identificatie bij Javanen in diaspora'. *Oso: Tijdschrift voor Surinaamse taalkunde, letterkunde, cultuur en geschiedenis* 13(2): 173–183.

Gowricharn, R. 2015a. 'Naar een diasporabeleid voor Suriname'. *Oso: Tijdschrift voor Surinamistiek en het Caraïbisch gebied* 34(1/2): 50–63.

—— 2015b. 'Creole Hegemony in Caribbean Societies: The Case of Suriname'. *Studies in Ethnicity and Nationalism* 15(2): 272–291.

Hoefte, R. 1998. *In Place of Slavery: A Social History of British Indian and Javanese Laborers in Suriname*. Gainesville: University Press of Florida.

—— 2014. *Suriname in the Long Twentieth Century: Domination, Contestation, Globalization*. New York: Palgrave MacMillan.

—— 2015. 'Locating Mecca: Religious and Political Discord in the Javanese Community in Pre-Independence Suriname'. In *Islam and the Americas*, ed. A. Khan, 69–91. Gainesville: University Press of Florida.

Hoogbergen, W. and D. Kruijt 2005. *De oorlog van de sergeanten: Surinaamse militairen in de politiek*. Amsterdam: Bert Bakker.

Meel, P. 2011. 'Continuity through Diversity: The Surinamese Javanese Diaspora and the Homeland Anchorage'. *Wadabagei: A Journal of the Caribbean and Its Diasporas* 13 (3): 95–134.

—— 2014. *Man van het moment: Een politieke biografie van Henck Arron*. Amsterdam: Prometheus/Bert Bakker.

—— 2015. 'Iding Soemita: Politiek leider van de Surinaamse Javanen en de verlokkingen van het land van herkomst'. In *Reizen door het maritieme verleden van Nederland: Opstellen aangeboden aan Henk J. den Heijer bij zijn afscheid als hoogleraar Zeegeschiedenis aan de Universiteit Leiden*, ed. A. van Dissel, M. Ebben and K. Fatah-Black, 223–241. Zutphen: Walburg Pers.

—— 2017. 'Jakarta and Paramaribo Calling: Return Migration Challenges for the Surinamese Javanese Diaspora?' *New West Indian Guide* 91(3/4): 223–259.

Mitrasing, F. E. M. 1959. *Tien jaar Suriname: Van afhankelijkheid tot gelijkgerechtigheid: Bijdrage tot de kennis van de staatkundige ontwikkeling van Suriname van 1945–1955*. Leiden: Luctor et Emergo.

Mulder, N. 1978. *Mysticism and Everyday Life in Contemporary Java: Cultural Persistence and Change.* Singapore: Singapore University Press.

Oostindie, G. J. 1988. 'Caribbean Migration to the Netherlands: A Journey to Disappointment?' In *Lost Illusions: Caribbean Minorities in Britain and the Netherlands,* ed. M. Cross and H. Entzinger, 54–72. London: Routledge.

Patmo-Mingoen, H. K. 1990. 'De Javaans-Surinaamse keuken en de volkscultuur'. *Oso: Tijdschrift voor Surinaamse Taalkunde, Letterkunde en Geschiedenis* 9(2): 56–72.

Pertjajah Luhur 2010. *Visie en beleid: Pertjajah Luhur 2010–2015: Samen werken is samen winnen.* Paramaribo: [Pertjajah Luhur].

—— 2015. *Samen vooruit: Surinamers voor Suriname: Partijprogramma 2015–2020.* [Paramaribo]: Pertjajah Luhur.

Redactie *Parbode* 2015. 'Van ruziemakers tot inhoudsloze bankzitters: Parlementsleden scoren belabberd'. *Parbode* 10(109): 36–41.

Reeve, D. 2014. 'Diaspora Power'. *Inside Indonesia* 115 (January-March). [www.insideindonesia.org/diaspora-power]

Sedney, J. 2010. *De toekomst van ons verleden: Democratie, etniciteit en politieke machtsvorming in Suriname.* Paramaribo: Vaco.

Snijders, A. 2015. 'Javanen en de politiek: Kibbelen en knarsentanden'. *Parbode* 10(112): 32–35.

Suparlan, P. 1995. *The Javanese of Suriname: Ethnicity in an Ethnically Plural Society.* Tempe: Arizona State University. [Orig. 1976.]

Vruggink, H. 2001. *Surinaams-Javaans – Nederlands woordenboek.* Leiden: KITLV Uitgeverij.

Wengen, G. D. van [1972]. *De Javanen in de Surinaamse samenleving.* [Leiden]: s.n.

Willner, A. R. 1984. *The Spellbinders: Charismatic Political Leadership.* New Haven: Yale University Press.

Woortman, R. and A. Boots 2009. *Anton de Kom: Biografie. 1898–1945/ 1945–2009.* Amsterdam: Contact.

Index

f=figure; n=footnote or caption; t=table

Chungli 167, 175
Ciceri, Reverend B. 182
Cilacap (Java) 139
Citra (company) 87, 99
Clifford, J. 1, 23, 88n, 89, 101
Club Jeunesse Indonesienne 99
Cohen, R. 88n, 101
collective bargaining 10–11, 114
colonialism 1, 4–9, 12, 14, 19, 20,
22, 27–36 *passim*, 50, 54, 56,
61–67, 82–84, 104–120 *passim*,
209, 241–242
construction sector 17, 20, 87, 103,
122, 123, 128t, 133, 163, 171,
173, 189, 261n
corruption 12n, 136, 170, 255, 262
Côté, I. 47, 51
Creoles 239n, 240, 243, 244, 245,
253, 261n, 263n
cultural boundaries, maintenance
of 3, 20, 82, 101
cultural hybridity 20, 54, 56, 57, 78,
82, 100
cultural identity. *See* identity
cultural markers 20, 82, 90–99
language 90, 91–93
neighbourhood and kinship ties
95–96
preservation 96–98
selamatan ritual 90, 91, 93–95,
96, 98
cultural pluralism 20, 82
cultural politics 19, 28, 29, 30, 35,
39, 44, 46, 49, 50
culture shock 215, 222, 226.
See also migrant workers:
communication
Cultuurstelsel (forced cultivation
system) 30. *See also* colonialism
Cyberjaya 127

dance/dancing 175–180, 186

Dayaks 46
days off. *See* rest days
De Kom, A. 243
De Vries, E. 61, 81
debt-bondage 107–108, 170,
173, 179
decentralisation. *See* Indonesia
Declaration on Protection of Rights
of Migrants (2007) 132
Departments. *See* Ministries
deportation 98, 125, 127–128, 157,
170, 177, 185, 207, 218. *See also*
dismissal
detention camps 12, 125, 126,
127–129
Dewey, A. G. 90, 91, 94–95, 101
diaspora
common features 88n
concept 28–29, 88n, 101
terminological issues 88–89
see also Chinese diaspora;
Indian diaspora; Javanese
diaspora; Jewish diaspora;
Malay diaspora
diasporic identity. *See* identity
diasporic practices 35–45
dirty (3D) jobs 160–161, 162, 168
dismissal 31, 169, 170, 215, 220,
221. *See also* deportation
djadji (substitute family) 95n
djagongan (secular feast) 94
Djintar Tambunan. *See* Tambunan
docility 6, 16, 83, 112, 162, 172,
178, 183, 255
dogs 172
domestic service sector 11–12,
15–18, 20, 103, 124, 127, 133
domestic workers 21, 123, 128t,
129–132, 146, 162, 163, 169,
170, 172, 173–174, 185
contract versus reality 219–220

Sex Discrimination Ordinance
(HK) 141
sexual harassment 12–13, 218, 223,
226–228, 232. *See also* women
shopping malls 18, 225, 233
Siban, M-J. 95
Sido Dadi (village) 67
Silvey, R. M. xiii, 13, 22, 56, 80,
188–208
Sindang Kasih (Sulawesi) 58, 59, 67
Singapore 8, 8n, 9, 10, 11, 13,
14, 15, 105, 107n, 110–111,
115–117, 124t, 133, 134n, 161,
194, 195, 201n, 202n, 210
Chinese diaspora 139
Employment Act 147
Indian diaspora 139
Indonesian embassy 155–156
Javanese diaspora in 137–159
Javanese domestic workers 21,
137–159; ~ (demographics)
138–145
Labour Association 111
Malay diaspora 139
migrant meeting places 140
migration systems (impact on
life and work) 146–149; ~
(Javanese identity, essential-
ism, stereotypes) 153–156.
See also identity
Ministry of Manpower 141, 147,
147n
Singarimbun, M. 56n, 80
singing 175–176, 176f, 177–178
Sister Anne 165
Sister Lenny 167, 169n, 179n
Sita, Ibu 43
slavery 4–6, 7n, 25, 179, 185, 219,
219n, 223n, 240
social class 3, 19, 76, 83n, 143–145,
162, 190, 212, 231, 239n, 243, 262

social mobility 20, 55, 57–58, 59,
76–77, 78, 146, 233, 244. *See
also* socio-economic status
social networks 123, 190, 203, 220,
224–225, 232, 233
social status 6, 16, 17, 32, 35, 38,
51, 104, 150, 223n, 230, 241, 259
social system 68, 78–79, 153
social workers 162–165, 167. *See
also* caregivers
sociality 193–204
socio-economic status 75–76,
78–79. *See also* social mobility
Soekarno Samadi 63–65, 68–71
Soemita, I. 23, 240, 246–250, 253,
254n, 264
Soemita, W. 23, 240, 250–257, 261,
260n, 264
Soeropawiro, S. 251–252n
Soetina 99
Soewarto Moestadja. *See* Moestadja
Somohardjo, P. 23, 240, 250–261, 264
South Africa 4, 4n, 6. *See also* Cape
of Good Hope
South Korea 161, 210
space 57, 67, 75, 77, 78, 79, 182
sport 97
Sri Lanka (Ceylon) 4, 5, 6, 128t,
134n, 139
Sri Margana ix
stereotypes 15, 21, 137, 138, 146,
153–156, 158, 171–174, 264n
Straits Settlements 105, 107, 119.
See also Malaya
Suharto 14, 30, 36–37, 42, 44, 45,
48, 143
Sukabumi (West Java) 22, 194–197,
201–202
Sukarno 14, 243, 247, 255n
Sulawesi 4, 7, 10, 13, 20, 27, 54–81,
256n. *See also* resettlement

improved bargaining
position
inequalities faced by 113, 190,
240. *See also* wages
life outside workplace. *See*
migrant workers: socialising
among
mainly caregivers 184. *See also*
caregivers
majority of international
migrants 2, 16, 194, 196.
See also labour migration:
feminisation of
marriage, to Javanese migrants
88; ~ to locals 117. *See also*
marriage; intermarriage
migration ambitions and
motivations 13, 16, 22, 210,
229, 232, 234
mistreatment of. *See* abuse;
migrant workers: mistreatment of; sexual harassment;
violence
rights 192
sexuality 12, 205, 225–226, 228
survival strategies 118, 232–233.
See also migrant workers:
protests and resistance
see also domestic workers; dress;
feminism; identity: gendered;
pregnancy; runaway maids

Wong, D. 125, 136
Wong, L. 181
wong anyar (newcomers) 87
wong baleh (returnees) 88, 99
wong baru (newcomers) 87
wong jukuan (New Caledonia) 88,
99
wong kontrak (contract labourers)
83
Woodward, M. R. 94, 102
work permits 12, 111, 121, 126, 127
working conditions 11, 12, 14,
21, 22, 86, 113–114, 118, 131,
143, 150–151, 161, 174, 179,
182, 232. *See also* Saudi Arabia;
wages; working hours
working hours 146, 147, 150–151,
165, 169, 170, 175, 224, 228. *See
also* rest days
World Bank 122, 136
World War I 112, 114
World War II 8n, 83, 85, 117, 244,
246

Yemen 203, 204
Yilan County 171
Yilan County Fishermen's Union
184, 185
Yilan Harbour 183
Yogyakarta ix, 31, 33, 48, 54, 66,
68–71, 74, 73, 258n